the
unexpected
SPECTACULAR

A Faithful God. A Journey of Hope.

Cathy Atkinson
with Andrew Atkinson

Disclaimer

I wrote this book based on my own and Andrew's memories as well as notes, scrapbook entries, photographs and journals. I used the actual medical records when possible and interviewed people who were there to witness the events as they happened, as well as those who have been part of our lives all along. I have made every attempt to document the events, locales and conversations as accurately as possible to maintain the integrity of the story.

I changed the names of some individuals and places for their protection, and in a couple of instances, I shortened the timeline of events for the reader's benefit. However, these changes in no way alter the truth of the story.

Printed in the United States

Dedication

DEDICATED TO my brother-in-law, Ken Atkinson, who lost his life while saving another. He was as humble as he was brave, and we miss him terribly. Thank you, Ken, for walking this road with us even as you faced your own difficult journey, and for truly living the legacy you left behind—an unshakable faith.

We are forever grateful.

Cathy Atkinson

Acknowledgments

I T'S IMPOSSIBLE to thank everyone—family and friends— who has bolstered my spirit, read drafts, offered suggestions and encouraged me along the way to finishing this book. To each of you who has had a part, I am so very grateful. I owe a special thank you to my friend, Vicki Kuyper, who many, many years ago mentioned rather casually, "You should write a book." At the time, I laughed at the impossibility of it all, but the idea settled deep in my heart, and I did not forget. To my dear friend, Susan Fuchtman, who willingly read and edited the first horrible drafts and had vision to see possibilities through the fog, thank you. Your encouragement has meant the world to me.

Thank you to the countless doctors, nurses and medical professionals who stretched themselves above and beyond to make this journey even possible. A special thank you to Dr. Mary Beth Deering, whose sensitive insight and fearlessness made a forever imprint in our hearts.

If it weren't for my husband, Tom, who walked beside me through it all—the actual events and then the writing—none of this would be a reality now. He helped me remember details I wanted to forget. He patiently put up with long stretches of my crazy, focused writing, allowing me time to continue uninterrupted. He laughed and cried with me and was brutally honest when I needed it and gracious when I didn't. He never gave up on me, and he is the reason I was able to complete this manuscript.

To my children David and Amy who lived through the frightening uncertainties and fears, feeling it all deeply, as only a brother and sister can, I am humbled and amazed and thankful. As siblings, they never faltered in showing compassion, yet fulfilled their roles perfectly when the requisite teasing was in order. Both David and Amy are invaluable spirit-lifters and encouragers and were not afraid to dive to the depths emotionally to help me with the accuracy of memories and the endless editing.

And, of course, there are no words to adequately thank Andrew, who actually lived this story and whose bravery knows no bounds. I do thank you, Andrew, for your willingness to share your story, including your own vulnerable thoughts. All three of my children are an inspiration to me, and I am blessed to be their mom.

Ultimately, it is my faith in Jesus Christ that compelled me to write this book; He is an amazing God and deserves all the credit for getting our family and me through each day. I wrote this simply to share the miracles He has done and to bring hope to others struggling with difficult situations. My faith is a work in progress, but I am thankful that He is forever faithful and unchanging. He is peace in the storm; He is all we will ever need.

One

The Lord directs the steps of the godly.
He delights in every detail of their lives.
Though they stumble, they will never fall,
for the Lord holds them by the hand.
– Psalm 37:23-24 NLT

To love at all is to be vulnerable.
– C. S. Lewis

THE RAIN ran sideways from the sky that afternoon, muddying the dusty roads, bouncing down the washes and drumming a muffled backbeat against my foggy kitchen windows. It was darker than normal, which made me want to take a nap or curl up next to the fire and escape into a book. I'd made a quick run to the grocery store earlier, though, and the results of that trip, still in plastic bags piled on the counter, were not going to put themselves away. I pulled out the old kitchen stool from its spot next to the fridge and, with a bag in one hand, climbed its wobbly steps to unload items onto the upper shelves of the pantry.

Just then, around the corner from where I perched, the front door exploded open in an unruly blast of wind and rain, sending papers and mail whooshing haphazardly down the hallway, setting pictures crooked on their nails. The door slammed against the entryway wall with such force that even the kitchen floor shuddered. I grabbed the cupboard door to steady myself. *What in the world...? I must not have closed the door all the way,* I thought. *Or was Andrew already home?* I glanced at the clock and then, leaning way out to the left, tried to get a quick glimpse of what was happening in the entryway.

"Andrew, is that you?" I called, although it was earlier than he typically arrived home. The heavy door closed with a careless thump and then a click of the wall switch sent a flood of warm light pouring down the length of the hall. Yes, okay, it was Andrew blowing in and not simply the wind playing tricks on me. *I wonder why he's home so early?* I thought.

Dripping a rainy trail down the hallway, he crutched past the kitchen without a word. Gypsy, our old black lab, leisurely roused from her nap on the cool kitchen tile and stretched, bending low on both front paws with her backside in the air. She stood up slowly and trotted around the corner to greet her best buddy. Still balancing on the upper step of the stool, I took one step down and squatted to turn off the music before climbing all the way down. I picked up another bag of groceries and caught sight of the back of Andrew's jacket as he headed into the living room. The rhythmic chink-cha-chinka of his aluminum crutches came to a halt and then his backpack, heavy and wet, slid off his shoulder and landed on the hardwood floor with a startling smack.

Had I glanced at him in that moment, I might have seen something in his eyes and perhaps been more prepared. But, busy with the groceries, a million ordinary things occupying my mind, I was focused on the task at hand, with no clue that the burden Andrew carried this afternoon wasn't weighing heavy in his pack.

For me the day had been gloriously routine; I'd made a promise to myself months ago—I'd even said it out loud—"You will not take one minute of any day for granted, from here on out." I decided to enjoy the regular days and the ability to accomplish ordinary tasks. How often over the years had I simply slogged through the routines, rarely taking time to appreciate the everyday miracles. Usually, I'm booked to the hilt, overwhelmed and busy with the daily schedule of life. And then the day is over, and the next day is gone, then a week; and before I even realize it, a whole month has passed. Our time in the hospital had given me more of a "slow-down-and-appreciate-the-simple-things" perspective, so I'd made a conscious decision to be aware and present and thankful. Even grocery shopping, my least favorite of household jobs, seemed more tolerable after not being able to do it for so long.

With my head poked into the kitchen pantry, I called out, "Hey, Andrew, is it still pouring out there? Are you completely soaked?" Then I added, "Grab a towel so those floors don't get all wet and muddy." Waiting for his response, I grabbed a jar of peanut butter and slid it onto the shelf. "How did it go today?" I asked. No answer. The box of spaghetti noodles tipped over in the bag, and I reached for it, cocking my head, listening for his voice. *Maybe we should have spaghetti for dinner,* I thought. And then, *Why isn't he answering me?* Is he even still in there or am I talking to myself? I stepped out from behind the pantry door and looked through the large, arched entryway that opened from the kitchen into the living room.

Yes, he was there…standing very, very still in the middle of the room. He stared straight at me, this blonde, curly-headed, blue-eyed son of mine. Barely twenty years old with a hint of stubble shadowing his chin, he was what I'd describe as "tallish"—at any rate, tall compared to me. Andrew was five ten or eleven and naturally muscular.

"Hi?" I offered questioningly, wondering about his silence. I reached for a head of romaine, waiting for him to launch into a comical rundown of the day's events. Andrew, always a great storyteller and easy to listen to, can find humor in even the most mundane happenings. He'd have usually had me laughing by now as he recounted some funny story from his day. But he stood silent—no grin, no goofy raised eyebrow. I thought maybe he'd gotten a bad grade on an assignment, so I stopped rinsing the lettuce and gave him my full attention.

A flicker of emotion trembled across his face as he worked hard to compose himself. He started to speak, then stopped. I waited, my concern increasing. Staring down at Gypsy *thump-thumping* her tail on the floor at his feet, he looked back at me and blurted out, "Mom, I'm going to get my leg amputated. I decided to do it." This time, he didn't hesitate at all; the sentences tumbled out one on top of the other. It took me a minute to process—as if the words themselves had actually emerged from his mouth in slow motion and hung suspended in midair between us, and I wasn't quite able to grasp them. Maybe I'd heard him wrong. Maybe he was kidding. But I looked again, saw the determination in his eyes and knew he meant exactly what he'd said.

I watched him fight to control his feelings, and my own emotions rose instantly to the surface. I couldn't think of what to say. It's not that we hadn't ever talked about the possibility of an amputation; we had actually discussed it on several occasions. I just wasn't expecting the subject to come up today. He'd worked so hard for so long to keep his leg. Why give up now? His declaration left me surprised and devastated for him, and, as selfish as it sounds, for me. I tried not to let my thoughts fly ahead to everything I knew this would mean, the bigger picture of it all. I didn't want to acknowledge the fear beginning to grow inside me or the sadness that had moved in and clouded my eyes.

Then I started coming to my senses. *What does he mean, he decided? How exactly did he come to this so-called decision, and how could he possibly think this is a good idea? We haven't even talked about it recently. Sure, he turned twenty last month—but really, what twenty year old makes this kind of decision? This is absurd. Get his leg amputated? Who does that on purpose?* Jumbled thoughts whirled around in my head, and I couldn't distinguish one from another. I felt as if someone had grabbed my throat from behind, and I wasn't sure if I could draw a decent breath again. I needed to take a step back emotionally and think through the circumstances logically, but I didn't know how. What's more, I didn't want to. I wanted to stomp my feet and hit something and scream and cry that this was *not* going to happen. That none of this was happening. Could not and would not happen.

I closed my eyes and forced myself to find a slight sense of calm. Mentally I managed to climb to a vantage point where I could view the situation from a different angle. Obviously, this had been a tough decision—Andrew was finding it difficult to speak. I didn't want him to shut down altogether. I had a pretty clear idea of what *not* to do, and I coached myself: *first of all, don't launch into your panicked-mother mode* (I have this one perfected), *and second, don't start with the military-grade interrogation tactics* (tempting, but never a good idea). *But what should I say to him? How can I convince him that this is not a road he wants—or we want—to go down?*

"Really?" I said, trying hard to lower my squeaky voice and exude a sense of calm. "You are?" I am learning that with my adult children, it's better if I don't talk too much. I try to bite my tongue and let them gradually fill me in on the details at their own speed. Rather than cutting them off at the pass with my racing thoughts and questions, I pause and breathe and listen. A better outcome usually results that way, with the operative words being "try" and "usually." *Focus on Andrew,* I told myself, *deal with what's right here, right now.* While I waited for him to tell me all about it, my head buzzed like a swarm of angry bees, ready to attack this amputation plan and kill it. My mind jumped from one thought to another and another. *Isn't there a less...drastic idea? Surely there must be another choice, someone else to talk to, something we haven't tried yet. He is not getting his leg amputated. That's all there is to it. The answer is flat out no.*

Around my house, I am your go-to girl for the latest in Internet up-dates. Given the situation, it would have been the expected norm for me to immediately log on to the computer and research what I could about the most recent advances in nerve and muscle reconstruction or ampu-tation. In fact, I do this regularly, hoping to discover some new bit of information or positive results from a test study somewhere—anything we can cling to for hope. Today, however, I didn't even think about get-ting on the computer. Leaving the lettuce in the sink, I walked around the island and into the living room, wiping my wet hands on a kitchen towel. "Are you sure, Andrew?" I said. "Really and truly sure?"

"Uh-huh. I'm sure." He pushed his hands deep into the pockets of his jeans, looked at his feet and then back up at me, resigned, borderline desperate. "I have to, Mom. I've been thinking about it for a while, and I really want to do it. I can't take this anymore." His voice, pleading, dropped to a whisper. "You don't know what it's like. I can't take the pain. I have to get it done as soon as possible."

At that moment, my heart broke for him all over again, and I choked with emotion as memories flooded over me. *How did we ever get to this point?* I hugged him, wishing I could squeeze away the anger and frus-tration and hurt that threatened to consume us both.

All during the morning before this conversation took place, I had watched as the enormous billowing clouds deepened and spread, gray upon gray across the sky. I'd headed to the grocery store before the worst of it hit and pulled into the driveway just as the first fat splashes began pelting my windshield. Grabbing bags from the back seat, I dashed to the front door and leaned on the doorknob with my elbow until it popped open. Just inside the doorway, I set the bags on the hallway bench, then turned and stood on the threshold for a moment. Filling my lungs with that delicious rain-fresh smell, I surveyed the valley stretched out before me. Underneath the mountainous base of steel blue clouds, ragged edges of the impending thunderstorm streaked downward like a watercolor painting until nearly touching the ground. I shivered and pulled my sweater close before stepping back inside.

Our home is a hundred-year-old farmhouse that sits on a hill in the middle of orchards and farms. Okay, before you start imagining how lovely that sounds, let me clarify a few things. This house began its life in the 1800s as an apple barn. Sometime in the late 1880s an outhouse was added, and the barn became a bunk house for the farm help. The back shed became a chicken coop. A few years and several haphazard renovations later, a family moved in and called it home. If you're a hopeless romantic like me, born with the optimistic cup-is-half-full gene, and if the idea of restoring a fruit barn turned run-down cottage into a beautiful and livable home sounds adventuresome and dreamy, let me stop you now. You'll have to trust me on this—living in any structure that is over a hundred years old is not romantic. It's drafty, creaky and cold in the winter, and horribly hot in the summer. If there are any closets, they are teeny tiny, so boxes pile up in most corners because there's nowhere to put things. Don't even get me started on the plumbing and electrical. The insulation is pretty much nonexistent, and though I could go on, let's just say it is much more of a challenge than an enchantment. The simple fact that the house started out as a barn, well, that says it all right there.

I will say, however, that though it's old and rough around the edges, our house has a few positive points, and initially we fell hard for this old charmer. It's in the perfect location, outside of town but not too far out, sitting on a rise at the end of a country road. The apple orchard is long since gone, but we have five huge, hundred-year-old cottonwood trees flanking the west side of the house. My kitchen windows provide a prime vantage point to survey the whole town and surrounding area, and I've grown to appreciate that I have ample warning when a car is heading our direction. I like that the trains come in every day, whistling and dependable—we can set our clocks by them. It's beautiful out here and peaceful. One of my favorite things about living in the country is sitting on the front porch just after sunset listening to the night creatures chirp at one another, allowing myself to be captured by the vastness of the stars. Our sky feels so big and so full around me that some nights I feel as if I'm the one "sailing on a river of crystal light" like Wynken, Blynken and Nod.

From the beginning, I wanted to buy this house. Tom, being the practical one, was not easily persuaded, but I happen to have a soft spot for old castoffs, and Tom has a soft spot for me. I tend to collect treasures unwanted by others like gnarly old wood and creaky houses; I like old oak doors and farmhouse tables and windows with the sashes still working. I've discovered a particular kind of pleasure in the character and quirks of an old house, but I found out pretty quickly that a person must be blessed with an extra dose of gumption to be able to live comfortably in a fixer-upper. It's one thing after another, and you never know what's going to go wrong next. If my windows sense the tiniest change in humidity, they fog up. They also rattle in the wind and stick in the heat, and it doesn't take too much of this before I'm all about trading in quirky for something a little less so.

Twenty-some years ago, before Andrew was born, we lived in the city and my life perked along as comfortably and predictably as my great-grandma's coffee pot. After I graduated college, I met and married Tom, and we had our first son, David. I loved being a wife and mom and had every hope and intention (as new parents do) to raise our child(ren) to live happy and well-rounded lives; we'd focus on the whole child—physical, intellectual, emotional and spiritual. We'd invest in quality toys and experiences, and we'd eat healthy foods. And so, with endless optimism, when David turned a year old, I comprised a checklist of objectives—a plan— for what I believed would create a healthy child. I included specific ideas to reach those goals and boxes to check off. I wrote out a daily plan and set objectives for myself, too. Short term, long term, you name it; my philosophy was, write it down, get it on "the list" and make it happen. I thought this was normal. Doesn't everybody make a list of objectives for their one year old?

Spiritually, my faith—and Tom's, too—had seen ups and downs, but we felt that we had grown through the bumps; we believed we had matured and were ready to fit in and follow the Christian "rules." After all, it was important to put more focus on the spiritual aspect of our lives now that we were parents. I was comfortable with rules. With rules, things were settled; one knew what to do and what not to do.

Growing up, I'd learned my church lessons well. The church we attended taught that if we obeyed the guidelines (Bible), God would love us, and we'd receive His blessings (good stuff would happen). Tom and I were committed to following what we assumed were our normal Christian responsibilities. We joined a weekly Bible study, attended church regularly, had our kids baptized, made friends in the young couple's group and even started praying together at night. Truth was, underneath all the activity, I didn't understand why it mattered that we were doing these things. I grew more and more frustrated; the harder I tried to keep doing it right, the more out of control I felt. One night when we were praying together, Tom fell sound asleep right in the middle of my prayer. That sort of killed the whole praying together idea for me—I mean, he was snoring. I didn't completely give up, though; I kept trying to do it (whatever "it" was) right. So, I kept on consulting my list and following along with the rest of our friends. I wanted our little family to have all the fun and good times that I saw happening in the lives of other "normal" families.

However, in the days following Andrew's birth, my life—and our family—took a drastic turn away from anything we might have thought of as *normal*. We were forced to abandon many of the activities we'd been busy with, the routines we'd hoped for and any sense of an ordinary life. Every day I would find myself in situations where I needed faith to simply take the next step. We've been on a "road less traveled" ever since, and it's taken us in and out and up and down, over and into situations so far away from normal that they could be straight out of a movie. The bottom line? Andrew certainly has lived a spectacular life. Not spectacular in the sense that he is unusually spirited or compliant or extraordinarily gifted like a prodigy kind of spectacular. He's not spectacular in a razzle-dazzle, drawing attention to himself or a wow-wee, Cirque-du-Soleil kind of way. When I say spectacular, I mean it in the sense that every moment of Andrew's life has been completely and altogether unexpected. And, consequently, so has mine.

That stormy afternoon as I sat with Andrew, listening to him share the hows and whys of a possible leg amputation, I realized again that I have new opportunities to act on my faith each day. That day I did what I learned to do many years ago: take a step into the water, paddle as hard as I can, hold on tight and catch the wave. Sometimes I crash head first, but other times the ride is exhilarating. What has changed for me is that somewhere along this journey I stopped trying so hard to work it out according to other people's rules because those rules are as dynamic as the tides. I know now that the best thing is to keep my eyes focused on the only unchanging point in my landscape—God. I trust that God knows what He's doing, that He will keep Andrew in His hands and that I will not drown trying to keep up with him…I mean, Him. In God's hands, our lives become part of His story, one that's different, so much deeper and far more spectacular than we could have imagined on our own—of that I'm absolutely sure.

Two

You made all the delicate, inner parts of my body
and knit me together in my mother's womb.
Thank you for making me so wonderfully complex!
– Psalm 139:13-14a NLT

I love these little people; and it is not a slight thing when they,
who are so fresh from God, love us.
– Dickens, *The Old Curiosity Shop*

ANDREW'S BIRTH day began on a cold Colorado morning in the middle of a blizzard. None of us knew then about the miracle God was about to set in motion. The fact that this little guy decided to make his first brave appearance on New Year's Day, three weeks early and with more than a smidgen of difficulty, should have sent up at least a tiny red flag, but we were blissfully unaware. Even after we settled into a routine at home with our new baby boy, we never saw it coming; life played out for a little while as normal as could be.

We've always just been regular folks, nothing even remotely fancy or special. At that time, we lived in a tiny blue ranch-style house on Norfolk Street, smack-dab in the middle of the block. It could have been pretty much Anywhere, USA. We were twenty-somethings, just beginning our careers as well as our own family. We thought our lives were on the right track, moving forward toward our goals. Then, right in the middle of our regular life, everything came to a startling halt.

We all experience those defining moments—an event that changes our perspective and becomes pivotal to the rest of our life. We didn't know it, but we were on the cusp of one of those moments. Like a Broadway show playing out in my mind, it's easy to step back into the memory of that night. It could have been yesterday, I remember it so clearly. We'd gone out during a snowstorm to celebrate New Year's Eve with friends.

"Mmmm...I can smell Chinese all the way out here," I remarked, as Steve opened the door to their apartment.

"Come in, come in," he invited with a smile. And then, turning to Tom, "You're just in time for the kickoff." Tom and I stood squished together on the entry tile next to the front door as we peeled off our coats, hats and gloves and hung them on the wall hooks so the melting snow would drip harmlessly onto the linoleum.

"Come here, honey," I said, bending down to David's level. He turned around like a stiff little snowman, cheeks icy and cherry red. I unzipped his coat and took off his hat and mittens. "You're going to have to help him with his boots," I said to Tom, moaning as I grabbed my lower back and stood upright again. "I can't bend over that far any-more." Distracted by the football game, Tom moved in to take over as I went to find my friend. Walking around the corner into the kitchen, I said dramatically, "I'm star-ving, Barb," as if I hadn't eaten in days.

"Oh, you," she teased, "you're always hungry. That's nothing new. Here you go," she said, handing me a plate as she unloaded the dish-washer. "Help yourself. I'm almost done here."

"No, no, that's okay," I waved away the plate. Pointing to the boxes of food, I said, "I'll just eat it like this."

"Oh, you will, will you?" She began to laugh.

"Mm-hhmmm, yes, I believe I will. Fewer dishes to worry about, you know," I drawled in my fake Southern accent and grinned back as I perused the variety of takeout boxes, looking for the Sesame Chicken? Barb knew it was my usual. Finally, I spotted it—with SesChic scribbled across the side in black grease pencil. I picked a fork out of the drawer, scooped some sticky rice into the box, and sat down at the kitchen table.

"You're sure?" she asked, holding out the plate again.

I nodded, my mouth already full of rice and sweet, spicy chicken. "How can this possibly taste so incredible? I think I'm in Chinese heaven," I said.

Laughing at my antics, Barb closed the dishwasher and turned to the table. "Okay, okay then. I'll join you." She grabbed chopsticks and another box of Chinese deliciousness and lowered herself carefully into the chair across from me. "Ugh," she moaned, "I feel enormous." Barb, pregnant with twins, was due in about three months.

"That makes two of us." I had only one baby on board, but I was due in just two weeks.

Barb broke her chopsticks apart and began rubbing them together. "How was your day?" she asked. "Here, want some chopsticks?"

"No, thanks. This works for me," I grinned. "I'll stick with my trusty fork. Chopsticks can be rather unpredictable, you know." I took another bite. I was famished, and I didn't have the patience tonight to mess with chopsticks. Oh, I'd tried on numerous occasions to make them work, and I could—sort of—if I really tried. But I'm the type that wants to be pretty confident about what I'm doing, and I like knowing the food is actually going to make it to my mouth. Safe. Easily controlled. I had absolutely nothing against the Asian culture or whoever invented chopsticks, they just didn't happen to be my cup of…oolong.

I prefer what's predictable. If there's any way possible, I want to know who, what, when, where, why and how ahead of time. I like to operate with well thought-out and, if possible, written instructions. Without my planner close at hand, I'm lost. I do not like to be unprepared or caught off guard.

As a little girl, I wanted to be invisible. I figured that by being invisible, I could learn what was safe and what wasn't, and I'd be less likely to make a mistake or get in trouble. I have always been shy and quiet, and it wasn't unusual to find me hiding in my closet reading books. I grew up liking predictable because you know the rules. And if you know the rules, you can follow the rules, and it's possible to make sure you never get in over your head. Even as a child, I'd make lists of things to do, and then figure out a plan—and those tendencies followed me right into my adult life.

That evening as we celebrated the beginning of a brand-new year, I had no idea how much my predictable little world was about to change or that I was already in way over my head without a clue. It's probably good I didn't know. I enjoyed that New Year's Eve without a hint of worry. Even if our husbands were completely into the football games, Barb and I were determined to celebrate New Year's with all the gusto that two very pregnant women could muster. So we ate our Chinese takeout and watched the New Year's Eve Special on TV (alternating with football, of course). David had long since fallen asleep, firmly clutching his yellow blankey and teddy bear, Bob. Barb and I played a game of Rummy and watched the time tick slowly by.

All along we'd been adamant about staying up to watch the ball drop in Times Square. After all, it's a "tradition," and I was all about keeping traditions. Pregnancy does funny things to you, however. By ten o'clock, I could hardly keep my eyes open, and the Chinese food wasn't settling quite right. I wanted to go home and get in bed. I was willing to forget the plans we'd made because I'd expended all the energy I had. Promising each other we'd do the New Year right next year, Tom packed up our gear, bundled our sleepy toddler and drove us home where I immediately collapsed into bed.

An hour or so later, I awoke with a very odd and yet oh-so-familiar gripping sensation wrapping its way around my belly. *Oh, no. Oh, no, no, no. This can't be happening now. It's not time yet. But, oh, yes, it most certainly is happening now.* I began to panic. "Ummm, Tom? Are you asleep?"

He jumped out of bed when I told him it was time.

"I don't have a bag packed," I said. "This isn't supposed to happen tonight."

"Well, just throw some things in a bag,"

"I can't! I don't have my list of what to bring."

"Oh, for crying out loud, this isn't a beauty contest! Just grab some clothes, Cathy," he commanded. "It's no big deal. I'll bring whatever else you need tomorrow." He called my mom to come over and stay with David while I grabbed a few things, and we headed to the hospital a little after 1:00 a.m. We checked in, got situated in a room and waited.

Time passed slowly as the straps around my gigantic mid-section measured every heartbeat and the contractions, which were five minutes apart. Then, they became more intense and came at three-minute intervals. Then…nothing. My labor came to an abrupt halt. Tom and I had a deck of cards, so we whiled away the next few hours playing Casino, waiting for labor to start again. More cards and more waiting. Tom kept winning, and I felt like throwing the cards at him—I was just completely frustrated. We walked around the labor and delivery wing of the hospital. I tried sleeping. I tried sucking ice chips.

Clearly, things were not progressing the way I had imagined. This was my body, and I wanted to be in control. I had already worked it out and had a plan in place. But I hadn't anticipated delivering this baby early, and I was feeling a bit panicky. Our little nursery wasn't ready, and

I'd been wanting to make a tape of music to play during the delivery. All the latest experts suggested that moms in labor play soothing music during contractions to guarantee a smooth-flowing, low-stress, natural delivery. I had been excited to make a tape of my own favorites. This scenario was stretching me way out of my comfort zone. I didn't know what would happen next, and I didn't enjoy the feeling of free falling in unfamiliar territory.

Beep-beep-beep-beep... the machines jolted me out of light doze. Almost instantly the room filled with nurses and doctors, bustling around my bed, adjusting the monitor straps, watching the readouts and talking amongst themselves. The little heartbeats on the baby monitor had suddenly slowed, and a quick consensus of obstetrical specialists took the situation right out of my hands. It was decided that this baby needed to be born. Now.

So, there it was. Another Cesarean was coming my way. I sighed, completely aware of the irony. I'd been through a C-section before. I knew exactly what to expect. I hadn't planned it and didn't want to do it, but at least I knew what to expect! *God, You have such a sense of humor!* I took a deep breath, said a quick prayer and found myself in the operating room almost before I knew the decision had been made. *Time to do this,* I thought, scared but excited to be just minutes away from meeting our new baby.

You can imagine how carefully I had studied the meanings of names, poring through the latest baby name books. The naming of another person is an important responsibility. Like most parents-to-be, Tom and I talked through a million possibilities and had finally decided on a boy's name and a girl's name. But, after months of certainty about the name, something very odd happened on the way to the hospital—I felt an overwhelming conviction that if this baby was a boy, his name should be Andrew. That was not the name we had decided on, but I was sure of it. I asked Tom what he thought, and he liked it. What's strange is that it's not at all like me be so impulsive. I'm not one to change my mind about a decision like that on a whim. Some people won't understand why it's so unusual, but I know myself, and I believe it was God who put that thought in my heart. I believe He already knew Andrew, and He chose his name before he was even born. In Psalm 139:13, the Bible says that God knows us before we are born and that He "knit us together in our mother's womb." God was making sure that I knew that He was—and is—a Mighty God.

I truly believe God cares about names. Many times in the Bible, God is involved in a name change or the giving of a new name. He *knows* our names and will give us a new name in heaven (Revelation 2:17). He has written our name in the palm of His hand (Isaiah 49:16). When the angel appeared to a pregnant Mary, he told her to name her son Jesus (Luke 1:31). God didn't just leave it up to the innkeeper or the shepherds or even to Mary or Joseph to choose a name. God didn't open the Book of Heavenly Names and randomly plop down His finger. The name *Jesus* existed before the beginning of time and was part of a family lineage that was set in place long before Jesus was born on this earth.

I believe that God named Andrew on purpose. I could never have done research on the meaning of the name *Andrew* in between contractions on the way to the hospital just to make sure I agreed with God's choice. I went with my gut. Later, I discovered the name *Andrew* means *strong, courageous, manly* and *warrior*. God already had intimate knowledge of Andrew's life, and His plans will not be thwarted. He is, after all, the Author of Life. It only makes sense that He would have chosen that particular name for our little boy.

Draped and drugged, I was more than ready to meet this baby. My sister-in-law, Jeanne, came with a video camera in hand. We tried to act calm but were completely giddy as we eagerly anticipated the first glimpse of our new little one. Lying on the operating table, I felt like an unopened Christmas present. I was now surrounded and covered by sterile blue drapes, except for a small square of exposed belly. Tom kept me updated on what the doctor was doing while I chitchatted with Jeanne and the video camera, and we all awaited that beautiful little squall, the cry of life. After the incision had been made, I felt intense pressure on my abdomen—as if someone had decided to knead a loaf of bread dough on my belly right then and there. I heard my obstetrician saying, "Suction, ok, clamp, now here…" Over the sound of the surgical instruments, I heard the doctor say, "Pretty little head," and then…"It's a boy!"

Jeanne, through her tears, captured the moment Andrew was born on film since I couldn't see over the drapes. Excitedly she said, "Oh, it's Andrew! Oh, Cathy, he's so cute, he's got dark hair." And she and Tom began exclaiming about his adorable ears and nose and how much he looked like David. Tom cut the cord; the doctor held him up for me to see over the curtains of surgical drapes, and then they whisked him to the bassinette behind me. Everything happened so fast and, after all these months of waiting, I was disappointed that I hardly even got to see him.

I kept waiting for that unmistakable newborn cry but heard nothing. People were still talking around me, but it all became a verbal blur. My mother's radar tuned in to catch that first little wail. I turned to Tom. "Why isn't he crying? Is he okay?" I waited. "What's happening?" I tried to crane my neck around to see him, but they were working directly behind me. The nurse dried Andrew while the pediatrician worked to clear his lungs. Tom took pictures and then came back over to my side. "They're suctioning his nose and mouth with one of those blue bulbs. He's getting oxygen, too."

Oh, okay. Hmm…what? He's getting oxygen? Why would he need oxygen? Prior to that very moment, it had not occurred to me that anything might be wrong. I simply hadn't considered that possibility. David had been fine, a perfect baby; I had assumed this baby would be healthy, too. Incredibly presumptuous on my part, I know. So naive. But since the possibility that he might not be fine had now surfaced, my mind started whirling with questions. *He will be okay, right? Still no cry. Is he okay? He's probably just getting a bit of a slow start breathing. Well, that's not that abnormal, is it?*

"Tom? Is he breathing?" Jeanne, still videotaping, asked me how I felt; I smiled and chatted it up for the camera, but now, with all the questions bouncing around in my head, an unsettling nervousness crept in. I remember feeling nauseous, worried because no one was saying anything about the baby.

We all had expected to hear a lusty, life-proving, lung-filling wail, but the operating room suddenly became very quiet. I couldn't see a thing lying flat on my back under the blinding lights. Paralyzed from the waist down and frustrated from the waist up, I wished for eyes in the top of my head. *Can't we just get this surgery over with, so I can hold my baby and go to sleep?* I wondered. I had no idea what was playing out on the table behind me. I could hear vague murmurings as the doctor and nurses worked on Andrew. I wanted to scream for someone to please tell me what was going on. Only later, watching the video play back, did I get to see what really happened—how that tiny baby struggled to breathe, all the while receiving oxygen, his little chest heaving up and down, his skin a not-quite-pink color.

Then I heard it, a quiet little *waaa,* and then again a little louder. A pause and then a real baby wail. I grinned underneath my oxygen mask. The whole room cheered, and everyone started talking at once. My obstetrician, still hovering over me, laughed and said, "Well, *there* he is." The pediatrician working on Andrew added dryly, "It looks like he's getting a little more excited about being here all the time."

I breathed in pure joy.

Wrapped in soft, muslin-colored flannel and a tiny knit hat, the now calm and swaddled bundle was handed to a very proud papa by the nurse. Tom grinned behind his surgical mask as cameras flashed. He was such a proud daddy with his brand-new son. He walked over to the operating table and held Andrew down next to me so I could see him. "Oh, Andrew! Oh, baby!" That overwhelming mother love filled me to the brim. I wanted to hold him close, but my arms were strapped down. I looked at his beautiful little scrunched-up face and talked to him, cheek to cheek. The doctor unstrapped one of my arms, and I touched Andrew's soft chin. He still had some white waxy-like vernix in the wrinkles of his skin, on his tiny hands and fingernails and around his little ears. His hair was wet, dark and curly. I inhaled deeply, filling myself completely with the intoxicating smell of a newborn. I never wanted to let go of that moment.

The pediatrician, standing behind me, watched Andrew carefully. "I think maybe we need to get him to the nursery to be examined. He's getting a little dusky."

Dusky? What? Did he say dusty or dusky? I wasn't familiar with that word. What exactly was dusky? Was that his coloring, or did it mean he was getting cold? I did notice he wasn't as pink as David had been, but I figured he must still be in the normal range. After all he'd just been through, who wouldn't look a little ragged around the edges? Whatever the doctor meant, I thought Andrew looked fine. I wanted to remember this fresh newness forever—my baby, perfect and beautiful, content just to be next to me.

Before I could say anything, the doctor took him from Tom and said, "We'd better get him down there so they can check him over." And just like that, they were gone with my baby again. Too groggy to read between the lines on that one, I asked Tom to follow along to take pictures and mental notes so he could report back with every delightful detail. Then, feeling the dragging, exhausted lethargy that comes post-surgery, I let myself drift in and out of la-la-land as my doctor finished all the details. He sewed me up with a nice, neat row of stitches identical to the ones he had made barely two years earlier.

In recovery, I tried to fight the nausea and headache, but I still wasn't feeling very perky when Tom came back with glowing reports of Andrew's length and weight and near perfect Apgar scores. I nodded. Good. We'd be heading home the next day with our second healthy baby. The doctors had given him a thumbs up, mentioning only that he had a slight heart murmur, as many newborns do. They said it's just part of being born at a higher altitude and goes away as the baby grows. Tom and I were both as thrilled as we could be.

We left the hospital the next day, arms full of balloons, flowers and a beautiful baby boy. Being home with the two boys turned out to be more challenging than I had anticipated. Tom took two days off to help, which I appreciated immensely. I knew that "Stiff" and "Sore" would be *my* faithful companions during the next few weeks of recovery, but I looked forward to slowly getting back to a comfortable norm with my boys.

Smitten with his new baby brother, David loved holding Andrew and helping me with him. He shared his toys, "read" him stories and helped me give him baths in the plastic baby bathtub. Like any baby, Andrew had his fussy times, but he loved snuggling up in the baby carrier. His two-week checkup showed nothing unusual. The doctor commented on how extremely responsive he seemed and ended our visit with, "He's doing just great!"

Winter days flew by, and we found ourselves in February, the usual baby and toddler routines keeping us busy. Andrew's personality was delightful; he loved us, and we loved him right back. He interacted with everyone and watched us as we walked around the room, babbling and cooing for attention.

With his dark, curly hair and deep-set eyes, a flawless complexion and a tiny dimple on his chin, he was the prototype for Adorable. Smiles and laughter came early and easily for Andrew, spreading baby joy to everyone around like frosting on a cake. For seven wonderful weeks, we enjoyed being a new family of four—two little boys and a mama and daddy who cherished them to the moon and back.

Three

Just as you cannot understand the path of the wind or the mystery of a tiny baby growing in its mother's womb, so you cannot understand the activity of God, who does all things.
– Ecclesiastes 11:5 NLT

A person who lives in faith must proceed on incomplete evidence, trusting in advance what will only make sense in reverse.
– Philip Yancey, *Reaching for the Invisible God*

S EVEN WEEKS into his brand-new life, Andrew got sick with a stuffy nose. Normally it wouldn't have been a big deal, but several days later he wasn't getting any better. I pulled out my trusty *Baby Medical Encyclopedia*, flipping to the section about upper respiratory infections and followed the protocol exactly. We did everything we were supposed to. As each day passed, though, he seemed a little bit sicker, more uncomfortable and fussier. In addition to struggling with a plugged-up nose, he now had a cough. Still, I didn't want to be one of those overly worried, ultra-protective kind of parents. After all, I'd been through this before—I'd experienced kids with colds. Plus, even I could tell it wasn't much of a cough. David had had plenty of coughs and colds—it comes with the territory.

By Friday of that week, Andrew's fussiness had not let up. He was agitated and uncomfortable in a different, persistent kind of way. I carried him around all morning and into the afternoon, snuggled close against me. I tried nursing him, changing him, laying him down and shifting his position. I checked his body for any sign of a bug bite or rash. Every hour I checked his temperature. I sang to him, talked to him…I tried everything to ease his discomfort, but nothing seemed to soothe this little one. By late afternoon I had exhausted my reserves. *Why is he so inconsolable?* He slept fitfully and kept waking himself up with that nagging cough. I wondered if I should take him to the doctor but, still not wanting to overreact, decided to wait and keep my eye on him. I finished a few chores around the house while arguing back and forth with myself about what to do. *After all, babies get sick,* I reasoned, *just like the rest of us. No need to panic. Taking him out in this snowstorm would probably make it worse even if I could get a doctor appointment at this late hour. All the same, he is only seven weeks old. Why don't kids come with their own "How-To" manual?*

Picking up the phone, I called my friend, Cheryl. "I'm so sorry, Cheryl, but I think we have to reschedule getting together for dinner tonight because Andrew is just too sick," I said. "He's been fussy and coughing, and I think he's got a slight fever."

"Oh, I'm so sorry," she sympathized. "I hope it's not serious."

"I don't think there's anything to worry about, but we'd better just stay home tonight." I tried to sound calm and reassuring as much for my own sake as for hers.

"That's okay," she said. "No problem at all. We'll reschedule when we're all feeling better, and it isn't so cold and snowy."

I glanced outside to see big, fat flakes still falling from the sky. Thank goodness for understanding friends—she had little ones too, so she knew about needing to be flexible.

Next, I called Tom. "Could you pick up pizza on your way home?" I asked. "Andrew seems pretty sick. He's been fussy all afternoon, and

I haven't had any time to think about dinner." I took a deep breath and settled in for what I figured would be a long night.

By 8:30 that evening, both Tom and I were struggling to keep Andrew calm, and I thought he might be getting worse. At the time it was hard to tell. Looking back, it seems like we should have known what to do—like it should have been obvious. But it wasn't. When we were in the middle of it, we couldn't see a direct answer. We just kept asking ourselves questions. Should we be alarmed, or should we hang tight and get through it? Were we overreacting? And why, oh why, do these things always happen on Friday nights? He was still so tiny we had no idea what medicines we could give him, or how much to give an infant his size.

This "sick baby thing" was clearly not something we were used to. Fear and frustration enveloped me, making my voice sound shaky and tight like someone else was talking. "I don't know what to do," I said, looking at Tom. "He's been like this all day."

"Me, either," he said, taking his turn with Andrew, walking and rocking and trying to soothe.

Cold pizza sat on the counter, hardly even touched. David whined as he followed us around because bedtime had long since passed with neither of us thinking about putting him to bed. Finally, we decided to bundle Andrew up and take him to the emergency room. *So what if we're overreacting? Better to be safe.* I called my sister who came right over to stay with David, and then we scraped the snow and ice from the windshield and piled in the car. By ten o'clock, we were standing bravely in a busy ER, baby in arms, like two cold pilgrims having just landed in the New World.

༄

A nurse ushered us into one of the examining rooms, and I laid Andrew on the raised bed; then two more nurses stepped in, and suddenly

I was on the sidelines watching as they began undressing my baby, taking his temperature, listening to his tiny heartbeats and looking into even tinier ear canals. One of the ER doctors walked in and introduced himself. He began to check Andrew's ears and listened again to his heart and lungs. Our little peanut was almost lost under the doctor's hands. Tom and I huddled in the corner waiting for someone to say something, not having a clue what to do.

It seemed like forever before the doctor turned to us to say, "Well, your little guy is pretty sick. It looks like he has pneumonia and double ear infections."

My stomach tightened and then did a double flip. *You're kidding,* I thought, but I knew better. "Double ear infections?" I managed to squeak out.

The doctor continued, nodding, "He has a fever and, in a baby this young…did you say he's seven weeks?" He looked over his glasses at the chart.

"Yes," I said, nodding and fighting back tears.

"We need to be sure that he doesn't have meningitis. I think we should do a spinal tap so that we can check the cerebrospinal fluid around his brain and spine."

"What?" I had no idea what he had just said, what it meant, or why things suddenly sounded so serious.

"A spinal tap is the best way to determine if there is an infection like meningitis. But it isn't without risk. We need both your signatures before we can proceed." The nurse offered us a clipboard with the forms.

I looked at Tom. Had we just been transported to an alien planet? We were totally unprepared for all these medical words—I mean, we're about as ordinary as two hats on a rack. We are runny nose and tummy ache kind of folks. We do Tylenol and Tums. The words *meningitis* and *cerebrospinal fluid* were terms you heard on the Discovery Health Channel, not spoken directly to you in a sentence concerning your baby.

As naïve as we were about medical things, we could sense the urgency in the doctor's voice. We hadn't realized this could be a life-and-death situation for Andrew, as tiny as he was, but we gave our permission for the spinal tap and stood shaking in our shoes as they prepared him for the procedure.

Finding a vein for an IV proved to be nearly impossible. The nurses tried everywhere on his little body, with poor Andrew having to endure one needle poke after another. That, in addition to his ear infections and gasping-for-air-pneumonia, added insult to injury. He ended up having little bruises all over his body from their attempts. They finally put the IV into a vein in his head. I was horrified. I'd never even heard of that. He looked like a funny old man with a top hat made of gauze and tape with a little plastic medicine cup upside down on top to protect it from getting bumped. Although it looked comical, this IV would be his lifeline, feeding him the lifesaving antibiotics and fluids he desperately needed, so I tried to think of it as a good thing as I held him close and comforted him.

The actual spinal tap was another story—they wouldn't allow us to watch or hold him, and that was the hardest part. We handed Andrew to the doctor who admonished us not to worry, and then he and a whole convoy of medical staff took Andrew into a room across the hall. Within a couple of minutes, we heard Andrew screaming behind the closed door. "Oh, God," I breathed, "What are they doing?"

"He'll be okay," Tom whispered. It was excruciating to hear my baby screaming and not be able to do anything. We didn't know whether to stand up or sit down, to walk around or stare out the window into the darkness. No matter what we did, though, it seemed wrong. I kept shivering, and Tom kept trying to put his arm around me, and I alternated between wanting him to touch me and not wanting to be touched. I was restless and couldn't stay still. We were both incredibly tired since it was well past midnight. I looked out the window as the snow fell and blew, drifting and making its quiet bed in the glow of the streetlights. I wanted to lie down in that soft, quiet snow and sleep.

Finally, they brought Andrew back to us, whimpering, trying to cry, but too exhausted to make much of an effort. I decided right then that he would not be leaving my arms again that night—as if I had any control. In my heart, I prayed and pleaded with God. *Help us, help Andrew not be sick. Please, God.*

One of the scariest parts about the traumatic experiences we go through is that they can seem so random. One day we're ecstatic and celebrating over the best possible news, and the next day we're handed a pink slip that completely devastates. One day your child is perfectly fine, and the next he's hooked up to an IV in the hospital. Sometimes it feels like God might be sitting on His throne, squashing one ant, leaving the next one alone, squashing the next, leaving two or three. How does He decide or allow or choose or…or why does He? I know that believing in God doesn't guarantee someone a better life—a Christian is not any less likely to be crushed by the blows of life than anyone else. So why believe at all? Is prayer real, or is it just a ritual we go through to make ourselves feel better?

I wanted answers I didn't have. All I knew was what I experienced day to day. It does seem like there is a universal tendency when faced with life and death, to cling to hope that a loving God is out there somewhere, hearing our heart's cry. It is normal and natural for people to turn to God in the midst of a crisis. Even those who have never prayed before drop to their knees. It's as if we all have some inborn knowledge that God is. But later, when we step back from the immediate trauma and battle it out with our brain, we wonder if our prayers have made any difference? Is God real? We sit and wait for life to work out our way. If it doesn't, we blame God and turn our backs on Him. I've done this—I'm guilty of it all. But I keep coming back to Him, and I want to understand. It seems like God has been okay with my insecurities and doubts because He hasn't left my side.

I have questions for God to which I may never get answers. Why does one baby die from meningitis while another survives? Why does life not seem fair? Why do children suffer? It seems like I have to be okay with not knowing the hows and whys because I'm not the one in charge. I know I'm not able to understand all that God does, and He doesn't expect me to. I just need to believe. Believing without seeing the proof and trusting God even when I don't know or understand—that's called faith.

Prayer is hard to understand. I think of it as a conversation between God and me. Sometimes it feels like I am talking to myself…like there isn't a God who hears me and cares. Sometimes I wonder if I've gone a little loopy. But most of the time I feel His presence inside me. I want to quiet my inside self and spend the time it takes to really know Him, and so I pray. I don't pray through a list as if He's a heavenly Santa Claus. Instead, I talk to Him about what comes to my mind. I usually start with thinking about who He is and focusing on Scripture that acknowledges His attributes. I talk to Him about what matters to me, how I'm feeling and what is happening in my life—as if I am talking to a friend. But, I confess, I can get so distracted, it's embarrassing. Using a prayer journal helps me stay focused. Sometimes I doodle or draw or write my thoughts as I pray. I don't think about prayer as something that worked or didn't work. I know He hears me, and if He chooses to act, I am delighted and grateful. I cannot allow circumstances to determine my belief in God, and neither should the results of my prayers—answered or unanswered.

In the Bible, we are instructed to pray. God isn't bound by time as we are, and I believe that His answers to our prayers might be on a timeline that is beyond our understanding. We pray and then we trust that He hears us and will take care of our worries in the perfect way at the perfect time. I know He answers prayer because I have experienced it myself. I've seen my own heart change course, and I've seen God intervene and transform a situation in a miraculous way. But there have also been times when I've prayed for something desperately, and He didn't answer my prayer—at least, not the way I wanted. Pacing the hospital hallway that night with Andrew in my arms, I wondered if God was listening and if He would answer our prayers for Andrew.

Finally, the results came back from the spinal tap—negative for meningitis. We were so relieved. Bowing our heads, holding Andrew in my arms, we took a quiet moment to pray. Thank you, Lord. Oh, thank you! I felt so happy I wanted to sing, but the tune got caught tight in my throat and came out in tears instead.

The doctor admitted Andrew to the hospital that night with all kinds of IVs and a plastic oxygen tent that covered the bed like a mosquito net. We pulled one of those big vinyl recliner chairs into the room so I could sit next to him. Along with two IVs, he now had a nasal oxygen cannula and an oxygen saturation monitor—and I was learning all kinds of new vocabulary words. The nurses called him the "darling of the unit"—he was smothered in coos and coddles. He improved a little bit each day, but our pediatrician mentioned that a pediatric cardiologist from Children's Hospital would check Andrew to make sure everything was fine. I nodded and said that sounded like a good idea. I knew the doctors would want to cover their bases, so this seemed pretty routine to me, which is why when the pediatric cardiologist from Children's stopped in and introduced himself on Tuesday afternoon, I wasn't the least bit concerned. I was delighted to show off my new baby boy and looked forward to seeing whatever an echocardiogram was. It sounded interesting.

The portable echocardiogram machine rolled into Andrew's room with so much presence it may as well have had its own beating heart. I'd never seen one before, and it looked to me like a taller version of the movie character R2-D2, the little robot-droid with blinking lights and noises. I'd never seen an echo performed on a heart and was fascinated by the pictures and sounds as the cardiologist moved the wand across Andrew's goopy chest. It produced static that sounded kind of like a waterfall with rhythm. The fuzzy pictures of his throbbing heart went in and out of focus on the screen and, try as I might, I could not make out anything that resembled parts of a heart.

The cardiologist calmly explained it all as he went along as if I was supposed to understand what he was saying. He pointed out the details of what he was seeing, but I still couldn't tell what was what. He started his explanations with, "Okay, and here we have the right atria. Now when I move over here, you can see the..." and his words all just faded into a distant blah blah blah. *Really? O-K.* I could see on the monitor that something was beating, but everything else appeared as if we were looking through a gray kaleidoscope. I felt really stupid, and I wasn't sure if it was just me, or if other parents had trouble figuring out this stuff, too.

Even if I *could* have identified the particular parts of the heart, I didn't understand the details of how a heart worked. I knew the basics. It's a muscle that pumps blood through four chambers, then to the lungs for oxygen, and then to the body...sixth-grade anatomy stuff. But that was it. Since I had no idea what the doctor was seeing or talking about on the ultrasound monitor, I just kept nodding and smiling. I figured sooner or later he'd say everything looked fine and that Andrew was doing great considering his infections. But this doctor took his time.

Sometime during that cardiological photo op, Tom arrived from work and stood next to me, quietly watching. I could tell he didn't understand the wiggly gray pictures either, and that made me feel a little better.

The doctor finished the echo and, wiping the sticky goop off Andrew's perfect little chest, he was quiet. I smiled as I waited for him to wrap up the exam with some final comments, but instead, he casually suggested we walk next door to the children's playroom to talk about the results. *Hmmm. Okay, maybe these doctors want to make sure we're aware of good heart health and that kind of thing.* Nine steps. It was nine steps from Andrew's hospital bed to the playroom next door. I had no idea that the direction of our entire lives was about to change with those nine steps.

Nothing can really prepare you for the moment you get devastating news. It's like someone changes the channel, and you suddenly find yourself on a different planet. Everything looks and feels and tastes different. It's like having the wind knocked out of you when you're not even playing the game. Right next door to Andrew's room, the hospital playroom had only one place to sit down—a short round table with four kid-sized chairs. So that's where we sat. Like giants perching on miniature furniture, we bumped our knees awkwardly on the table's edge. The doctor took out two pieces of paper and began to draw a heart on one.

"Do either of you know how a heart works?" he asked as he drew. I knew right then that my own heart was pounding, but did I know exactly how it worked? At that point, I couldn't have told you how a hammer and nail worked. We shook our heads side to side in unison. "This is a normal heart," he said, proceeding with Anatomy 101 for parents who don't also happen to be cardiologists. Then he took the other sheet of paper and began to draw. "This is Andrew's heart." He paused and waited for us to breathe…and comprehend.

I'm thinking. Think, think, think. I'm really trying to think, but, like Winnie-the-Pooh, there seems to be a bit of fluff in my ears. It's hard to process what this man is saying.

The doctor continued, "You can see that Andrew doesn't have a pulmonary artery, here. And he is missing the valve, here." He pointed to each part in his drawing with his black felt tip pen, and then he looked at us. "There should be a wall to separate the ventricles, right here." Trying to be gentle, trying to explain so we could grasp the meaning, he talked with extra pauses. "Andrew has a rare and serious congenital heart defect called Truncus Arteriosus." Then he started going on about the different types of Truncus defects, Type 1 and Type 2 and…

Suddenly, it was more than I could take. I heard bits and pieces, but my brain stopped taking it in. I became hyper-focused on the doctor's hands as he pointed with the pen—his fingernails, trimmed short and neat, his gold wedding band, his grip on the pen. The picture and his words started to blur and slur, and my head was fuzzy, and I wasn't quite sure but I thought he might have said that Andrew's heart defect…very serious…life-threatening…would require open-heart surgery…and, if he *did* survive…*A heart defect? Wait a minute. What? No. No, no, no.* My Andrew was perfect—ten little fingers and toes, little button nose, little ears innocent of the scary words that I was now hearing like "anomaly." A funny kind of mistiness pooled around me, denial and confusion taking over. *I think I am in the wrong room. That doctor is wrong. He must have read the results wrong. He's talking about a different baby. I'm sure there is a mistake.* My stomach churned, my mind suddenly short-circuited and my legs wanted to take me somewhere else—away from that table and that doctor and those words. I didn't *want* to understand. *Let's go back about five minutes, could we, and start over. Don't say it. Please, please don't say those words that will change our lives forever. Because I don't think I can take it.*

As if in a faraway dream and unable to see my way through the foggy landscape, I wanted to escape. It was more than my brain could take in. I interrupted the doctor mid-sentence, "I…I think I might hear Andrew crying. I, um…I'm going to go check on him." I stood up and started walking toward the door, leaving Tom sitting there wide-eyed, trying to focus and talk at the same time.

I just got up and walked out. I didn't know and didn't care what the doctor thought. I had to get out of that room. Normally I consider myself to be fairly strong emotionally; it's not like me to go careening off the edge. But when I stood to leave that playroom, I felt incredibly helpless and weak. The little blue table legs and the doctor's black slacks and his shoes, the pen and the paper and the little red chairs suddenly grew and grew in my mind until they loomed huge above me. Like Alice in Wonderland, I grew backward until I felt very small and was shrinking even smaller, lost and frightened in the nightmare. Was I dreaming? I could only hope.

I walked stiffly toward Andrew's room, around the corner to the left with the door wide open, and the silver doorknob far above my Alice-in-Wonderland reach. I wanted to go in to him, close and lock the door and protect him. But then I noticed to my right the long, sterile hallway that led out of this black hole, out and away from all the excruciating horribleness. It crossed my mind that I could turn and walk out. I could leave right now and pretend this wasn't happening. It didn't make sense. Some stranger had just informed me that my baby might not live? Might not survive? How could he say that? How could this be?

In the space of about a nanosecond, my mind raced around and around in confusion and even anger. *Okay, wait a second. Whoa, whoa, whoa. Just hold your horses, and let's get this story straight. I was the one that carried him for nine months. I did everything I could to ensure that he was a healthy baby. In fact, I was over-the-top diligent. I gave up my* morning coffee and never touched a glass of wine, drugs or medicines the whole time I was pregnant. I exercised and ate a garden full of salad and took my vitamins faithfully. How could this happen? I started thinking about my neighbor across the street, who I knew enjoyed a drink or two pretty regularly, smoked and who knew what else. I doubted she'd ever had a prenatal vitamin. Yet she'd had a beautiful baby who was absolutely perfect. Not a thing wrong with him. I'm not saying I want her baby to be sick, but what's the matter with this picture? It's not fair. Why didn't the doctors catch this supposed heart defect when Andrew was born or at his first check-up? I felt betrayed by my own ignorance and naiveté and by the doctors who I thought should have known better. And even by God.

So, okay, I reasoned, this is probably just a simple mistake. Has to be. The machine must be out of whack. I don't know anything about heart stuff, and I don't really want to know. Someone else can do this. Not me. Not my baby, thank you very much. I want out. There was a moment when I really wanted to walk down that hall and right out the door. Just leave. I actually wanted to. It was going to be too painful. I wanted to disassociate myself from the doctor, from this hospital, from Andrew and the whole situation. For a second I thought it would have been so much easier.

Then I was shocked and angered by my thoughts. Had I really just thought that? How could I have even considered leaving? Everything in me wanted this diagnosis not to be true. I felt like screaming it away. But I couldn't ignore the part about this being my baby and how he needed me now more than ever. I couldn't leave—that motherly instinct kicked in, and I knew I couldn't turn away. Andrew would not travel this road alone. No matter what happens, I thought, I will stay by his side. Shaking inside from anger, hurt and fear, I realized there was no other option for me.

So, I stepped into Andrew's room and felt my grip on reality beginning to return. He looked so tiny and sweet lying under that plastic oxygen tent. I had to step forward into the pain. I cried for him and for me and for the dreams that were never going to be. I cried for what he was going to suffer through in his life. I cried because I didn't know what was going to happen, and I was scared. Then I settled down, wiped my tears and picked him up. He was still the same baby I knew and loved…the very same one I had given birth to seven weeks ago. He hadn't changed, and this wasn't his fault—I was the one who had changed. In the course of the last five minutes, my entire world had flipped upside down.

For a few days after that, my inner pendulum swung all the way back in the other direction. I fiercely took up my battle shield for him. Now I was fighting mad. I wanted to feel and experience this heartache as intensely as he did. I wanted it to hurt me like it was hurting him. I didn't even know where to begin with all my questions. I was grasping for God in the dark, my eyes tightly closed, afraid that I might not be able to see Him, and then afraid that I might see Him and be paralyzed in fear.

Four

O our God…we are powerless against this great multitude which is coming against us. We do not know what to do, but our eyes are on You.
– II Chronicles 20:12 AMP

Sometimes our circumstances reduce us to complete dependence upon the Lord. Then we find out there is no one quite like Him. We can hang our weakness upon His strength, our inability upon His power, our helplessness upon His help, and prove Him mighty indeed to save.
– Jill Briscoe, *Songs from Green Pastures*

ANDREW BECAME stronger every day, and he was ready to be discharged by the end of the week. We'd had our lessons on heart defects and learned that even if Andrew's heart could be fixed, it would not be *easily* fixed and would require multiple open-heart surgeries over his lifetime. The onslaught of information left us feeling as if we'd been thrown into an Olympic-sized pool without any idea how to swim. We were figuratively dog paddling in the deep end, gasping for a breath of air when we could.

Hospital carts loaded with smiley face balloons, get-well cards, little pink pitchers, meds and instructions to follow up with the pediatrician and cardiologist followed us to the hospital entrance, where everything was stuffed into our brown Corolla for the drive home.

Andrew needed supplemental oxygen all the time now. His lungs had taken a beating from the pneumonia, and now the effects of his heart defect were threatening to damage them even more. A medical supply store employee came to the house that same afternoon and wheeled an enormous gray metal oxygen tank into Andrew's bedroom. It was as big as the changing table. I sarcastically dubbed it "The Elephant" (in the room). David was going through a circus animal phase, and we'd been reading all about elephants, so it seemed appropriate—or maybe just the first thing that came to my weary mind. We'd been to the library and checked out *Clifford Goes to the Circus* multiple times, and it was the favorite story these days. We read it over and over till I finally bought a copy. David would play circus, pretending to be ringmaster for our own three-ring show. Carefully he'd lay out a few washcloths on the floor around the room. Then he'd run around the house with a plastic turkey-baster directing the stuffed lions and tigers to their places on the washcloths; sometimes he'd become the wild animal, growling and leaping from washcloth to washcloth, wanting me to direct his tricks. Having our own "elephant" was perfect as far as he was concerned. No worries that it was imaginary.

In the days immediately after arriving home from the hospital, the three of us played circus in Andrew's room many afternoons. David would place the stool on the floor next to Andrew's crib and stand on it, holding onto the crib railing while he directed the circus acts. Andrew's stuffed monkey and teddy bear were propped on the floor next to David's plastic horses and the oxygen tank elephant. I'd sit on the floor holding Andrew, pointing the spotlight (flashlight) from one circus performer to the next. I'd announce (per David's instructions) in my best circus voice each exciting event. "Ladies and gentlemen, I bring you the greatest ringmaster of all time!" I'd say, followed by a pretend drum roll. Then, "May I present, for your enjoyment, Mister David Atkinson!" He'd step up on the stool in his diaper and t-shirt, looking solemn and important.

"Yea!" I'd clap and pretend to be the excited audience.

"And now," he'd say in his best two-year-old voice, trying hard to be big and booming, "The monkeys and the bears!" We made the stuffed monkey and bear do tricks, working hard to coax a smile from Andrew with our antics.

We snatched every happy memory we could every chance we got during those months. It was an intense time. Seeing my baby at the end of that long plastic tether could bring me to tears. But if we were in the right frame of mind and could laugh a little, we'd tease together about him being a kite way up in the air, or a dog on the end of a leash trying to get away. It sounds so cheesy now…maybe our sense of humor was a bit off during that time, but we were in our own little world, and you really had to be there to understand the humor. Luckily our house was only about 850 square feet—small enough that the oxygen tubing could easily stretch from one end of the house to the other, so we carried Andrew everywhere. He was never in his room alone unless he was sleeping; wherever we were, he was with us—in his baby swing, in the bouncy seat, carried in the snuggly, in our arms…but always attached to that plastic tubing. He was a member of the family, and although the tubing was a hassle, we made sure he took part in our activities.

We also had a small, portable oxygen tank. I called it Baby Elle. It was also gray—a small oxygen tank that fit inside a plastic case with a nylon strap attached that allowed us to carry it over our shoulders like a purse. I had a love-hate relationship with Baby Elle because she was very, very touchy! If she got bumped or tipped to the side, she'd sound an alarm so loud someone in the next county would wonder what was going on. It actually sounded a bit like an elephant's startling, obnoxious squeal. This alarm could prove to be very embarrassing, like when someone's car alarm goes off, and it takes a while to turn it off. Juggling the tank plus a baby in a car seat, my purse and a diaper bag while holding the hand of a two year old and walking anywhere should have landed me Olympic gold.

One afternoon we stopped at the pharmacy to pick up a prescription for David, who had an ear infection. Andrew started crying, and I could tell it was going to be bad. As I reached for him, I tipped the portable tank over, setting off the alarm. I tried to get Andrew out of his car seat quickly (of course the buckle was sticking) and simultaneously reach down to set the oxygen tank upright when David burst out crying and stood with his hands over his ears because the deafening noise hurt his ears. I needed three arms, a nanny and a degree in oxygen tank management. I was simultaneously trying to push the reset button on Baby Elle, balance Andrew in one arm and pull David into my other arm to calm him down. Everyone in the drugstore turned to stare at us, gathering in groups at the end of the aisle. It took forever to get the alarm turned off and, by that time, it appeared we were the highlight of the drugstore day. I was mortified because of the ruckus we were causing and frantic to get my kids calmed down. I fully expected to hear an announcement over the loudspeaker, "Bad mother warning in aisle five; security has been notified." I wanted to disappear like the woman in the "Calgon, take me away" commercial. I finally got everyone settled down, but Baby Elle and I had a rather prickly relationship after that. You had to tread carefully around me in those days anyway. I was looking to pick a fight (even with an oxygen tank). My emotions ran high, and even little things caused my cranky side to surface.

The oxygen tubing Andrew had in his nose was a big frustration. I hated taping the cannula to Andrew's soft baby cheeks to keep it in place. It was hard to put it on, knowing I'd have to basically rip it off again in a couple of days. His skin became chapped and tender from that stupid tape. It made me angry, since it felt like kicking a man (albeit a *little* man) when he's down, and my thoughts rebelled with each removal and application. *Surely someone could have figured out a better, softer skin adhesive than that stupid, sticky, skin-ripping tape! Doesn't anyone know how difficult and painful this is? It's appalling!* I knew I was overreacting, and I'm sure it was the best product out at that time, but I needed to vent, and that tape was my "enemy." I could hate it without repercussions.

The two and a half months between Andrew's diagnosis and his first surgery were an absolute and complete nightmare. His life hung in such a precarious balance. When he looked at me with his big eyes, it seemed like he was begging me to do something to help him feel better, and I was constantly in a state of panic trying to figure out what to do. Watching him die a little every day was an experience that is impossible to put into words.

We were administering five to seven different medications—different doses at different times, all around the clock. I finally drew up a chart and taped it to the kitchen cupboard so we could cross off each dosage because, after a while, it was simply impossible to remember. The days and nights and medicines all ran together.

Then there was his nutrition. Our goal was to get him to gain weight before surgery. We tried. We tried so hard. He was just so small, and his skin seemed to hang on him. When I looked at his tiny little frame, it was like a punch in the gut. We had to track how many ounces of formula or breast milk he drank. I began to pump because breastfeeding was just too much work for Andrew. Even sucking on a bottle was hard work, and he'd work up a sweat while eating. We used all kinds of protein supplements and extras to help him put on weight. He was so weak and ate so little that we were constantly trying to feed him. A feeding schedule was nonexistent. He had no appetite due to the meds, so feeding on demand didn't work. A little here, a little more there. By April we were feeding him as much as we could with an eye-dropper, just letting it trickle down his throat. It's no wonder he wasn't gaining weight.

Technically it was still wintertime, but Tom and I started sleeping with a big box fan in our bedroom to drown out the sounds, which traveled easily in our house. Both of us were now hyper tuned to every little noise—which was both good and bad. It was good because we needed to be aware of even the slightest change in Andrew, but bad because realistically we couldn't get any sleep. Every cough, sniff, toss and turn woke us up in fear for his life. Plus, he was fussy, and we were feeding him at least every two hours. So, when Tom was home in the evenings, at night and on the weekends, we started taking four-hour care shifts around the clock when pretty much all one did was take care of Andrew so the other person could sleep. We knew we *had* to sleep during our allotted time because our turn with him would be next. So, we'd go into the bedroom and turn on the fan. It blocked out the distractions and became our emotional cue to try to relax and sleep. Somewhat Pavlovian, but it worked.

My mom and sisters came to help during the day when they could, but nights were the scariest because we felt very alone. One night just after that first hospital stay, I carefully measured out all Andrew's meds and gave them to him. Then I looked again at the instructions the doctor had written out and totally panicked. I had just given him all his meds measured out in cc's, but the directions said to give it in ml's. How could I have been so careless? Both Tom and I had been nervous bringing him home from the hospital, and now I felt like I had no business being a mom. I couldn't even measure out the right amount of meds! What was I thinking? I felt nauseous. I thought, *I probably just killed him. Now we'll have to go back to the hospital and try to save his life again.* I was so tired and so scared that I could hardly think straight. It was about 1:00 a.m. when I called the doctor and explained through my tears, "I just overdosed Andrew. He won't die from my mistake, will he? I didn't mean to do it. It was an accident!"

Thank goodness our own doctor was on call that night. He knew me pretty well already and had to interrupt my blubbering to tell me to calm down, that everything would be fine. He explained to me that ml's and cc's are the same. I stopped crying. "Oh. They are? Oh, right. Of course they are. I knew that. So, I didn't just kill my baby?" I was so relieved I didn't even feel stupid for calling him. "Thank you, doctor. So sorry to have bothered you." I cried even harder when I hung up the phone. Tom and I just held each other. It was like that so much of the time—always on the cusp of fear, afraid that something horrific was about to happen.

Life for me was an adrenaline junkie's dream. Anything remotely predictable was ancient history. I was long past imagining I could control or plan out even the slightest detail of our lives. It was as if we lived in a blurry, terrifying, alternate universe. We did everything we needed to do to survive, everything we could to keep Andrew alive, but none of it seemed real. It just didn't seem possible that we were the ones living this horror. We went through the motions and tried not to miss a step. Going anywhere outside of the house was a huge ordeal, but we had to go out almost every day. We practically lived at the doctors' offices; I could drive the routes in my sleep. David had a permanent nametag in the sibling play area at Children's Hospital, and the workers there all knew him. I kept track on the calendar that month—fifteen out of the twenty-two weekdays in March, we made a trip to either the hospital or one of Andrew's doctor's offices.

One day that month Andrew had a heart catheterization, so we spent the entire day at Children's Hospital. We learned that a cardiac catheterization (cardiac cath or heart cath) is a procedure that allows the doctor to examine how the heart is working and discover exactly what is not working and why. The cardiologist threads a very narrow, hollow tube called a catheter into a blood vessel that leads to the heart. In Andrew's case, the femoral blood vessel in his upper leg was used. The doctor injects a dye into the catheter, and an x-ray type machine takes pictures of the heart, so it can be analyzed correctly. Andrew's cath went well and was over within a couple of hours.

Tom and I sat in the cardiologist's office and listened as he described the results of the test and gave us some further information about the defect. The cath confirmed what the doctor had known from the first echocardiogram, what he had explained to us that day in the hospital. Andrew's heart defect was called Truncus Arteriosus, Type I, which is rare. Including all three types, Truncus occurs in fewer than 1 out of every 10,000 live births, less than 1% of the time. Including all the variations, there are only about 300 cases of Truncus each year in the United States.

During the first eight weeks a baby is developing in the womb, the heart forms. Around week four, the aorta and the pulmonary arteries and valves are supposed to separate and take on their distinct jobs within the heart. When a baby has Truncus, the aorta and pulmonary artery don't separate as they should, but instead stay fused together as a single large vessel, or "trunk" (as in tree trunk). Also, the wall that is supposed to develop between the ventricles in the lower part of the heart doesn't get the message and doesn't show up to keep everything in the right place. This means that the blood flowing back to the heart from the body gets all mixed up with the blood coming in from the lungs, preventing needed oxygen from reaching the rest of the body. As a result, it isn't uncommon for babies with Truncus or other heart defects to develop a bluish coloration around their lips and fingers or toes. I realized now that's what the doctor meant in the delivery room when he'd said Andrew was looking kind of dusky just after he was born.

Babies with Truncus that are fortunate enough to have and survive the surgery will need additional surgeries after the initial repair because they either outgrow the new artery, or the new artery and valve fail after a period of time due to a variety of reasons. The doctor told us once again that Truncus is fatal if not surgically repaired. He also said the initial surgery to repair Andrew's heart would be complicated and reminded us that the correction and repair of this defect wasn't yet perfected. We were told that the surgery was still being developed, having been performed successfully only a handful of times.

Andrew's cardiologist went on to explain that the surgery wasn't available in our area and that we would have to travel to a different major metropolitan area if we wanted to pursue surgery.

What? What does he mean, if we want to pursue surgery? I was furious at that suggestion. *Do we not live in the 20th century? Doctors fix things like this. Of course we want to pursue surgery.*

The doctor gave us four location choices for the upcoming operation: Boston, Houston, Philadelphia and San Francisco. The decision was up to us, which was overwhelming—how were we supposed to know what was best? This was before the days of easily obtainable information from the Internet. Tom's brother, Ken, a family practice doctor, did some research and recommended that we take Andrew to Boston's Children's Hospital—the most Truncus surgeries had been performed there, and they also had the best track record for survival. So that was that. Our cardiologist made arrangements for the operation. It would be performed by the world-renowned Dr. Aldo Castenada, a pioneer in the area of pediatric cardiac surgery. Somehow, we just needed to help Andrew get bigger and strong enough for the surgery.

Andrew had another bout of pneumonia during April but was not admitted to the hospital. I don't know why because it was touch and go for him. Every day, every office visit was something different; blood work, change of meds, EKGs, echos, more blood work, more meds.

Meanwhile, I was trying to be a good mommy for David who was not even two and a half. He was a little trooper, tagging along to appointments, being a "helper," and learning to entertain himself while I endlessly tended to Andrew's needs. All the other Moms of two year olds were talking about the ups and downs of potty training. I knew David was ready to start potty training, but I just couldn't take on the extra work. I wished so much that it didn't have to be this way—that I could be a better mom, attentive to David and his needs. As I talked with another mom one day, she casually mentioned how unfair all this was for David. I knew she was trying to be sensitive and thoughtful toward him. "He could probably be potty trained by now," she remarked.

"Well, I'm doing all I can," I replied, feeling a bit defensive. I knew she was right, but I didn't think I could deal with one more thing. I did feel for David, though, and later that week I went to Walmart and bought a little potty chair. So many times I found myself overwhelmed with guilt. You name it, I wasn't doing it right. I wasn't the wife that Tom needed, I wasn't spending time with my extended family, I had dropped out of Bible study. I was insecure about taking care of Andrew. It seemed like all I was doing was taking, taking, taking and not giving back anything at all. I felt like a failure. Yes, I knew the situation wasn't fair for David, but it wasn't exactly fair for Andrew either. Or for any of us. The harder I tried to make things better, the worse the situation seemed. Most people were very sensitive, but some just didn't get it, and the negative or judgmental comments (although few) loomed larger than life. I didn't yet have the thick skin that comes from experience, which really would have helped me brush it off and not take what people said so seriously.

Our extended family was, of course, anxious to help in any and every way they could. More than ever before I began to see and appreciate the incredible support system that family can be. Gone were the petty family irritations and arguments. Everyone rallied to be there for each other. Some days my mom came over and stayed with David, or I'd take him to her house, or she'd help take care of Andrew. She and my dad spent a lot of time at our house that month. On Sunday mornings they'd come over after the first service at church to babysit so Tom and I could go to the second service. My sisters and sisters-in-law were a huge help, too. They would drive David to the park to play and take him on play dates with his cousins; they helped care for Andrew and babysat so Tom and I could have a break once in a while. Aunts, uncles and cousins rallied and supported us financially, babysat when possible and were loving and considerate. We knew we were cared for by a divine provider.

Friendships that were dear and deep held the umbrella for us as well. It literally wasn't possible for us to do this alone—I needed friends, and they were there for me. During those months, when I was making almost daily trips to the doctors' offices, my good friends helped baby-sit David. My friend Cindy watched David for me so many times I lost count. Her daughter Jill was David's age, and they were buddies. One day I came to pick him up, and Cindy caught me at the door. Putting her finger to her lips, she whispered, "Shhh." I looked across the living room to where she pointed to see David and Jill sound asleep, buried in of a pile of toys and books. It looked like they might have fallen asleep mid-sentence. We left them sleeping, and while Andrew slept in his car seat, Cindy and I shared a cup of tea at her kitchen table.

One of the best gifts for me was not having to worry about David. I knew he could be cranky sometimes. He was dealing with all of the up-heaval in our lives as any two year old would. He didn't like being away from home all the time, and he sometimes threw a fit. He'd always done better with a set routine. However, both David and I were learning to go with the flow, and this current schedule was simply not a choice. When he knew he was going to play with a friend, he was happy and content, and I felt better, too, because I knew he was in loving hands.

For an entire month before Andrew's surgery, people from our church brought dinner to us. We were new attendees at a large church, and we didn't know many of the people bringing the food. Having people who didn't even know us go to all the trouble of making dinner and bringing it over was a humbling experience. I appreciated it because I knew I really couldn't do it all and truly needed the help. Being on the receiving end is much harder than a person imagines, but those meals meant so much to us—a hot dinner on the table gave us a chance to sit together and do something semi-normal. It meant that Tom and David and I might have a minute or two to re-fuel and connect with each other.

It's hard to find words to express how appreciative we were of the outpouring of concern. Acquaintances, neighbors and even people we didn't know well would send word or drop by or call. We received cards and notes from people who had been in our shoes and from some who had not. I found that even if someone had not experienced dealing with a sick baby of their own, a listening ear was enough. We weren't looking for anyone to move mountains. A touch or hug, a smile, the words didn't really matter. Just being there spoke volumes. I wanted to be able to reach out to people, to give back somehow. However, I felt as if I was suspended in a cocoon that was my world, and I couldn't break free to reach the rest of the world that seemed to be moving on a different plane.

At that point in this journey, I felt as if my heart was splayed open, top to bottom, completely vulnerable and exposed. I was raw, and I was bloody, and I was not very patient. I certainly wasn't interested in listening to clichés. I had no time for that. I did *not* want to hear, "I'm sure it will work out," or, "It's all going to be okay." When those words were offered, I smiled and nodded, but inside I was crying out for someone to understand the real truth. There *weren't* any guarantees. I wanted to say, "It might *not* all work out. We don't know. He might die. Don't you *get* that?"

Spring is a busy time of year. Everyone is getting flowers put in, gardens planted, spring cleaning completed and vacations planned. People need to get things done around the house and, for most people, work is also demanding. Only a couple of men were able to call Tom during that time, but it was a lot to expect, and we understood. It was hard enough for normally chatty women to talk with me about how it was going with Andrew—I could understand how difficult it would be for men. Most men have no idea what to say to each other on a good day, unless it's about sports or work. They usually leave it to their wives to deal with the difficult conversations.

As a result, some people avoided us because it took a great deal of emotional commitment to enter into a conversation. Our lives were not the walk-by-and-wave kind of hi-how-are-ya-fine that most people prefer. We understood, but we just couldn't respond that everything was fine when someone asked how we were. Instead, we'd nod and just not say anything. When people didn't know what to say, conversations could be strained or awkward. We've all done it—panicked and blurted out whatever comes to mind without thinking first. One friend said to me, "Even if he (Andrew) dies, you know in your heart it will be fine because he'll be in heaven and the angels will be rejoicing." I can see why she thought that was a comforting thing to say, but it stung. *Even if he dies?* That sounded awful. We were doing our absolute best to keep him alive. I didn't care about angels rejoicing. I did not want to be told that it would be fine if he died. It wouldn't be fine with me.

I wanted someone to feel the real, anguished pain that I was feeling and hear my angry questions and not be repulsed or frightened away. I wasn't faltering in my faith, but I did not want to be reminded that, "God has a plan," or "God works everything out for good." Of course,

I knew those things in my heart of hearts, but it wasn't comforting to hear someone say it, and I was too weak to hold onto those truths at this point anyway. I needed someone to be close enough to hold those truths for me through a gentle hug, a real human person to cling to. The people who weren't afraid to be scared along with me were the ones I let into my world. These were the people who called, who took the time to come to see us, who held Andrew, oxygen tubing and all, and cried with us. I know it's natural to recoil at the horrible sight of a sick baby. No one wants to go there. But that was our life, and we needed friends who were not afraid to look fear in its face and stand shoulder to shoulder with us.

After Andrew came home from the hospital, I had been on an unpaid maternity leave for eight weeks when my boss came over to see the new baby and me and talk about when I could go back to work. As we talked, though, I realized that he did not understand the reality of caring for a very sick baby. I couldn't just hand Andrew off to a teenage babysitter; he'd need a nurse to care for him if I went back to work. Even if we could have afforded that, I could not have handled it emotionally. He was too sick to leave. Sitting on our brown hand-me-down couch holding Andrew in my arms, his oxygen tube running down the hallway, I knew in my heart I couldn't go back to work. The more we talked, the more apparent that became to Tom and my boss as well. I would not be able to return to work even part time. I think I had known this deep down, but it was a shock hearing myself say the words out loud. In one way, I was relieved. I knew it was the right thing, and really the *only* thing, to do. But in another way, I felt responsible for our tight finances—we needed the money now more than ever. A heavy burden entered our world that day, and we have not recovered financially even to this day.

It's hard to talk about the financial devastation that hits you as a result of a situation like this. It's hard, first of all, because you don't ever want your child to feel responsible for the difficulty. It is not his fault, but he wouldn't understand that and would likely be upset and confused. Kids automatically feel guilty for things that aren't remotely their responsibility, and they are not ready to wrestle with the tough questions of why life isn't "fair." Most adults have a hard time with these issues. At some point, your child is going to get it even if you never say a word. Then you reassure and remind him, "We're a family, and we'll get through this together." You will say that even if you have no idea how, because financial hardship is not your child's burden to bear.

Additionally, it's hard to talk about financial issues because you don't want to sound whiny and ungrateful for all the financial help you have received. When someone chooses to help financially in any way, we know that it is above and beyond, that it is a sacrifice for them, and we have appreciated every amazing gift. That's why lamenting over our lack of resources during hardship is inappropriate—it's our fear getting in the way. It's God's job to provide for our needs. He's the one we should be talking to.

In the early days, during and after Andrew's first heart surgery, we were so overwhelmed by the costs that it was almost laughable. We owned nothing of any significant value. What were they going to do, take our fifteen-year-old car? Confiscate our 13-inch TV? Tom used to joke that he could have made a full-time job out of our health insurance issues. That wasn't really a joke—for him, every lunch hour was dedicated solely to dealing with our finances and insurance issues. The costs were mind-boggling, and afterward he usually felt like he'd faced a den of lions blindfolded. Many times we were overcharged or denied payment by the insurance company for something that should have been covered. It was crucial that someone go over the bills carefully, and we couldn't afford to pay for that kind of help. We were drowning as it was.

For me, our financial issues were bigger than anything I could imagine. I'm not good with money, and the enormity of bills for thousands and thousands of dollars put me way over the edge. I dealt with it by ignoring it. After all, why worry about something so big when there was nothing we could do about it? We were looking at debt that far exceeded what we would probably make in our lifetime. It was beyond my ability to comprehend.

In desperation I prayed for help and direction and for some way to just get through it. I knew God was ultimately the Provider, and trusting Him was our only option. I guess that's a good place to be—really, it's where we should be all the time. We've seen God work miracles to meet our needs. But we've also seen God use an anxious situation to stretch and mold us. We've kept on trusting Him when the need went unmet for a time. This step toward trusting God, it's not easy. It's strictly a decision to trust Him no matter what, good and bad, hard and easy, seen and unseen. I'd made the decision that I wanted to follow God back in high school, but I was finding that I needed to choose to trust Him now every day, sometimes every hour. I was determined that my faith would not be dependent upon my circumstances or other people.

Andrew was uncomfortable. He didn't feel at all well and became increasingly irritable as the weeks wore on. Who could blame him? He was in congestive heart failure. I felt bad for him, but when he started crying it would often escalate into an all-out panic attack (as we called them), and when that happened, he was a tough little cookie to handle. Something would set him off, and he'd start crying *hard*. It would take me several minutes of intense care to get him calmed down again. And I was the only one who *could* calm him. He would cry so hard—I mean out-of-control crying—that it was scary. And you never knew when or where it would happen. We always had to be on alert and prepared.

When he started into that panicky cry, I would strip him down to his diaper, and then massage his little body firmly, but not too hard. I'd put my face right up next to his and talk to him. I would just keep massaging and hold him up close, skin to skin. Pretty soon he'd calm down. It must have looked odd, this mother stripping down her screaming baby in the middle of well, wherever, and then talking to him face to face as if he could understand her.

Usually Andrew would have these crying attacks when his senses would get overloaded—if he was suddenly too hot, if it was noisy or crowded or bright, or if there was a loud sound, he just went ballistic. We dealt with episodes at the pharmacy, in the pediatrician's waiting room, in the car, at the grocery store. People would start whispering, and though I really didn't know what to do, I just followed my gut instincts. I had to do *something*, and half the time I was nearly crying myself because I was so desperate to calm him down. I felt like saying to all those staring people, "Fine. You think you can do better? Come on over and try!" But, in spite of my anxiety and the questioning looks of others, I did whatever I had to do to help my baby.

All the spiritual questions I had been wrestling with were setting up their own little chat sessions in the back of my mind. Subconsciously, I was trying to process what I really thought about God, birth defects, children in pain, prayer. But none of that was on a conscious level for me; everything was percolating just under the surface. During those gut-wrenching months, as I helplessly watched my tiny baby's life slipping away toward death, I had no time to wrestle with those questions. I was either too busy to think, too exhausted to sort through my thoughts, or too afraid to actually face reality. Somewhere inside I knew the answers were not going to be easy, but right then I figured God had to take me as I was, doubts and all. I was at the same time both exceptionally vulnerable and wildly defensive. Like an injured mother animal crazy to protect her young from danger, I was singularly focused on saving Andrew's life. I couldn't talk about the deeper questions, although I knew they were there. But, oh, I wanted answers. I wanted real answers from real people who had walked this path ahead of me. I needed to know we weren't alone; I just didn't know which way to turn.

I wondered, *Where is the Ever-Present God in all this pain? God, can You hear me? Are You there? Can You hear this baby crying? Why don't You do something?* In my mind this wasn't supposed to happen to a baby. This was sacred ground. I was confused, and I wanted to reach for God. But, how *do* you trust God when you're scared of what He's allowing to happen?

Five

Have I not commanded you? Be strong and courageous.
Do not be afraid; do not be discouraged,
for the LORD your God will be with you wherever you go.
– Joshua 1:9 NIV

God's grace may be unnoticed. But usually those who are
suffering will notice even its lightest touch
and will hold it a precious and incalculably valuable thing.
– Elisabeth Elliot, *Twelve Baskets of Crumbs*

ONE DAY in mid-April I stood in the cardiologist's examining room. Andrew, with his big blue eyes and skinny arms and legs, lay fussing on the table as the doctor listened to his heart through a stethoscope almost as big as Andrew's chest. He had not gained any weight again, and I felt almost hopeless, almost out of any ability to make it happen. I was focused intently on the small details of the every day, trying so hard to do everything possible to keep him alive. I kept track of his meds, his feedings, his oxygen saturation levels. One day and one hour at a time, every single day and night I did all I knew how to do—but I couldn't get even another ounce or two of weight on him. My eyes pooled with tears.

The doctor interrupted my thoughts with, "Well, I think it's time for Andrew to make a cross-country trip to Boston."

"You do?" I jumped to life at this suggestion. Tom and I had sensed for a couple of weeks that it was time, but we needed our cardiologist's go-ahead before we could make the trip. It was what we'd been living for, but also dreading—confirmation that Andrew was now so sick there was nothing else we could do. Our insurance wouldn't cover a cross-country flight-for-life trip so with a financial gift from my parents, we bought tickets on a commercial airline. It was scheduled for the day after Easter Sunday. A pilot friend made arrangements for Andrew to have oxygen during the flight. While not generally allowed, the airline made an exception. We were nervous about the trip, but Andrew was so sick that we didn't have much time to think about it.

Both Tom and I grew up in modest, hardworking families. There was nothing fancy or even slightly upscale about our lives. We didn't go on lavish vacations; our families went tent camping. We walked to the bookmobile and the public pool, and sometimes ate Spaghetti-O's or oatmeal for dinner. We were thrilled with hand-me-down clothes. Going out to eat was a rare special occasion, and if you needed to visit the relatives for a funeral, you took a Greyhound bus. In our teens, we worked as soon as we could find someone who'd pay us for something we could do. It was up to us to save our money if we wanted anything special. It was a no-frills life, but we didn't feel deprived or resentful; that's just how life was.

As you can imagine, neither of us had much experience traveling cross-country. In fact, we had no experience. We didn't know a soul in Boston and had never been to the East Coast. Neither of us had ever even ridden in a taxi before or tipped a valet. If it sounds like we were a couple of high mountain hillbillies, I guess we were—we'd just never had the opportunity to travel. We looked into staying at Boston's Ronald McDonald House, but it was completely full, so we made reservations at a hotel near Children's Hospital. At first the traveling part seemed to me like it could be exciting. I had grandiose ideas that the hotel would be beautiful, and I could take bubble baths and order room service and it could be a sort of vacation for us. Ha! What was I thinking? I could not have been more out of touch with reality. We had a very sick baby, and that took center stage.

Then there was also the problem of the price of Boston hotels. We could no more afford a hotel than we could afford open heart surgery. Even one night was beyond our meager budget, but my parents offered to pay for one night. We had no idea what we would do for sleeping arrangements after that. Tom was taking an unpaid leave from work to be able to go. We knew the whole thing would be financially overwhelming, but we couldn't think about that. The finances would have to take a back seat to getting Andrew the help he needed. We had to trust God and step out in faith. This was all uncomfortably unplanned, but we didn't have a choice. We *had* to go now and solve the money problems later. We would do absolutely anything to save Andrew's life.

For a rather quiet person who likes my predictable little ducks in nice, neat rows, the journey on which we were about to embark was akin to dancing on the moon. Crazy. People like us don't do this. I could never have anticipated the scenario that was about to unfold in front of us.

Life had changed completely, but my relationship with God was solid. In fact, He was the only thing that hadn't changed. My everyday life looked different, but my faith was intact, and I was trying to trust God with each frightening, uncertain step. I didn't feel that my entire relationship with God was in jeopardy simply because I had questions and doubts. I figured we'd work through it. I found I was having a conversation with God in my head pretty much all the time. Prayer no longer happened at a set time of day, recorded in my prayer journal. I talked to Him—cried out to Him—on an ongoing basis. I was not always happy with Him either. I taped some Scriptures on the fridge and the bathroom mirror. That was it. Neither Tom nor I could concentrate on Bible study or regular devotions. We actually had no time to read the Bible or have extended prayer sessions. We tried to go to church when we could, but many times it felt like we were only going through the motions. Life was too uncertain to schedule or plan anything. Reading and re-reading the Scripture verses on the fridge and the bathroom mirror was the best (and only) spiritual thing I could do. It got the message into my heart and mind and, after a while, I could repeat those verses from memory. A couple of verses from Psalms and a sentence of encouragement were God's words to me, and it was enough.

On the morning after Easter, as we waited in the terminal for the airplane prior to boarding, Andrew had one of his panic attacks. It was snowing outside, but his little internal thermometer was all over the place, and it sent him into one of his awful crying fits. Experience had taught us that I was the only one that could calm him. Here, in the middle of the airport, with the loudspeaker announcements blaring every few minutes, people bustling, beeping transport cars, our own emotions on high alert, an oxygen tank and a screaming baby, getting him calmed down was going to be very challenging. Tom gave me that look—that panicked this-can't-be-happening-and-I-don't-know-what-to-do look. I was beyond caring what people thought. I carefully lifted my tiny, sick, screaming baby out of my husband's arms, grabbed the oxygen tank and a baby blanket, and headed to a quiet corner away from the crowd. We were only a couple minutes from boarding time. He was screaming as I stripped him down. The few people that were around stopped what they were doing and stared. I know they wondered, what in the world…? I didn't care. I rubbed his arms, legs, hands and feet, and I massaged his tummy and head. I talked to him up close by his cheeks and wrapped him snugly in a soft blanket. He calmed down right before we had to board the plane.

Thankfully, we were able to board early and get settled. We laid Andrew on a blanket, snuggled into the space between us on the seat. The oxygen tank turned out to be a big deal. Even having it on the plane made the attendants uncomfortable, so they were polite, but not exactly helpful. Because it was against the regulations, they probably had no idea what exactly to do. They thought we would know, but we were clueless. I never figured out why they wouldn't let him use his regular oxygen tank. The one they provided under the seat turned out to be for an adult—the cannula was huge, and the oxygen flow would have been like a fire-hose for a baby. We had to think fast and wing it. With only a couple of minutes for us to make it work or get off the plane, we improvised, managing to force his baby-sized cannula and tubing into the large tank's spigot so there wasn't as much oxygen blasting through. We turned it down as low as it would go and then held the cannula near his nose, so he was getting the oxygen without it being forced into his tiny nostrils. The next time the flight attendant walked by, we smiled and said everything was fine.

I was nervous that he was going to have another panic attack on the plane. I believe that God in His mercy gave Andrew peaceful sleep and us a couple hours of calm before the storm. I have no idea how people found out, but word spread through the airplane that we were flying to Boston so that Andrew could have a life-saving heart surgery. By the time we were disembarking, fellow passengers wished us well and offered their prayers for Andrew. I was embarrassed by all the attention, but we knew we would need all the prayer support we could get.

So, yes, the two country bumpkins did get lost in the Boston airport. We managed to stay together, though. It was crowded and loud, and there were so many people! While we were trying to locate the baggage claim area, Andrew had another crying fit that we had to deal with. "Oh, God, help us," I whispered. I went through the routine and got him calmed down again.

We were standing there lost, looking for some kind of sign that might point us in the direction of the baggage terminal, when an older couple in long coats with gray hair and glasses walked up to us.

"You look like you could be lost. Can we pointcha in the right direction?" The tallish, somewhat distinguished-looking man smiled. "This airport can be confusing. Where are you headed?" I looked at Tom. How in the world do people understand that accent? The woman was smiling at Andrew in my arms.

"Um, yes, thanks," Tom responded. "We're looking for the baggage claim area."

"We're headed there, too. It's over here." He motioned with his brief-case hand, and we followed. They introduced themselves, but I was so nervous and exhausted I don't remember their names. We told them Andrew was having surgery the next week at Children's. Standing at the baggage carousel, we quickly spotted our suitcases waiting for us. Another blessing.

"He's a beautiful baby, but he looks pretty sick." This woman had a caring way about her. It turned out that she'd been a nurse, and she suggested that we take Andrew straight to the hospital instead of going first to the hotel. *Yes. Yes, that actually sounds like a good idea to me.* They helped us find the taxi lines, carried part of our luggage for us and encouraged us to move to the very front of the line. I was hesitant, but Tom walked straight up to the front of the extremely long line of people anxiously waiting for a taxi. He yelled over the deafening noise outside the terminal, "We have a very sick baby and need to get to Children's Hospital right away. Could we please have the next taxi?" People parted the way for us, and no one even batted an eye. When I turned around to thank the older couple, they were gone. I looked through the crowd but couldn't spot them anywhere, and we never saw them again. They had been such a help to us. I came to believe they were angels—real human angels or real spiritual ones, I don't know, but it didn't matter. We were just thankful to God for sending them to help us. Everyone else was incredibly kind and helped us get our luggage up to the curb as the next cab pulled forward.

You haven't experienced Boston until you have ridden in a cab. That's what everyone had told us and, after that day, I can testify that it's true. I don't think words exist that can describe that ride. *High-speed, harrowing, shocking, knuckle-biting* maybe come close, but it was an experience I'll never forget. We didn't have a car seat with us, so we had to hold Andrew. Luckily, he was exhausted from his crying fit and not interested in fussing. After the driver threw our luggage into the trunk like bags of garbage, we settled into the back seat for the ride of our lives.

Our driver was a crusty older guy with massive biceps and black curly hair that stuck out from under a black baseball cap. He was Italian, which we discovered shortly after our zero-to-sixty getaway from the airport loading area. Almost immediately he began yelling and cursing in his native tongue as we sped down the streets. At first, we thought he was talking to us. We looked at each other. Were we supposed to understand Italian? Finally, we realized he was yelling at the other cars. I had no idea why, but we were going so fast, how could I tell? Speeding down the incredibly narrow streets (have you *been* to Boston?) with literally one or two inches between us and the cars parked on the sides of the streets, I was petrified we were going to hit them. Every so often I'd let out a nervous laugh that sounded a little like a high-pitched bark. I couldn't believe this was really happening. He took the corners so fast and sharp that I was clinging to Andrew for dear life as we slid back and forth across the slick brown vinyl seat. I'd be practically cheek-to-cheek with the window and then, around another corner we'd go and I'd find myself cheek-to-cheek with Tom who was holding tightly to the back of the front seat. The driver continued shouting in Italian on his two-way radio, livid about the road construction or the red light or the pedestrians. At one point, he actually stopped the car, got out, shook his fist and cursed at another driver stopped on the opposite corner. I am not joking. The other driver started shouting as he moved toward us, and I thought they might get into a fistfight right then and there.

All this boisterous verbal jockeying was somewhat shocking to us mild-mannered westerners, and my heart was pounding. We had no idea what to make of it; I wasn't sure whether to burst out laughing or be downright scared. It was like we'd been thrown into the middle of a mobster movie set and ended up in the car with the stunt man. I hoped upon hope he was taking us to the hospital and not some seedy section of town where mob bosses would emerge from the buildings with guns, wearing black fedoras and trench coats. We screeched and swerved and sped our way through the Boston traffic as if it wasn't there at all. After this ride, I thought to myself sarcastically, *heart surgery should be a breeze.* Anyway, I count it as a miracle that we made it to the hospital alive and in one piece, taxi driver included.

We had not been expected to check into the hospital until the next morning, so they told us to go to the Emergency Room. Three hours later Andrew was admitted, and we were shown to room 3520 on the cardiac unit floor. Andrew's crib was one of four in the small, square room—one crib in each corner. The cribs had tall chrome bars on the sides and back and front bars that lowered down and out of the way. I situated Andrew in a comfortable position, and he fell asleep almost immediately. We rounded up a couple of chairs and attempted to get comfortable ourselves while we waited for the nurse to come in. An eighteen-month-old boy occupied the bed to our right. His mom didn't speak English, but that was all right with me, really, because I didn't have the energy to do any chitchatting. The next bed over held a tiny baby, but we saw no parent. The room seemed crowded and awkward, even though one bed was pushed into a corner, empty.

The nurse came in and checked Andrew's vitals, asked us more questions, jotted notes in the chart. She brought us a stack of diapers and a little bottle of formula for Andrew. Evidently, we were still his primary caregivers at this point. Obviously the "rules" and expectations in this hospital were different than in Denver. I remember the nurse that helped us get settled, Ashley, was as cute as a button, but barely understandable. I wasn't used to the Bostonian accent yet, and she spoke very fast and used phrases I didn't know. I was kind of in shock when she spoke. I felt like we'd landed on some exotic island and were trying to decipher a new language, so I'd watch her mouth. She had the most gorgeous teeth. At first it took all my concentration to translate what she was saying. I'd look at Tom with raised eyebrows and a "did-you-get-that" look and he'd be looking at me the same way, neither of us having any clue what she'd said. Then I'd ask her to repeat it again. In addition to her thick accent, she talked at lightning speed. Our lack of understanding became comical. Once she realized what was happening, she laughed with us and tried to slow down or repeat phrases or pronounce a word more carefully. She had a great sense of humor and was understanding of us newbies.

With only a few exceptions (like Ashley), we found the doctors and nurses to be more reserved than in Denver, pretty much straight business with no time for smiling or chitchat. They also were not as open about sharing details about Andrew and did not offer any information we did not specifically ask for. It seemed so different, and we felt a little out of the loop. On the upside, though, it was a privilege to be here. Andrew was in the hands of the best pediatric cardiac surgeons, cardiologists and nursing teams in the world. When he was first diagnosed, his doctors in Denver had said they could not and would not perform the surgery, and when we had talked to our cardiologist, I could tell he didn't hold out much hope for success. Surgery to repair Andrew's defect had not been performed for very long anywhere and was still in experimental phases in the few places that would attempt it. Surgeons had performed the procedure, yes; but it wasn't happening very often anywhere, and not at all in our city. What's more, as with anything experimental in its early days, the results were iffy at best. In the beginning, our doctor had not recommended straight out that we should take Andrew home and love him until he died, but what he did say was close to that. I had immediately dismissed his suggestion, of course, but it was sobering.

With its renowned pediatric cardiac intensive care unit and an entire wing dedicated to cardiology, Boston was one of the best cities in the country for what we needed. This is where the sickest babies were taken; this was their last hope of help. This was *Andrew's* last hope of help.

Andrew was assigned a cardiologist for his time at the hospital. This doctor would communicate with our doctor in Denver and do all the things cardiologists do. He walked in with a crooked smile and twinkling eyes, and we liked him that very second.

"Hi, I'm Jim Lock, one of the Cardiology Fellows, and I'll be taking care of Andrew while you're here." He smiled as he reached out to shake hands. How are you all doing after your trip out here?"

"Oh, we're fine. Nice to meet you." Tom replied. I smiled and shook his hand.

Dr. Lock turned to Andrew, "So here's our little guy. Looks pretty wiped out right now." He bent over the bed where Andrew lay asleep and untied the little hospital t-shirt carefully so as not to wake him. Then, ever so gently, he laid his hand on Andrew's chest and held it there, like he was feeling the beating with his hand. He touched Andrew's cheek and then, pulling his stethoscope from around his neck, he glanced up at us and smiled as he began listening to Andrew's heart.

Tom and I waited nervously. We knew this could be the end of the road, and we were anxious to know what was next for our son. I had butterflies. He was taking such a long time. Then Dr. Lock gently rolled Andrew onto his side, so he could hear the heartbeat from the back. Andrew slept through it all. "I spoke with your cardiologist in Denver this afternoon," he said as he stood up again, his tall frame unfolding to full height. "We had a good visit. He said you are wonderful parents." We smiled, and he continued. "Everything looks as we expected with Andrew. We need to check his blood cultures for any signs of infection before we go ahead and schedule his surgery. But it looks like it will be either Thursday or Friday." He paused and looked down at Andrew. "He's sure a cute little guy." Another pause. "Do you have any questions?"

We couldn't think of any.

"Okay, well, we'll let you know for sure when we find out about the blood work. I'll stop back by tomorrow morning." He shook hands with us again, and we thanked him before he left the room. Then we settled back into our chairs in the corner. Relief flooded over me; he cared, he knew what to do and had it all under control. Sometime later, a woman we had never seen before walked into the room, looked around and then walked toward us. "Are you Tom and Cathy Atkinson?" She was careful to whisper to keep from waking the sleeping babies.

"Yes," I stood, and Tom stood up behind me.

"Hi, I am Diana, a friend of a friend of some of your friends back in Colorado. In, I think it was in...um, Evergreen? It was through my Bible study. Do you know a Melanie who lives in Evergreen?"

"Oh, yes." My brain was spinning trying to put these puzzle pieces together. A friend of a friend? Somewhere in the farthest reaches of my mind I remembered that Melanie had said she might have a contact here in Boston. "Hi, Diana," I smiled and put out my hand to shake hers. "Yes. Yes, we know Melanie. She's a good friend of ours."

Diana continued, "My Bible study group was alerted to your situation and that you might need a place to stay while your son is here in the hospital. I wanted to offer you our home if you still need somewhere to stay."

"Oh, my," I said. I looked at Tom. We were flabbergasted. We literally could not believe how God had orchestrated this one. "Really? That's incredible." I didn't know what to say. "We do have reservations at a hotel for tonight," I said. "But after tonight, we don't have anywhere… we actually hadn't figured that one out. I think we planned on staying here at the hospital, but we weren't sure…"

She stepped forward, holding out a key. "Here is the key to our back door, and let me give you the address." Digging in her purse for a pencil and paper, she kept talking. "You can come and go as you like. We have lots of missionaries that are in and out. Help yourself to the food in the pantry." She found a pen. "Your bedroom is the first door on the right as you go up the stairs." She scribbled a map and wrote the address on a little slip of paper. "Our house is near the T—the commuter train line. There is a station close by, easy to walk to, that would bring you back down here to about six blocks from the hospital." Her words seemed to be flowing out at a hundred miles per hour—we had to concentrate to keep up with what she was saying. I wondered whether everyone on the East coast talked so fast.

"This is incredibly thoughtful of you. I don't know what to say." We were overwhelmed. Here we were, total strangers in a strange city and she was willing to open up her house to us. It meant a bed to sleep on, a shower (even a bath if I wanted), a washing machine so we could do laundry and somewhere to take a break away from the hospital. It made me feel like visiting royalty.

"Oh, don't worry about it at all. It's available for you whenever you need a place to get away," she said.

We thanked this gracious woman profusely, and then she was gone.

All afternoon in that hospital room we held Andrew, played with him, walked him to keep him calm, fed him, and rocked him in those big wooden rocking chairs they always have at hospitals. The window in our room faced west, and I watched the sun's rays grow long across the floor, and then the bright street lights of Boston blinked on for the night. It was early evening when we realized we were completely exhausted. Andrew was quiet now and sleeping again. The nurses assured us he was in good hands and that we could leave him for the night. I hesitated to leave, but we were so tired, and the tiredness won out. In the midst of deciding what we should do, saying good-bye to our sleeping baby, answering questions from the nurse and just being so weary, we made one big mistake. We forgot to leave a phone number where the hospital could reach us in case something happened with Andrew during the night.

Six

God is our refuge and strength, an ever-present help in trouble.
Therefore we will not fear, though the earth give way and the
mountains fall into the heart of the sea, though its waters roar
and foam, and the mountains quake with their surging.
– Psalm 46:1-2 NIV

But pain insists upon being attended to. God whispers to us
in our pleasures, speaks in our conscience, but shouts in our
pains: it is His megaphone to rouse a deaf world.
– C. S. Lewis

THE NEXT morning popped up suddenly, like a piece of toast, a bit overdone. We had meant to be up and about earlier, and when we did wake up, the time startled us, I immediately began rushing around in high gear, feeling panicky and out of control. It was only eight o'clock as we crossed the street to the hospital, but it felt much later to me. It was the first time I'd been away from Andrew, and even though I knew he was in good hands, I speed-walked, antsy and anxious to see him.

Navigating the maze of hallways in any hospital takes forever. Why do hospital halls and wings have to be so complicated? We finally found our way to the cardiac care unit, then down the hallway to his room and around the corner, happy at the prospect of seeing his little face, and… Andrew wasn't there. His bed and all his things were gone. The spot where we had left him sleeping soundly just the night before was empty. My stomach flipped and stayed in that upside-down position. The floor had obviously been mopped sparkling clean. There was no indication of Andrew ever being here—no leftover bottles half filled with formula, no bed linens, not even the crib. I was dumfounded.

"Are we in the right room?" I whispered to Tom. I turned to the mother who was calmly rocking her sleeping baby. Yes, she was the same mother that was here yesterday. "Where's Andrew? Where is he?" I asked, with exaggerated motions and pointing and raised eyebrows. She shook her head, unable to offer any ideas, "No habla Ingles." My panic button was officially pushed.

"Well, I don't know where he is, but I'm gonna find..." Tom spun around and started toward the door, nearly running head-on into a nurse coming around the corner, arms full of clean bed sheets. "Whoa..." he said, stopping just short of a collision. "Hi, we are wondering, um...Do you know where Andrew Atkinson is?" She had a blank look on her face. Tom continued, "Our baby...he was here yesterday—the crib, he was...he was right here," Tom motioned to the empty space.

"Oh...oh, are you Mr. and Mrs. Atkinson?" Sounding all aflutter, she set the linens on the end of the counter.

"Yes," we spoke in unison.

"Oh, I'm so glad you're here. We couldn't reach you last night, and we needed to move Andrew."

"Move him? Why? Where is he?" I asked, relief flooding my body. At least he was alive.

"He's down the hall, but let me get you the other nurse so she can take you over there." She darted out of the room leaving us standing there with our hearts in our throats and no idea what was going on.

"Mr. and Mrs. Atkinson?" A different nurse came bursting around the corner with the first one.

"Yes."

"Hi, I'm Penny. If you'll just follow me, I'll take you to Andrew." We shadowed her on either side as we walked the long hallway towards the big green swinging doors that said Intensive Care Unit. She chatted with us in a friendly, upbeat voice, asking how we were doing and we learned about Rule #1: Parents must make absolutely sure to give a number where they can be reached if they are going to be leaving the hospital. We kept nodding. I felt sick inside. How could we have messed up like this? Why weren't we here for Andrew when he needed us?

Penny continued, "Last night your little Andrew gave us a run for our money. After you left for the evening, he had an episode where his breathing and heart rate were compromised; we felt it was best to move him to the ICU. He was in quite a bit of distress, so we put him on a ventilator and sedated him to help him stay calm." She paused to let this information sink in as we kept walking. Then she continued, "The Cardiac ICU is right here, through these doors." She hit the large round metal button on the wall, and the green doors swung open into the ICU. A few steps further brought us to the nurses' station.

After the initial speechless fear of not knowing what had happened, we had questions. What did she mean compromised? Why did they have to intubate him? I can't say we were completely shocked. Surprised, yes, but not shocked. We knew that he was sick, and I was glad he was here to get the care he needed. What he needed was beyond what I was capable of giving him. I knew that. Penny wasn't giving us many details, and I couldn't figure out exactly why he had to be moved—I mean, what exactly was an episode? What had she meant? All Tom and I could figure was that he must have had one of his out-of-control panic attacks, and the nurses couldn't get him calmed down.

I was about to ask her more about it when Penny introduced us to several nurses at the ICU nurses' station. "This is Mr. and Mrs. Atkinson, Andrew's mom and dad." One of the nurses stood up and put out her hand to shake our hands. "Hi, I'm Stacy, Andrew's nurse. I'll be taking care of him today." This young nurse was warm and friendly, smiling as she talked to us, leading us over to his crib. I liked her immediately. Her hair was the color of maple syrup with hints of red and gold in the long braid that hung down her back. Her voice was understanding and positive.

"How is he doing now?" I asked, "Is he okay?"

"Oh, yes, he's been doing great since he got here last night. So, that big tube sticking out of his nose, that's the ventilator." She pointed it out to us as we approached his bedside. "It's hooked up to the machine that's breathing for him in order to give his body a chance to relax and not have to work so hard to breathe. He gave us quite a little scare."

"He did?" I thought I might be having an out-of-body experience as I looked at him lying there. Is this my baby? All these tubes…and he looks so, so different, and…

"Yes, he did. He really got everybody around here hopping."

I wish I had asked her what she meant by that, but I was speechless when I saw him. "Umm, wow," I managed. We were just so shocked even though we had tried to be prepared. I mean, obviously we were here for heart surgery. We knew he was going to be on a ventilator at some point, but we weren't expecting it that day. I tried to take it all in as gracefully as possible, but seeing my four month old in that condition was very surreal. He had white adhesive tape crisscrossing his mouth and cheeks to hold the ventilator in place and another tube coming out of the other little nostril. He was lying on his back in a little white t-shirt and diaper, with his arms straight out flat on each side of the bed. They had taped splints around both arms to keep the IVs in place. You could see his little fingertips poking out from the end of the splints, but that's about it. He had heart monitor patches on his legs and feet and

stomach, and an oxygen saturation clip on his foot. He was heavily sedated, and his skin looked ashen. Though he always had tinges of blue
and gray around his eyelids and mouth, they were darker than usual. I
forced myself back into the moment.

Stacy was saying something—oh, still talking about the episode last
night, "Yes, but we were able to get it all under control, and he's doing
really well now. All his vitals are stable. Would you like to hold him?"
Of course I want to hold him. I can't wait. Best idea ever. I was glad we
had Stacy. She wasn't patronizing or trying to impress us, and I appreciated that. It seemed as if she truly looked at us as actual people and understood how emotionally drained we were by this experience. We were
trying to take it all in, process the big picture, understand the details,
and it was tough to handle. She was doing her best to make it easier all
the way around.

During the weeks we were at the hospital, I grew to love Stacy and
the other wonderful nurses that spent their days and nights saving these
babies' lives. Sometimes they needed to be no-nonsense; that was the
nature of the job. But Stacy was special to us because she was Andrew's
primary nurse, and we could tell that she grew to love him. In the midst
of this awful experience, her sweet, caring spirit was genuine and I often
found myself comforted by her presence.

"Yes, I'd love to hold him," I responded, nodding as she pulled the
rocking chair closer to the crib. It would feel good to have him in my
arms. I needed to hold him.

"Ok, let's see…" She picked up Andrew, being careful not to disturb
the tubing and IV lines as I situated myself in the chair. "I think this
will reach over there." She lifted him over the crib's edge and out to me.
"Here you go," she said, as she laid my little son in my arms and then
made sure the vent was adjusted correctly. I finally breathed a little.

"You can hold him as long as you want; I'm going to go check on some other things. Let me know when you're ready to lay him down again or if you need anything else."

"Okay," I responded, trying to snuggle Andrew closer in my arms, but all the paraphernalia attached to him felt awkward and staged. He did open his eyes about half way to look up at me, but he was so medicated that he only managed to keep them open for just a second. "It's okay, Andrew, you just go to sleep," I soothed my child. I knew he needed all the rest he could get.

Tom pulled a chair close, and we took turns holding Andrew, talking to him and rocking and wondering quietly to ourselves what exactly had transpired the night before while we were sleeping soundly right across the street. We felt terrible that we hadn't been there with him.

Dr. Lock, Andrew's cardiologist, popped in to check on Andrew that morning and brought us up to speed on the latest developments. Andrew had had a spinal tap after we'd left the night before because he was running a slight fever. The initial results came back good—no infection, but his fluid level was way down. He had received two transfusions during the night, but the final blood culture results wouldn't be in for another day. After consulting with one another, the doctors decided to move the surgery back at least one day. We were disappointed. If it turned out there was an infection, we'd have to wait even longer. If he couldn't beat the illness quickly, he'd become weaker and unable to survive a surgery. We could do nothing but wait and pray.

Andrew had a team of three cardiologists and a gazillion other doctors and fellows and residents…I hadn't realized before we came that we were in the teaching hospital for Harvard Medical School. At some point that day a couple of the staff cardiologists stopped by to see if we had any questions about the actual surgery. They walked us through exactly what would be happening in the operating room if we got to that point. We learned he would be put onto a heart-lung machine which would do the work of his heart while the doctor was operating. His chest would be opened, and the doctors would first assess his specific situation more closely because every baby's heart is different. The surgeon would basically try to replumb his heart by connecting the aorta to its normal spot, placing a new aorta and valve (from a pig) where Andrew's pulmonary artery and valve should have been, and putting a patch in where the septum (ventricular wall) should have been. Then we would pray. The first forty-eight to seventy-two hours would be critical.

We were thankful to be in Boston, surrounded by remarkably skilled and passionate physicians from all over the world. The cardiologists had discussed Andrew's case in their weekly meeting and had done another echocardiogram the night before, but Dr. Lock said they had not discovered anything new; his condition was exactly as they had anticipated. The surgery would take a good part of the day, they thought.

Since Andrew's surgery was postponed a day, it turned out to be a rather quiet day in the ICU for us and for Andrew. We needed that bit of downtime, and since we weren't about to leave his side again, we sat kind of in the background all day long and held our baby. We were able to observe it all—the sights, smells and sounds of the ICU. We watched the nurses hustling here and there and got a feel for the rhythm and flow of this critical care unit. It was much more intense and incredibly different from our previous hospital experience.

The bassinettes were spaced out in a semi-circle around the nurse's station—small, raised beds with bright spotlights above each one, with larger beds for toddlers or older children,. Looking at the beds from the nurse's station, the children were placed in order, from the sickest baby on the far left around to the least sick on the right. Of course, that categorization was all relative. The least sick baby in the cardiac intensive care unit is still very, very sick. Curtains hung between each bed to divide the spaces, but they weren't pulled out far enough to separate the parents sitting next to each baby's bed. This meant no privacy; we could all see each other. Each baby had his or her own nurse, with the babies in the first two or three spaces having two nurses each.

We felt like the new kids in school. Andrew's bed was in one of the last spots on the right—he wasn't very sick in comparison to the others, and he didn't demand a huge amount of attention since he hadn't had surgery yet. We were kind of on the outskirts of all the major action. We watched, wide-eyed, the goings on around us with a mixture of curiosity and horror. The nurses ran a very tight ship and, if there was a crisis, (which happened often), *everyone* had to leave the area and go out to the ICU waiting room. When that happened, it was usually because one of the babies coded, and those intervals out in the waiting room were very scary for us parents. When a baby returned to the unit from surgery, all the parents had to leave. For procedures like removing chest tubes, curtains were pulled, and everyone could stay except for that baby's parents. Everyone also had to leave when the nurses changed shifts between eight and nine each morning and between seven and eight at night. And if you wanted to spend the night, you could not sleep in a chair or fold-up cot next to your child; you had to sleep in the waiting room. Though we understood parents not being allowed in the CICU overnight, we hated having to leave Andrew's side. Even one room away felt too far.

Once when a newborn arrived on a life-flight helicopter from California, the staff was so busy getting her settled that they forgot to tell us all to leave. We had front row seats to the whole transfer process because she was assigned to the bed right next to Andrew's. We watched in awe as the flight nurses and doctors coordinated with their hospital counterparts, wheeling her in, relaying all her vital information and transferring her from portable machines to the hospital machines. It was very intense, and we could see the passion they had for their jobs, and the care that they had for that little baby and her parents. This baby girl, only one day old, had Transposition of the Great Arteries—her aorta and pulmonary artery were reversed and plugged into the wrong spots. She had surgery the next day and actually was able to go back home before we were.

One of the hardest parts of the CICU for me was the whiteboard. As you walked from the waiting room through the doors and past the nurse's station, a large whiteboard on the wall had all the patients' names written on it. I know almost every hospital floor and unit has one of these whiteboards, but this one was different. When a baby died during the night, his or her name would be erased from the board. It wasn't an everyday thing, but it did happen. All these babies were so very close to heaven. Leaving the unit every night meant we had to walk back past that board every morning, and I was always scared to look, afraid that someone's name would be gone. Because these were the sickest babies, the truth is that many of them did not live. The doctors and surgeons were trying to give them a chance—a chance they wouldn't have had anywhere else. But it wasn't always successful and some of the babies and children just didn't make it. It was devastating and frightening for everyone, not only because we cared about the other families and babies, but also because we knew that missing name could easily be our child. We were all in the same boat.

Finally, Andrew's lab results came back negative for infection, so the surgery was scheduled for Friday morning, right before Mother's Day. The papers had all been signed, the final testing done, and everything was a go. We both stayed the night on cots in the waiting room. It was uncomfortable, but I wanted to be close by and not miss a single possible moment before he went into surgery the next morning.

Seven

Now faith is the assurance of things hoped for,
the conviction of things not seen.
– Hebrews 11:1 ESV

At the timberline where the storms strike with the most fury,
the sturdiest trees are found.
– Hudson Taylor

I GRABBED a cup of coffee, then headed through the doors and into the unit. It was 5:45 a.m. Stacy helped me pick up Andrew, ventilator and all, so that I could hold him on my lap. Then she handed me a box of Kleenex. "I thought you might need those," she said gently, and I nodded, appreciative but unable to speak because of the lump in my throat. I held him and cried quietly, my face close up to his. I looked at his perfect little chest that would never look that way again. My fingers memorized each unscarred bump and dip stretching from his belly button all the way up his breastbone and the little tracheal dip between his collarbones. I studied his face, his sweet cheeks and the soft curve of his eyebrow, his feathery eyelashes. The wrinkle that occasionally flashed across his forehead made me wonder if he was dreaming. Or could he hear my halting, whispered words? I fingered through his baby fine, curly hair and held those tiny fingers that just barely protruded out from under the splints still taped to his arms. "Oh, God," I cried through my tears, "please protect him." My throat hurt from holding back my sobs.

Tom came in about 6:15, anxious for a few minutes with our son too. Andrew was out of it because of being sedated, and I was glad that he wasn't in pain. He slept the next hour and a half as we held him, but a couple of times he opened his eyes like maybe he knew we were there. I ached for him to know how much he was loved because we could not possibly have loved him more than at that moment. I was filled with all kinds of mixed emotions: glad the day had finally arrived, scared for what was going to happen. I wanted to get it over with, I wanted to go home and pretend it wasn't happening at all, but most of all I wanted somehow for it to be me and not my baby who was heading into surgery.

This operation made me feel like I was jumping off the high dive for the first time. My stomach had been in knots with each step building up to this moment, but now, out on the end of the board trying hard to keep my balance, I faced the very moment when my faith had to take over. Petrified and wobbly and paralyzed thirty feet out over the water, I could do nothing but step off into the air. Even though we'd made it this far, relinquishing my baby into someone else's care, knowing the outcome would be unpredictable—it was truly a step of faith.

Taking that jump of faith with nothing concrete to hold onto is the opposite of what we're inclined to do. It goes against most of our natural tendencies, which is why it's so scary. But as far as I could tell, God was the only solid thing around. He was my Rock, and I knew I had to hold onto Him. So, as frightening as it was, when the time came, I handed Andrew to Stacy so she could lay him back in his bed and get him situated for the surgical team and doctors.

Dr. Castenada, the surgeon, stopped by to check in with us and asked if we had any questions. We'd met him a couple of days earlier, so he was just making sure we were doing okay. His heavy accent made him hard to understand, but he was wonderfully kind, and we were confident that he knew exactly how to take a tiny broken heart and make it work again. We were honored that Andrew was in the hands of one of the most skilled physicians in the world. If anyone could save his life, it would be this team. At 7:30 a.m., Dr. Lock and the nurses came to get Andrew. They unhooked the ventilator from the wall and connected Andrew to the portable vent. Stacy gave me a quick hug and said she'd see us later as we followed his crib out of the ICU and into the elevator. We rode down to the third floor with the team, kissed Andrew good-bye and then watched as they walked his little crib down the hall to the operating room. *And just like that, my baby is gone, heading into surgery without me.*

We found our way to the waiting area which consisted of a dozen or so chairs behind a partition in one section of the hospital lobby. It didn't feel very private, but there was coffee and a vending machine, and the phone volunteer promised to keep us updated when they called from the operating room with progress reports. We settled in for a long and anxious wait.

Everyone copes with stress in different ways, and even though we'd been married for seven years, Tom could still surprise me. Today he decided he wanted to take a nap. And, much to my chagrin, he did. Usually, that would have been fine. Sure, go take your nap, no problem. But we had barely settled into the waiting room chairs. I walked over to a table to get a magazine, turned back around, and he was out…sound asleep. He might have even been snoring. It ticked me off. How could he do that?

"Your son is in *surgery*," I whispered, leaning over and elbowing him quietly, trying not to make a scene. "*Heart* surgery, right *now*." He cracked an eye but closed it immediately and kept on sawing logs. Frustrated, I opened the magazine and randomly flipped through the pages loudly, not reading or even looking at the pictures. I know it was stupid to let it irritate me, but I didn't understand how could he just go to sleep while Andrew was in surgery.

Later that morning, in the cafeteria, I brought it up again. "How could you just go to sleep like that? That was so insensitive."

He kind of chuckled and said, "I was tired. I got up early this morning, and besides, it was all fine. I think you might be overreacting."

"I am *not* overreacting," I said under my breath. "I stayed awake in case there were messages from the operating room. That's what normal people do."

"Ohhh, is that right?" he teased. "Well, if something had happened, I'd have woken right up. I wasn't going anywhere." Then he put his arm around me as he said lightly, "Anyway, I don't think Andrew needed my fatherly sensitivity during his surgery."

"Well, maybe you could have been a little more sensitive to *me*, and maybe I needed you to stay awake." And then, just to tease him back a bit, I threw in, "Or, maybe you should have been *praying for him.*"

He cracked a smile, "Oh, so now the truth comes out." Pulling me closer, he said, "Do you think I haven't been praying?" He paused and held me back at arm's length, looking to see if I was really serious.

I gave him a half-hearted smile and looked down. "I know, but…"

"Cathy, you know I've never stopped praying—every second of every hour of every day since we found out." He kissed me on the side of my head and said that he thought maybe I needed a nap. *Yeah, okay. Very funny! Maybe in a few years…*

We watched the other families come and go throughout the morning, and every so often Andrew's surgical nurse would call from the operating room with an update:

- 8:30 a.m. — He was ready to go onto the heart-lung machine.
- 9:30 a.m. — He was on the pump, and they were putting the

new pulmonary artery in place and getting ready to repair the hole in his heart.

- 12:00 p.m. — He came off the pump without any problems, and they were closing his chest.

Sometime mid-afternoon Dr. Castenada found us in the waiting room. Still dressed in his blue surgical scrubs and wearing his scrub cap, he looked tired but pleased. He told us that the surgery was over and had gone very well—there were no surprises, and Andrew was doing fine. He crossed his arms and shifted positions as he continued. "I'm very happy with the outcome. He did well, and I expect that his recovery will be excellent." But then he said, "The next seventy-two hours will be critical, and that is especially true of the next twenty-four hours."

We nodded in understanding.

"I think he will do well. But we will see in the next few days." His accent emphasized the "we will see." "Yes," he continued, "this next phase is critical to Andrew's recovery, but I think he will do fine. Do you have questions?"

"No, I don't think so. But thank you so much," we both said at the same time. And as I said it, I realized how horribly inadequate a simple thank you was compared to what this doctor had just done for Andrew and for us.

He nodded his head. "Alright then, you should be able to see him in about an hour. I will make sure someone calls you here." He shook our hands, turned and walked back through the Authorized Personnel Only doors. I remember thinking that he was an amazing man.

It wasn't Mother's Day quite yet, but I felt like I'd been handed the best Mother's Day gift ever—Andrew had actually made it through surgery. We called our families to give them the good news. At that point, we both felt like skipping down the hallway, shouting out the news at the top of our lungs. Instead, we tried to control our exuberance as we walked to the cafeteria, excitement bubbling inside. We headed straight for the frozen yogurt machine and savored our moment of joy.

It was another hour and a half before we could see Andrew back in the ICU, but when they finally let us in, we were cautiously optimistic. He looked puffy, and his pale skin was in stark contrast to the vivid red blood that filled his chest tubes. I counted six IV lines, the heart monitor lines, the ventilator tubes, two catheter wires, two chest tubes, the oxygen monitors and a blood pressure cuff. Underneath all that, though, our little Andrew had a newly plumbed heart—a heart finally capable of sending blood to his lungs and oxygen to his body.

We pulled our chairs into place next to him, and I taped a silver banner across the foot of his bed that said *I Love You*. We had a photo of David with our dog, Cody, so we propped that at the head of the little bed and set his Paddington Bear music pillow next to his cheek, supporting the ventilator tubes. I got out my knitting, and Tom read. Now and then we'd turn on the musical pillow and let Brahms' Lullaby wander through our minds. Sometimes we talked to Andrew, but mostly we tried to keep busy with something. This was going to be our life for a while.

After a few days in a large hospital, you realize it's like living in a bubble. It has its own little biosphere, with unique habitats and communities. We were just one little part of the huge hospital world, inhabitants of the CICU and the Cardiac Unit. When we ventured into the hallways to head for one of the cafeterias, they seemed like tunnels taking us from one environment to another. We explored and found passageways leading to the hospital next door—Brigham and Women's—where the food selection was tastier and more appealing. We even found microwave popcorn in one of the vending machines and that amazing soft-serve frozen yogurt machine in the cafeteria.

Before long, we settled into a type of routine. When we were required to leave the unit during the CICU nurses' shift changes morning and evening, that's when we'd eat. I almost always had grilled cheese, with catsup for dipping, for dinner. I was totally unconcerned about the calories and fat. It was familiar, so for me, it was comfort food. Tom, being the risk taker that he is, would try some of the more exotic cafeteria choices like stroganoff and hamburgers and burritos. But we both loved that frozen yogurt!

Babies who undergo surgery for Truncus are kept sedated for quite a long time—longer than with other heart surgeries. The doctors had discovered that recovery was easier if the patient spent more time sedated and was awakened very gradually. Andrew was kept sedated for a full five days. So, during that time, we simply observed our son, his nurses, the doctors on their rounds and the families around us in the CICU. It was hard not holding him, not knowing how he truly was underneath all that medication.

Finally, one night Dr. Lock said Andrew was ready to be weaned off the sedatives. He also said it would be easier to assess his progress and get a better idea of the surgical outcome once Andrew was awake and alert. What we didn't know was that something serious had happened while Andrew was sedated, something the doctors weren't telling us, that may have had a drastic impact on his progress toward healing. But all I could think about was seeing his happy baby eyes again.

Eight

The LORD is near to those who have a broken heart,
and saves the crushed in spirit.
– Psalm 34:18 ESV

God does not willingly bring affliction or grief to us. He does
not delight in causing us to experience the pain of heartache.
He always has a purpose for the grief He brings or allows
to come into our lives.
– Jerry Bridges

I AWOKE early the next morning in the CICU waiting room, still weary because I had slept fitfully. I never could sleep well on those cots. I still hadn't figured out how to turn over quietly; every time I moved, the cracking plastic mattress and aluminum frame squeaked in unison like a sixth-grade orchestra. Plus, the legs didn't lock into place, so I was always nervous that the whole thing was going to collapse underneath me. We—and several other parents—slept almost every night on our fold-up cots tucked into the corners and along walls, trying to find a tiny sliver of privacy, not willing to leave the premises.

Tired as I was this particular morning, I wanted to get up and get going because today was the day Andrew would be weaned from the meds that kept him in a semi-coma. It had been five days—five long days that seemed to stretch on and on. We had waited, watched him sleep and worried, never knowing if he was out of the woods or not. We waited through moments when the alarms started buzzing and beeping and a rush of doctors and nurses tended to him, our stomachs flipping as we stood watching in the background. And we waited through days of relative quiet. We came to realize that *not* knowing what to expect is part of it all; every single moment held a distinct possibility of life or death. We hung on the doctors' words as they made rounds each morning and evening, but we were careful not to count on anything as one hundred percent stable or secure. Just like a roller coaster ride, our world could freefall right over the edge in a matter of seconds, and we knew it. When you're in that spot, it comes down to holding onto how things are right *now*, being thankful for God's mercies and being present in every moment. But today was finally the day he would wake up.

Folding and securing my wobbly cot, I pushed it into the corner. I felt claustrophobic; the room seemed small this morning, as if it had shrunk a bit during the night. I really needed some space and could hardly wait to see Andrew. After folding my blankets, I whispered to my snoring husband that I was going on in. I glanced in the mirror to make sure I was presentable and quickly brushed through my sleep-tousled hair. Makeup and the latest hairstyles were not a part of my morning routine anymore. Everyone here knew there were more crucial things at stake. We did the best we could and focused on what mattered. I hurried past the nurse's station, over to the half-circle of hospital bassinettes, my stomach doing cartwheels the whole way. You never knew what you would be facing. Since his surgery last week, Andrew's bed was second from the left. I saw Susan, one of his nurses, standing over him, checking his leads, talking softly. She glanced at me and said to him, "Look, Andrew, here's your mom," then, smiling back at me, she said, "He opened his eyes this morning."

I barely heard her, I was so happy to see him awake again. He looked a bit groggy, eyes at half-mast, but I immediately thought, *Hey, I'll take what I can get.* I leaned over the bed, kissed his forehead and looked into those dark blue pools. Chatting with him as if he had just returned from a long trip, I talked about how much we had missed seeing him and how happy we were that he was back with us. Soon Tom arrived and stood on the other side of the bed, just as delighted as I was. We took turns talking to our baby, elated by this giant step.

As I watched him, though, it began to dawn on me that something wasn't quite right. I studied his eyes and knew—as only a mother knows—that our little Andrew wasn't quite there. A parent *knows* their four month old, and that baby knows you. And I especially knew Andrew because he had been so sick, and I'd spent all day, every day with him. Yes, his eyes were open, but I couldn't tell if he was actually seeing me or not; his eyes emitted only a blank stare. Nothing inside them spoke to me—no recognition, no following me with his eyes, no personality shining through. A panicked tightness enveloped my throat as I whispered to Tom, "I think there's something wrong. He doesn't seem right. I don't believe he's seeing us; he's just blank."

Overhearing my concerns, Susan was quick to reassure us. "It's probably because the meds haven't worn off yet. Give him some time."

Oh, of course, I thought, and my throat relaxed a bit. So we settled in for the day, one half-worried parent on each side of Andrew's bed trying to get our minds on something other than our obvious concerns. Tom zoned in on a book while Andrew slept, and I tried to stay focused on a knitting project. Every so often, if Andrew stirred, we'd stop and talk to him, checking his reactions for any change.

About mid-morning, as the doctors did rounds, I was still worried that something wasn't right with Andrew, so I got up my nerve to ask the doctors about it. Since Children's is a teaching hospital, rounds always involve a large group of doctors, fellows, residents and interns walking around with clipboards, discussing the child in each bed in detail as if the parents were not there at all. They would talk quietly amongst themselves for a couple of minutes, and then the whole group would do-si-do to the next baby on the right. They all stayed very close together, only moving when the person next to them moved. Tom and I used to laugh and joke between the two of us that it looked like an amoeba square dance.

The doctors were polite, but distant, and somewhat intimidating. I know doctors aren't gods; they're just men and women trying to figure things out. And yes, I do realize they have other patients, other families…sometimes the expectations placed on those in the medical field can be way out of proportion. We tend to assume they can fix whatever is wrong, but sometimes they can't. They are trying their best, but sometimes it doesn't work, or they don't know what else to do. But we expect them to know, even though that's not fair.

However, I was my child's advocate, and I *had* to speak up for him. Even if the doctors didn't understand everything, I expected accurate communication and respect, and I felt they expected exactly that from the families of their patients. So, although I was apprehensive, I put on my best child advocate face and stood up when the amoeba-like formation of doctors walked toward us and encircled the foot of Andrew's bed.

I waited until it seemed like they were finished talking before I spoke. "I have a question." They all turned, startled, and looked at me. I went on, "This morning he was able to open his eyes, and that was good, but it didn't seem that he was responding to us when we talked to him. His eyes—they just weren't focusing or something." I felt like I had completely bungled all the words, that what I said might as well have been gibberish.

The doctor group stared at me or looked down at their clipboards.

They cleared their throats and shifted in place. A long few seconds passed. Had I spoken out loud or did I imagine it? Dr. Lock spoke up, "I'll come back over in a bit and check on him. I'll try to answer your questions after we're done with rounds." He seemed a bit more formal than his usual approachable, friendly self. It was probably because so many others were around, but it caught me off guard and made me embarrassed that I'd said anything at all. Something was amiss, but I couldn't put my finger on it. Maybe I broke protocol by talking to them. I probably shouldn't have spoken up. I wondered if asking a question to the group was taboo. I was only trying to find out what was wrong. I thanked him quietly and shrunk back into my chair wishing I could disappear completely. That seemed to be that.

Frustrated, I returned to my knitting. Of course, I found a dropped stitch and had to rip out a few rows. It felt good to rip it out. I wanted to rip the whole thing out. Everything else in my life felt ripped out. I felt close to being ripped out altogether. I shoved the yarn back into the knitting bag and just sat…frustrated and scared and embarrassed.

My emotions can be feisty and unpredictable—sometimes they quietly slip the reins on the horses and lead me off in the wrong direction before I even know what's happening. I don't think it's wrong to feel the emotion; I think it's how I respond to the emotion that can be right or wrong. I get angry at myself when I jump to conclusions or make judgments without the facts. Anger takes energy and causes frustration and, when the truth comes out, most times I've misunderstood what happened. But even when anger is justified, I find I can be overcome by disappointment, devastation or discouragement.

The thing is, when I allow my emotions—or my response to my emotions—to take over, I am not able to see the bigger picture of what God is doing. Like putting on a pair of glasses that block out what's true, I start listening to and believing the lies that gallop around in my head.

God doesn't love you. He doesn't hear your prayers. You just made a total fool of yourself. You must prove you are good enough. The intensity of my emotional response often makes me blind and deaf to His presence. It's strange, because I really do believe that He's there, but I can't feel His presence. I feel very alone. It's as if my emotional responses wipe out what's real. I forget that I already have God's guidance and comfort—His Spirit is right inside me. But I'm scared I'm going to have to handle everything all by myself. I can't see or hear or feel His presence, and I doubt His ability to help. I cry out, "God, are You there? Can You hear me, God? I need You!" Sitting in that chair, watching Andrew stare into nothingness that day, I couldn't feel God's loving arms around me. Confused and terrified of the unknown, I wanted to shut down.

Finally, Dr. Lock came back and began to examine Andrew. He checked his eyes with his penlight for any response. We could see for ourselves that there was none. His eyes did not move back and forth or dilate normally, and he didn't have a normal reflex response. I felt sick. After several minutes of testing, Dr. Lock picked up Andrew's medical chart and flipped back through. Then he looked at us. "Well, we can't be sure, but we feel that Andrew may have had a fairly severe seizure while he was sedated. Because of the meds, we weren't aware of the seizure until later when his labs came back, and it is possible that he has suffered some neurological damage as a result. At this time, we don't know how severe that damage might be."

"What?" The words I was hearing were hard to take in. "How could it...wait, what do you mean?" Fear suddenly grabbed hold of my vocal chords and threatened to choke me into silence.

Tom was on his feet next to Andrew's bed, his hand resting on Andrew's forehead. "A seizure? What...like a grand mal type seizure? How come no one told us? When did this happen?"

"Well, the thing is we don't know how his brain has been affected, so we don't want to make any assumptions." The doctor's demeanor was serious as he continued. "It could be almost nothing—hardly noticeable—or it could be that it affected his vision or another part of his brain. There is nothing we can do at this point; it is out of our hands. We will keep our eyes on it, but we'll have to wait and see. Right now, we need to concentrate on getting him healed up from this heart surgery. He is not out of the woods yet, and there is always the potential that he may have another seizure. We are doing all we can for him, so I wouldn't focus on the neurological outcomes just yet."

My mind was racing frantically. *What? You're telling me not to think about the fact that my son might have brain damage and could be severely challenged in some of his physical or mental abilities? How could I not think about that? Yes, I am glad he is awake, but have we come all this way for this? Of course we are going to think about the outcomes! What will this mean for him and for us? When will we know?* I suddenly felt a tsunami of fear, a wave of nausea rolling in; I stood up and walked to the waiting room. Only then did I turn my thoughts to God. A desperate question gripped me and wouldn't let go. "Lord, what is happening?"

I picked up the parent phone in the CICU waiting room and dialed Colorado. "Mom?" I paused. I didn't want to cry. "Hi, Mom. We need prayer. Something's happened, and Andrew's not doing that great," I told her. "Uh-huh, they think he had a seizure. We don't know, but there might be neurological damage. Please call your prayer chain and anybody else you can think of." I fought back tears while trying my best to fill her in on the latest. We said good-bye, and she promised to pray. I collapsed on that green vinyl couch and fell asleep for a while. It was a dozing kind of sleep, and each time I woke, I prayed.

I did believe that God hears our prayers and that He performs miracles. I knew that I had seen God intervene in supernatural ways in my own life, so I had that to go on. I also knew the Bible says, *"His thoughts* are not our thoughts and His ways are not our ways." Could I trust Him no matter what? Was I ready to trust Him totally with Andrew's condition? I didn't know. I felt like, *Okay, God, I gave You the heart defect, I gave You the surgery...but do I have to give You everything?* Accepting the fact that Andrew could have additional mental or physical handicaps brought mixed feelings, and I struggled to find the answers to my questions.

I finally rose from my fitful sleep and went back to sit with Andrew. This was so far from what I ever expected as a mom that it seemed almost unreal. I stared at him as he slept, cradled between wires and tubes and rolled-up blankets and beeping machines, and I knew in my heart that underneath everything visible, his real cradle was God's mighty hand.

Susan must have noticed my Mom-fears and stepped in. "Would you like to hold him?" she asked. It was the best thing I'd heard in days. We hadn't been able to hold him since before the surgery. Of course I'd like to hold him! He still was on the ventilator and had a million IVs lines, so it would again be awkward, but I didn't care. My arms were aching to hold my baby! Tom and I took turns holding our son for probably an hour. Bliss, I tell you, pure bliss.

Meanwhile, the outcome of my frantic phone call to my mom resulted in the human version of the Twilight Bark from the movie *101 Dalmatians*. Phone call after phone call to prayer chains and more prayer chains—from my mom's church to our extended families and all of their churches, from New York all the way to California; Florida; Washington, D.C.; New Zealand; England; the Philippines and even the Middle East. Word spread around the world to pray for Andrew. I still have letters and notes from people I didn't even know who prayed for him.

It seemed like I prayed all day. I was so sick with fear that I didn't know what else to do. At one point that afternoon, I went into a bathroom stall and prayed. It's funny now, but I wanted to be somewhere private and quiet, and that seemed as close to God as I could get! There just aren't very many private spots in a hospital. My heart was shattered by disappointment and grief, and I wanted my Andrew back. *I had such hope and now what? Will he be completely disabled or only partially? Will he be blind? Is he also deaf?* I felt like a robot, going through the motions, unaware and uncaring of what the next moment would hold.

Tom and I prayed together in the hospital cafeteria that night. It was late, past the regular dinner hour, so hardly anyone was there. The staff had turned off half the lights, and we were able to find a quiet corner. I ordered my usual grilled cheese, and the dill pickle that came with it smelled so good I went ahead and ate it while we prayed. We didn't know what words to say, but we were desperate for Andrew's healing, for help knowing what to do, for wisdom for the doctors and nurses. Although we knew our family and friends were praying for Andrew, we carried his burden as only parents can, and we felt helpless, scared and alone as we prayed in the cafeteria that night.

Later that evening, as I tried to get comfortable on the cot in the darkened waiting room, I let the tears flow freely and tried not to give myself away with uncontrolled sniffing. My hope was gone. I cried for the loss of my dreams for my son. I cried because I was scared and overwhelmed, and I didn't know where to turn or what was going to happen. I cried for the pain and struggles I saw ahead for Andrew, and for what we'd already been through.

My thoughts weren't organized enough to be able to focus on the logical. But I did remember a song and the lyrics that had touched me, reminding me that God, and God alone, creates, sustains and loves each of us. From the mighty to the small, every single one of us is in His hand.

Andrew was so small and helpless, and I felt that way, too. I needed reminding that even the smallest of God's creations is in His care. I *knew* that no matter what happened, and even in spite of what may have happened, God was able to bring something good out of it. That was His job, not mine. This would be for His glory; He knows what's going on. Although it *felt* to me as if everything was spinning out of control, I held on, white knuckled, to what I knew as fact—that God had not changed. At that moment, I knew that nothing else mattered; not one other thing in this whole big world mattered except my faith in God. It was God and me. My heart, laid bare, stripped of any cares for this world, finally understood the reality of trusting Him no matter what.

Andrew was God's creation, God's child and if God so chose, He could take Andrew's life or allow Andrew's life to take a different direction completely. I could not hold on to my own hopes and dreams for this small son of mine; he was in God's hands, the Author of Life. I believed that God loved Andrew much more than I could, so I chose to trust that He would do what was best. The glory in Andrew's life would ultimately be, as the song says, God's and God's alone. Through my tears, I surrendered my own will to God, even as I prayed that Andrew's heart and body and mind would be healed.

The next morning, I didn't hop up from the cot as soon as I woke. In fact, I lay there for a while, steeling myself for the day and willing my heart to be brave. I started contemplating the idea of neurological damage and what all that might mean. It occurred to me that if Andrew had indeed suffered brain damage, he was going to need me to be on top of my game. I had best stop pouting and get with the program. This was God's child, and we were his parents, regardless of the outcome of this surgery and his seizure. So, when I walked up to his little crib that morning, I was prepared to face the worst. "How are you this morning, sweet boy?" I asked, stroking his forehead. Then, miracle of miracles, Andrew opened his eyes and looked at me! The change was immediately apparent.

Our nurse walked over with a grin, "Andrew seems to be doing better this morning." She washed her hands, and a flood of joy washed through my whole being. "He is responding and alert and his vitals have improved. It looks like he may have turned a corner."

I was completely overwhelmed by what I knew could only have been God's mercy reaching down. Where others saw the doctors and the medicines doing their jobs, we saw an absolute miracle. And it really didn't matter if the miracle had happened through the doctors and the medicines they prescribed—God had been merciful to us, and we were thankful. The doctor's comments were "cautiously optimistic," but Tom and I *knew*. Andrew was one way yesterday, and now he was different. We didn't need to know details, but we did know that although Andrew's situation had been out of the doctor's hands, it was never out of God's hands. My eyes filled with tears of joy.

It's so funny how the same emotions that separate me from God can also connect me to Him in ways that are truly too deep for words. He shows Himself to me, and I am suddenly filled full of *Him*. A sunset, a sunrise, a shimmering mountain lake, the softest smell of a new baby, my children's laughter—the God of true emotion creates emotion in me. When I see Him in the gifts He gives, suddenly everything makes sense. My life is only a part, a story within a much bigger story. I live that little part of the story every day, and seeing His movements within my own story is exciting. I know absolutely that He's there, so I'm always watching for His miracles. When you witness a miracle, it's like standing on the edge of heaven and becoming tuned in to the reality of the spiritual world.

We got to hold Andrew again that morning, and neither of us wanted to take turns. He gazed at us like he was memorizing our faces. And we felt privileged to gaze right back. I imagined the day when I could tell him about the way God had miraculously healed him. About how our God is a really big God. In the Bible, God is called by several names that show different facets of His character. One of these names is *El-Shaddai*. In Genesis 17:1, for example, when God is talking to Abram about the many descendants he would have, the name *El Shaddai* is used. It means "Almighty—the Almighty One." That day in the hospital, I was clinging to the Almighty One, holding on tightly to the power in that name.

No matter what experience we go through, God will remain God. He is almighty, He is powerful, and He is good. Our emotions often fool us, but any fear that the enemy tries to throw at us is no match for our God; we can lay down that fear right before Him, and He will replace it with faith. I knew these things in my mind, and I wanted them to take over in my heart so I could be rock solid emotionally. But I struggled every day. I struggled with knowing that I really did not have control over this situation. Neither could I control God by being good enough or faithful enough or praying hard or long enough. Sometimes I'd feel a tremendous surge of faith, and then I'd turn right around and feel nothing at all.

One day a Catholic priest walked through the doors and straight over to our immediate neighbors, Mike and Shannon. They visited for a while. Their baby, Devin, who had been in bed number one the entire time we had been in Boston, was not doing well. The last couple of days had been especially hard, and his little body was starting to shut down. We had overheard the doctor saying there was nothing else they could do, and a decision had to be made about taking him off life support. Watching the anguish that this young couple (who could just as easily have been us) experienced was beyond words. The priest had come to offer a prayer for Devin and for them, and I knew that the Holy Spirit was the only breath of comfort there could be, if there could be any comfort at all. My heart broke as I watched them lay hands on him and pray quietly together. In that moment of grief, I almost felt paralyzed, and I turned away, giving them what little privacy I could.

A little while later, the priest walked over to our little spot—bed number two. I guess he was making the rounds. Right away I had my guard up. I felt defensive but didn't know why. He was obviously a caring and spiritually helpful man. Although we weren't Catholic, I had not been opposed to having a priest pray for us, and I thought it was wonderful that he had come for little Devin. But something inside of me did not want him here right now for Andrew. I resisted his presence, and I did not want him to start in on some rehearsed prayer. I didn't know him, and he didn't know Andrew or us. As far as I was concerned, Andrew was not going to die, and he didn't need this man's prayer. If it sounds like I was rejecting God, I wasn't. I was rejecting a final prayer.

My fears were totally irrational, but all our emotions were out of whack during those days. Subconsciously I associated the prayers of that priest with death; if he prayed for Andrew, it meant that Andrew was close to death. Although that fact would have been obvious to absolutely everyone else, at that moment, I couldn't handle it. I was all clamped up inside about Devin and thinking normally was a little out of my emotional reach. I had to believe Andrew was going to be okay. God knew my prayers and my needs, and we had been asking for His help, and that was good enough for me. I thanked the priest, but told him we'd say our own prayers. "It was very nice of you to offer," I said, "but we'll pass this time."

When we entered the unit the next morning, Devin's name had been erased from the whiteboard—he had died during the night. I felt sick inside and tried to focus on the fact that he was in heaven and had a perfect, pain-free little body, but it was difficult. His bed was gone, everything cleaned up and put away. There was just this big emptiness right next to us where he had been. Mike and Shannon's chairs had been pushed back out of the way; the floor was freshly mopped. Just like that, they were gone, and we didn't even get to say good-bye. We asked the nurses, but they couldn't talk about Devin. They did say he passed away during the night. An unspoken fear crept through the unit that morning, stretching its long, wispy ghost-like tentacles from one set of parents to the next like the plague on the firstborn children of Egypt. Its grip was palpable, and no one said much at all that whole gray day.

The next afternoon, we were still feeling glum, so the nurses planned a treat for all of us parents. They reserved one of the hospital's VCRs and rented a comedy for the parents to enjoy. It was exactly the medicine we needed. Every parent in there—and the nurses, too—laughed harder than we had in weeks. It lifted our spirits and the dark cloud that had enveloped the unit. It felt good to make a quick escape into another world, forgetting reality, if even for just a few moments. It turned out to be the perfect antidote. Our emotions could easily swing from one extreme to another, and most of the time we didn't know how to stop the craziness, so we just hung on.

All these happenings made me keenly aware that I had a tendency to live by my feelings much more than I should. But I also realized that I couldn't allow my faith to be driven by those feelings. Faith is a choice—it's a decision I made completely separate from any feelings or circumstances. And so, even faced with raw fear or intense grief, I can still trust Him. And to this very day, for me, there's nothing else to hang on to anyway—He *is* all there is.

Nine

This I recall to my mind; therefore I have hope.
It is because of the LORD's loving kindnesses that we are not
consumed, Because his compassion doesn't fail.
They are new every morning. Great is your faithfulness.
– Lamentations 3: 21-23 WEB

We need never shout across the spaces to an absent God.
He is nearer than our own soul,
closer than our most secret thoughts.
– A.W. Tozer

ANDREW BEGAN to thrive after his surgery. The doctors were pleased with every aspect of his recovery and, although it was impossible to predict exactly, the hope was that his newly rep-lumbed heart and the implanted valve (homograph) would last several years before he'd need his next surgery. Because our home was a mile above sea level, he was on oxygen for the first month at home, but he didn't seem to mind. He amazed me with his voracious appetite and pink cheeks and fingers. I watched him grow practically before my eyes; he learned new baby-play activities daily. He looked and acted and *felt* like a different baby than he was before our trip to Boston. Our lives as parents were changed completely, too. He ate like a ravenous baby bird, slept through the night and no longer had the sudden panic attacks we'd struggled with so often. He needed only a couple of medications now instead of the whole shelf that he'd taken before surgery, and we weren't driving to and from doctor appointments every other day.

In June, he was allowed to come off the oxygen. Hallelujah! That was a big day and a big deal. For the first time in months, it felt like we were an average, everyday family. I loved it. One day soon after that, we received a coupon in the mail for a free baby portrait. I got Andrew all dressed up in a cute little navy blue sailor outfit with red piping around the collar and took him to the studio. He looked adorable, and he was so happy. I mentioned that these were his first portraits because he had just had open-heart surgery, and the photographer couldn't believe it. Then he tried to get me to buy all kinds of picture packages that would have cost an arm and a leg. There was no way we could afford anything but the free ones, but that guy sure worked all the angles. He called in all his associates and, pointing to Andrew, said dramatically, "Look how beautiful he is! And he's just had heart surgery! Can you believe it? He's never had his portrait taken before, and now she doesn't want to buy the pictures of her beautiful baby!" And then all the others agreed what a pity it was that I wouldn't have the best pictures to remember him.

"Thank you, but not this time," I declined firmly. I was getting irritated. I felt these folks had a lot of nerve, trying to take advantage of the situation! But I stuck to my guns, and it turned out I didn't need all those specialty shots anyway. Andrew was a natural behind the camera. Even the proofs I got for free were darling.

Andrew needed physical therapy to help strengthen his upper body, which was underdeveloped and still sore from the surgery. Sometimes he would use his legs in place of his arms to hold things. He'd wiggle his legs up from under the high chair tray, so he was sitting in the shape of a V with his legs poking up, laughing and babbling and carrying on like it was the most normal thing in the world. If he was cradled in my arms or lying on his back, he'd hold his bottle with his feet. When he was in his swing, he'd bat at his hanging toys with his feet instead of reaching out with his hands. I wondered if it was because it hurt and took more energy to use his arms, or if it was just Andrew being Andrew. Even then he was a comic and a daredevil, and if he did something that got a giggle out of us, he'd do it all over again just for the laughs.

Sitting up requires strength and coordination of muscles in the neck, back, chest, and tummy, and his physical therapist knew how to get him to play so that he strengthened those muscles without realizing it was work. I learned all the exercises so I could do them at home with him, and he was able to sit up by himself by the time he was eight months old. He was still cautious about using his arms and upper body muscles, so a typical crawl was out of the picture. But he wasn't about to get left behind—he had to keep up with his big brother, so he used his legs to propel himself around in a most creative fashion. Back end up in the air and chest down, he'd stretch out with his arms, push forward with his legs and scoot like a little inchworm. He could go anywhere he wanted, and he was fast.

That summer we tried hard to recover. On the one hand, we were still processing everything that had happened, trying to take bits and pieces of the experience, thinking it through and dealing with our emotions. On the other hand, we wanted to forget the whole thing and pretend it hadn't happened at all. I wanted to blend in with other mothers, talk about normal baby things. But sitting and talking with other moms, I found I couldn't relate. Andrew was on his own timetable and wasn't doing the cute things the other babies his age were doing. We kept trying to be "normal," but what was normal for everybody else was no longer an option for us. But we did try—and the results of us trying to fit our old expectations into our new life put us smack dab in the middle of some interesting and hilarious adventures.

One of our attempts at "normal" started with our desire to recreate a fun camping experience—something Tom and I loved to do. We'd both grown up camping and, although getting ready to go can be a lot of work, it is usually just the ticket to a relaxing weekend that isn't overly expensive. So, when the cardiologist said that Andrew was not yet allowed to go to the mountains because of the altitude, I knew I had to get creative. We wanted to get out of the hot, sticky city and up into the cool, quiet breezes of the mountains, so I came up with a plan. We'd drive only as far as the foothills where I knew we could find some lovely areas with campfire pits and picnic tables, fishing ponds and shady spots where we could take a nap or read a book. We'd pack our lunch and head home in the late afternoon, so we wouldn't be biting off more than we could chew. I wanted to evoke the *feeling* of camping, so I planned that we would roast hot dogs over the fire and set a can of pork and beans on the fire to get bubbly hot. Then we'd have s'mores because you can't go camping without the deliciousness of graham crackers, toasted marshmallows and chocolate. Tom planned to take David down to the little pond for some fishing after our lunch. It sounded perfect.

Spirits high, we loaded the car with fishing gear, camp stove, picnic basket, cooler and camp chairs. We had a general idea of where to go and started looking for a pretty little spot to set up when we arrived, but it was certainly not what we'd expected. We couldn't find the little fishing hole we remembered, and the pine trees and cool breezes were conspicuously absent. This wasn't the camping we were used to, but we finally settled on a campsite space half way up the side of a steeply sloping hill, but it did have a tree...one tree. It was pathetic, and I was disappointed, but, *Okay,* I decided, *we are going to make this work, and we'll have fun anyway.* We parked our car in a lower parking lot and hiked up the hill—not that far really, but with a baby and a toddler, it felt like climbing a fourteener. Tom made two extra trips up and down the hill with the cooler and the camp chairs and blankets to spread out. By this time, we all were hungry, so Tom and David set out to find firewood.

I set Andrew in his car seat on the picnic table and looked through the cooler for the hotdogs and the can of beans. Tom came back quickly after he realized all the wood lying around was drenched from the rainstorm the day before. He tried, but had no luck getting a fire lit. While he was trying to get something to spark, newly potty trained David was mentioning he had to go—really bad. The outhouse was all the way around on the other side of the picnic loop, so—since I was busy with lunch and Tom was fully occupied trying to get a fire going—Tom told David to go potty over by the tree because it would be more private. I was pulling the rest of the lunch items out of the camp box when I glanced at Andrew playing happily on the table. My eyes immediately spotted a wasp circling the baby seat, and before I knew it, it landed right above Andrew's little knee. The next thing I knew, I was flying through the air like a super hero mother in a slow-motion movie shot, intent on rescuing her baby from the nasty, hurtful insect. But I was too late. It nailed him just before I got there, and he screamed bloody murder.

"What happened?" Tom leapt up at the sudden, earsplitting cry.

"He just got stung by a wasp." I grabbed a piece of ice from the ice chest and put it on the spot that was already turning red. "Oh, baby, I'm so sorry. I know that hurts." I tried to soothe Andrew while getting him out of the seat. "Tom, do you know if we have a first-aid kit in the car?" I was wondering, of course, how this might affect his heart. I remembered the doctor saying if anything unusual happened that we should call him. He'd said that sometimes the effects of the anesthesia can cause weird reactions to things even months later. I wondered if a wasp sting would be considered unusual.

"I don't know if there's any first aid stuff, but even if there is, there's not going to be a bee sting kit or anything like that," Tom replied. I tried to situate the ice on the bite by tying it around his leg with a bandana, but he kept kicking it off or grabbing at it. About that time, hearing David call my name, I looked over to see him still over by the tree attempting rather bravely to accomplish the task of going to the bathroom by himself. Neither Tom nor I had realized until that very moment that when he said he needed to go, he meant the whole shebang.

"Mooooom," David cried for help again.

"You've got to be kidding," I said under my breath as I headed toward him, leaving Andrew crying behind me. David was almost two and a half, and he had tried his best, but, well, let's just say it was not a pretty picture. I gagged and turned away. Andrew was screaming again. "Tom, I need your help over here!"

You'd have thought things could not possibly have gone any further downhill from that point—we were all hungry and couldn't get a fire started, there was really nothing to eat except marshmallows and graham crackers because everything else I brought needed to be heated up, and we had an unhappy, hurting baby, an unhappy, messy toddler, a frustrated dad and a mom with a weak stomach. But, wait, it got worse.

Tom had taken over toddler cleanup, and I was comforting Andrew when I looked down the hill and saw school bus after school bus rolling around the corner and parking in a nice neat row right next to our car. The entire Denver Parks and Recreation Summer Fun program had scheduled their "day in the mountains" for this very day. We counted five school buses full of elementary age kids. The kids poured out and proceeded to climb the hill to a group campsite that was just beyond our spot. Like an army of ants, they swarmed right past—actually right through—our site, probably ten feet from Tom and David. As hundreds of kids with their sun hats and brown paper bag lunches passed us, I stood there and stared. *I cannot believe this is happening. A quiet, relaxing afternoon in the mountains? What were we thinking?*

The hot pink welt on Andrew's leg had swollen to about the size of a half-dollar and had a white spot in the center with a little red dot where the stinger had gone in. He'd stopped crying temporarily, probably because the spot was numb from the ice, but I was nervous—what if he had an allergic reaction? We didn't know if he was allergic to stinging insects or not. I could have been overreacting, in fact, I probably was. But how do you know? So many things had happened the past few months, and I was skittish about taking any risks. It would be just our luck for Andrew to have an anaphylactic reaction while we were out playing camper family and pretending to have a good time. I decided it wasn't worth it. It did not matter to me if we ever had another camping experience or not. *Whose brilliant idea was this anyway,* I thought to myself sarcastically.

"Tom, let's just go home," I muttered. "I've had enough wilderness adventures for today."

"Sounds good to me." He began gathering the blankets and hot dog skewers and the lighter fluid he'd used to try to get a fire going while I put the food back into the cooler and box. We grabbed the kids, loaded the car in record time and were headed home well before the last of the Denver Parks kids had gotten up to their spot. He and I decided not to try anything that harebrained again for at least six months.

Everything turned out rather capital in the end though. Andrew was not allergic to the wasp sting, we were thrilled to find a change of clothes for David in the bottom of the diaper bag, and we enjoyed a five-star meal at McDonald's on the way home. Andrew slept in his car seat while the rest of us sat quietly devouring our food, no one speaking because we were so hungry, and it tasted so good.

As the summer and fall progressed, we took it a little easier on our family adventures. We stayed closer to home and didn't attempt any-thing that would have been considered even slightly brave. All the med-ical issues flowed together with all the non-medical parts of life, and that was our new normal. We went to the park and zoo, the cardiologist, the physical therapist and the grocery store—all safe, close and easy.

Ten

Yet I am always with you; You hold me by my right hand, you guide me with your counsel, and afterward you will take me into glory. Whom have I in heaven but you? And earth has nothing I desire besides You. My flesh and my heart may fail, but God is the strength of my heart and my portion forever.
– Psalm 73:23-26 NIV

The same everlasting Father who cares for you today will take care of you tomorrow, and every day. Either He will shield you from suffering, or He will give you unfailing strength to bear it....
– St. Francis de Sales

PARENTING ANY child can be a wild ride, but some kiddos... well, *some* take you right up and over the top. I'm not saying that's good or bad, I'm just saying it's true. Kids are different. Tom and I never expected to be parenting a child with a heart defect, and I'm not sure if it was that or simply Andrew's personality, but we never knew what was waiting around the next corner. Often, we'd find ourselves in over our heads, rushing pell-mell in unexpected directions and being exactly the kind of parent we'd said we never would be. It can be fun, but, oh so exhausting.

By about fourteen months, Andrew had started taking a few steps alone—we were ecstatic and got such a kick out of helping him take steps back and forth between our outstretched arms. Once he had gotten past the initial healing from the surgery, his physical development took off. He was a fearless climber, scaling everything he could pull himself up onto even before he walked. I called him my little Houdini because he could wiggle himself out of the most secure straps. He had figured out how to climb over the crib rail months ago, so I now left it down for his own safety.

Never content to sit still, we laughed that he was making up for lost time and that he needed his own personal lifeguard walking around behind him, picking up after him right and left, making sure he wasn't getting himself into danger or serious trouble. When it came time to explain what I did all day, it was difficult to wrap up in words. I worked hard every day, and I was always tired, but somehow I never ended up with much to show for it. Who would ever believe me if I were to try to recount all that I really did? I decided I needed proof that my life truly was crazy busy, so I came up with a brilliant idea. I would keep a journal of my day, moment by moment if need be, and it would be kind of my own proof-of-life statement.

That morning started out questionably since I was not in the best of moods, but I figured it might be the perfect day to start my journaling project. David was three, Andrew, fifteen months and I was pregnant again and fighting morning sickness. Hoping for a rare snippet of quiet time and a cup of tea, I had crept out of bed early only to discover the boys were already awake and playing. I quickly put on the water for tea and worked on a mental list of tasks I needed to accomplish. I knew most of it probably wouldn't happen (sigh), but one could always have a list. I planned to dive into some chores and get them done and out of the way—but first things first. Teakettle whistling, I poured myself a cup and glanced at the newspaper I'd laid on the counter. I walked over to the kitchen table with my tea in one hand and paper in the other just in time to see David dragging the bouncy horse around the corner of the playroom and into the hallway toward the living room.

"What are you doing?" I asked.

"I want this in there," he stated firmly, grunting as he pulled the horse while motioning toward the front room.

"I don't think so, kiddo, not today," I replied, walking over and reaching for the handle of the horse. "Today is cleaning up day. Do you want to help me?"

He looked at me and then dropped his head to his chest. "Noooo," he bellowed in a panicky voice. He threw himself to the floor and, in an Oscar-worthy performance, had himself an old-fashioned temper tantrum. "Oooohhhhh noooooo," he cried, kicking the floor and letting out another pitiful wail.

I rolled my eyes, but I was a little surprised. First of all, it wasn't really like David to throw a temper tantrum, and second, it wasn't even seven o'clock in the morning—I was still in my pajamas. *Do we really have to start the day like this? Can't there be a little calm before the storm?* I thought to myself hopelessly. I helped him (picked him up and carried him) to his room, deposited him on his bed and left the room, ignoring the outburst. I refused to put up with such antics.

I vacuumed the living room, the hall and my bedroom, then I opened the boys' door to check on the progress of the temper tantrum. David had calmed down, so I went in. I sat on the edge of the bed, and we talked, and he was sorry. Andrew sat contentedly making a tower with blocks. Maybe I could get that last bedroom vacuumed. But not even a minute had passed when I heard a rather loud bump from their room. *Oh, great, now what?* Peeking around the corner, I discovered Andrew sitting smack-dab on *top* of the dresser. He had emptied all the drawers and pulled them out to use as a ladder to ascend to the top. He somehow had managed to maneuver himself into a sitting position, but now he was stuck. The whole room was a total disaster from the contents of the drawers, but he'd also bumped the red-framed picture of Winnie the Pooh off the wall, and it lay broken on the floor. All the special books that I had carefully set up on the dresser because they were too beautiful to have down low had been pushed off and lay upside down in piles on the floor, and the basket of disposable diapers was dumped and scattered next to my feet.

"Oh, Andrew!" I admonished, moving him from the dresser top to the floor. "What in the world are you doing?" I picked up the books and broken picture frame, telling him firmly, "No, no!" as I returned the diapers to their basket and the clothes to the drawers.

Meanwhile, David decided to make a run for it back to the playroom to build a fort. He dragged blankets (which were neatly folded in the living room basket) into the playroom and attempted to drape them from the card table to the bookcase which didn't work and caused multiple books to tumble off the shelves. He was getting frustrated, and I did feel some empathy for him because he was trying so hard to make it work. I lifted the corner of the blanket and situated it across the top of the table, so he had a bona fide fort to play in. Happy again, he called Andrew, got his bucket of Legos off the shelf and ducked under the table to play. I gave up trying to clean and turned to leave while reminding myself to pick my battles—it was a playroom, after all.

A couple of minutes of relative calm (the key word here being *relative*) and Andrew was hovering at my feet again, holding onto my pajama leg for balance. I noticed he had chocolate all over his hands and face—*Wait, what? What is all this?* Chocolate covered the front of his yellow footie pajamas, and chocolate trailed back down the hall. I picked him up. "What have you gotten into? Hmmm?" The chocolate led back to the kitchen and to last night's cake mix package that had been in the trash. Except now it was all over the kitchen floor. I set Andrew back down and grabbed the broom and dustpan. Our dog was not about to miss out on the fun, so he took his place happily licking the chocolate from Andrew's face and hands. David came bounding around the corner to see why his little brother was giggling and thought it all hilarious. It was contagious, and we all ended up laughing. Maybe things weren't as bad as they had seemed.

Feeling more positive, I decided it was time for breakfast. I cleaned up Andrew's face and hands and buckled him into his toddler seat, then I helped David into his booster seat. I poured them each a glass of orange juice and a bowl of cheerios with milk. Everybody was happy and busy eating, so it seemed safe to leave them for a minute to get dressed. I quickly pulled on jeans and a t-shirt and headed back to the kitchen. I was fast, but not fast enough.

In the kitchen, bedlam reigned. Andrew had climbed out of his seat (that was the Houdini coming out) and up onto the table. He had poured his orange juice out of his sippy cup into his Cheerios, curdling the milk and ruining his breakfast, then dumped David's cereal and poured David's juice into the mess. Andrew thought it was funny, and David was crying.

Lifting Andrew off the table and onto the floor, I grabbed the sponge and proceeded to clean off the table and the puddle that had spilled onto the floor. Andrew decided it was a good time to get undressed, so he unsnapped the front of his pajamas and stepped out of them, leaving them on the kitchen floor. David wanted down because he had to go potty. Andrew wanted back up for more breakfast. I helped David down, lifted Andrew up, and poured them each another bowl of cereal. I loaded the dishwasher and got it filled and ready to go, then discovered we had no soap. That was it. I'd had it. I poured myself a bowl of cereal and milk and turned on the TV—and it wasn't even a kid show. So much for getting the chores done.

Later that day, I remembered my journaling project and took a minute to write down what had transpired that morning while it was still fresh in my head. I'm glad I did. It's funny to look back on that day, but it was exasperating at the time. It's no surprise that it was my one and only entry for that journaling project. My boys kept me busy, that's for sure.

In October of that same year, when Andrew was twenty-two months old and David had just turned four, we experienced a really scary incident. I was going through our regular nighttime routine before putting the boys to bed. I'd bathed them, helped Andrew into his pajamas, said prayers, and then laid Andrew down in his crib for the night. Cranky and tired, he'd been running a slight fever that day, and he seemed to settle down to sleep right away. I headed into David's room where he was choosing books for a bedtime story. We sat down together in our favorite spot on the floor under the window near a heating vent where it was always toasty warm. We'd just begun reading *Curious George Flies a Kite* when we heard a funny noise. Kind of half a cough and half a meow. *What was that?* I thought. *Was it something outside? A cat?* I cocked my head and looked at David. He looked up at me puzzled, wrinkling his little brow. "Did you hear that?" I asked.

"Uh-huh," he said, looking back at the book and turning the page, much more interested in the curious little monkey than in the curious noise.

I heard the noise again, "What was that?" I asked and decided to investigate. "I'll be right back, honey," I told David.

I stood and pulled back the curtains, peering out the window into the dark night. I couldn't see anything, so I walked around the corner into Andrew's room with David padding along behind me in his footed pajamas. I peeked over the end of the crib at Andrew. The light was dim, but he had scooted himself to the top corner of his crib and appeared to be sound asleep. Everything seemed fine here. I turned to go but then stopped and took one more quick look, kind of a last-minute second glance. Subconsciously I knew there was something odd and stiff about the way he was lying. I took a step closer and was horrified to see that his eyes were rolled back, and he was trembling slightly. I knew immediately he was having a seizure. Adrenaline instantly flooded my body.

Andrew had never had a seizure except for the one in the hospital in Boston. I'd never even witnessed a seizure. *Oh, oh, God, what should I do?* "David, go get Dad," I commanded, trying to keep the frantic tone out of my voice.

He turned and ran down the hall, hollering, "Dad, Dad!" He had no idea what was going on but, still clutching his book, ran as fast as his little legs could go.

The side of the crib was down, and only the faint yellow glow of the night-light lit Andrew's room. I grabbed Andrew under his arms and pulled him to the center of the mattress, yelling, "Tom, call 911! He's not breathing!" Tom came running with David right behind him.

"What? What's going on?" He flipped on the light, took one look, and ran back to the kitchen phone. Thankfully we had a small house!

Somewhere in the back of my mind I knew from First Aid classes that a seizure usually is not dangerous unless the person falls or hurts himself during the seizure. Or, if the person stops breathing. Andrew was unconscious and not breathing, definitely seizing, but not like the seizures I'd seen on TV. He wasn't shaking violently or making noises; he was only trembling a little and beginning to turn gray, his eyes rolled back. I could see vomit drooling out from between his clenched teeth and I knew that his airway must be blocked. I did exactly what you're *not* supposed to do. I forced, and I mean *forced*, my hand into his clenched mouth. I'm not recommending it, but I had to do something! He wasn't breathing, and I was desperate to get his airway cleared. I managed to get his mouth open part way, and the vomit came spewing out all over his sheet. I noticed later that the top of my hand was bloody and scratched with bite marks, but at that moment I just reacted and did what I thought I needed to do. He still wasn't breathing, though, and I didn't know what to do next. "Breathe, come on, Andrew, breathe…"

In the living room, Tom was on the phone with the 911 dispatcher who told him to have me bring Andrew in near the phone and lay him on the floor. This was before the days of cell phones. "Bring him in here!" Tom shouted from the living room. I was so scared I was shaking too, but I gathered Andrew's limp body in my arms and ran down the hall to the living room. When I laid him down on the floor, I really thought he was dead.

"Oh, God, oh, God, oh, God," I was out of my mind with fear, and I couldn't even begin to remember how to do CPR. Mind you, I'd had several CPR courses.

"Is he breathing?" the 911 operator asked Tom.

"No."

"Do you know CPR?"

"I think so. I'm not sure."

"Okay, I'll talk you through it," she said. "First, tilt his head back so his airway is clear."

Tom knelt down on the floor on the opposite side of Andrew and tilted his head backward.

"Oh, God," was literally all I could get out as the tears streamed down my face. Andrew's face was gray, almost blue, his lips were even a darker purplish blue, his eyes still rolled back, and he wasn't breathing at all. I could hear the sirens getting closer and closer, and I was frantic for them to arrive. It seemed unreal that they were headed to our house. I left Tom working on Andrew, ran to the front door and swung it wide open so the paramedics would know where to come. The moment I opened the door, Andrew kind of shuddered and took a slight breath. I'm guessing the cold gust of air shocked his system somewhat.

The paramedics rushed in, and we told them what had happened as they got out their equipment and knelt down next to Andrew. His little body, unconscious and still that sickening bluish gray color, lay motionless on the living room floor surrounded by grown men in their big black coats. I couldn't believe this was happening. The medics started oxygen, and Andrew took another slight breath. But he wasn't breathing regularly—only shallow breaths every now and then.

I stood by the wall watching as the scene played out before me and thinking to myself, *This is not real, this must be a dream.* And then I was mad. *Lord, You have got to be kidding! Surely, we haven't come all this way…Do You mean to tell me, Lord, that he's gone through everything he's gone through, and then he dies from a seizure?* I was practically shaking my fist at God. *This is NOT happening! You cannot let this happen, Lord!* I wanted to scream it out.

"Ma'am, ma'am?" A youngish police officer with a notepad and kind eyes started asking me questions, which helped me refocus and kept my tears at bay. "Is he your son?"

"Yes, yes, he's my son." I almost started crying.

"What exactly happened? Can you show me where you were?" He wanted to see David's room and Andrew's room, wanted the details of where and how I had found him. In a daze, I led him down the hall to the bedrooms, answered his questions, how it all happened and at what time and where. I showed him my hand and explained how I cleared Andrew's throat and airway. He told me I should get someone at the hospital to look at my hand, then we went back to the living room.

They continued to work on Andrew, who was still taking breaths only now and then. I called my mom and asked her to meet us at the hospital ER. David had been following me around, still clutching his book, grabbing hold of my leg when he could. I picked him up and hugged him tight. He had watched the whole scene unfold, and I knew he was confused and scared, utterly bewildered by what was happening.

"What's wrong with Andrew?" he asked.

"He's just a little bit sick," I replied, "and he needs to go to the hospital because he had a seizure, but I think he's going to be okay."

"Oh. He's going to the hospital with the policeman?"

"Yes," I said.

"Am I going to the hospital with the policeman, too?"

"Well, *you* are going to ride with Daddy in our car to the hospital, and we're going to meet Grandma there. Okay? How about having a sleepover at Gram's house?"

"Okay, can I take my book?"

"Yes, you can bring your book." I handed David to Tom, who was talking with a different police officer.

One of the paramedics lifted Andrew off the floor, still unconscious, wrapped him in a blue blanket and headed out to the ambulance. A police radio beeped on and static blared for a second. "On our way. Ten minutes to arrival." The paramedic's voice was serious as he spoke to the hospital ER staff. I started to follow the first paramedic right out the front door, but another paramedic stopped me.

"Ma'am, you can ride in the ambulance cab with me, if you like," he said, gathering up his equipment and bag.

I was so frazzled I couldn't find my purse or coat, and I remember running around the living room saying, "Where's my purse? Where's my purse?" I was shaking as Tom handed me my purse and coat out of the front closet. How could he stay so calm? I gave David a hug and told him to have fun at Grandma's, then I ran out the front door behind the paramedic toward the ambulance.

Our front yard looked like a television set. A gigantic ladder truck, even longer than our house, two ambulances, and a police car—with all their lights flashing—littered the driveway and curb. Several police officers and firefighters, black silhouettes against the brilliant lights, were talking outside, static and beeping blaring from police radios and disrupting the quiet night. Did we really need all this for a seizure? Whatever. I couldn't think about it. The neighbors were out, standing and gawking in little groups. I couldn't tell who was who because the flashing lights were almost blinding. I'd never been in an ambulance before, front or back. I didn't realize they were so high off the ground, like a truck. I guess I just never thought about it. The paramedic opened the door and helped me climb into the passenger seat before he ran around, hopped in behind the wheel, and shifted into drive. He flipped the siren switch and, with the lights still flashing, we drove off through the crowd.

"How are you doing?" he yelled at me over the blaring siren. I was not doing well.

"Well, I have had better days," I sarcastically snapped back. Instantly I felt bad for the way I spoke to him. It just came out. I didn't even know him. *Why would I be so acerbic toward a man who just saved my child's life? I need to apologize, to explain that I'm not normally so rude and that I truly appreciate everything he does.* On a good day, an ordinary day, I never would have said that. But this was not an ordinary day, and my emotions and mind were absolutely fried. I just sat there mutely. I *couldn't* say anything. My mind felt paralyzed. *Oh, Lord, help me. Help Andrew.*

Right then, in a moment when I couldn't *will* myself to think or talk, this Bible verse popped into my mind. I'm not kidding, and I'm not trying to sound hyper-spiritual.

> *He tends his flock like a shepherd; he gathers the lambs*
> *in his arms and carries them close to his heart.*
> *He gently cares for those who have young.*
> – Isaiah 40:11

I had been trying to memorize this verse, and there it was, right in the front of my mind just when I needed it most. It was crazy really. I could barely think straight, but I was remembering a Bible verse? Really? Only God could send His Word clearly into my mind when I was in such a panic. The Scripture calmed me and immediately helped to settle me inside. I kept thinking those words over and over as I craned my neck around to try to see Andrew through the little window behind me.

I have always believed it's a good idea to memorize Scripture, but, honestly, I hardly do it enough. Until that night, I'd never seen my own situation changed immediately because of a verse I had memorized. It's clear to me now why God tells us to treasure His Word in our hearts—it becomes a way that He can speak to us. If I hadn't already been memorizing that verse, the Holy Spirit could not have brought it to my mind and could not have used those specific words of Scripture to comfort me. It's a step of faith to work on memorizing verses, believing that someday God will use them in our lives. For me, that Bible verse got me through the fear that practically paralyzed me that night on the way to the hospital.

We arrived, and the paramedics pulled the gurney out of the back of the ambulance, snapped the legs into place and then rolled Andrew into the ER, spouting off his vital signs and the details of his seizure to the doctors as they went. I hurried in behind them. One of the paramedics was holding an oxygen mask for Andrew. Andrew's body was limp, so I knew he was still unconscious, but at least he was sort of breathing. They transferred him to the examining table, giving him oxygen through a mask that almost covered his whole face. By then I could tell that his color was beginning to return. By the time Tom arrived, Andrew was hooked up to an IV and fluids had been started, and his blood work had been sent to the lab.

The ER doctor kept saying, "Andrew, Andrew can you hear me?"

Finally, his eyes fluttered open, and I breathed a sigh of relief. After his labs came back, the doctor told us it had been a febrile seizure. We found out this kind of seizure is not uncommon in children his age, and it is caused when a fever shoots up quickly. A febrile seizure almost always resolves itself fairly easily. The more significant (and life-threatening) issue was that Andrew had choked on his vomit, and the concern was that he might have aspirated some into his lungs, but it turned out he didn't. The nurse gave Andrew some Tylenol, and he fell asleep. They monitored his fever and sent us home early the next morning.

For me, that seizure was the scariest incident in my life up to that point. I had flashbacks of it for months after that. I'd been so terrified. I truly thought Andrew was dead or dying. Yet, when we got to the hospital and no one seemed overly concerned, I was confused. I wanted to cry or scream or demand that someone clue me in. We'd survived Andrew's other serious medical issues, and this was by far the least life-threatening—but I hadn't known the facts, and what appeared to me to be happening (that he was dying) wasn't the truth. I realized that even in my mixed up ignorance, God was there and comforted me through the Bible verse.

That experience convinced me that memorizing Scripture should be a priority for me. God showed me that I need to remember to focus on Him. Keeping His Word in my head and heart is one way to keep that focus. I have to trust Him through the valley of the shadow of death. If I memorize Scripture, He can use it to comfort me when I am in a bad spot. He can bring to my mind just the verse I need at just the time I need it.

Eleven

Let everyone see that you are considerate in all you do...
Tell God what you need and thank him for all he has done.
Then you will experience God's peace, which exceeds anything
we can understand. His peace will guard your hearts
and minds as you live in Christ Jesus..
– Philippians 4:5-7 NLT

If you want your children to be intelligent, read them fairy
tales. If you want them to be more intelligent,
read them more fairy tales.
– Albert Einstein

OUR TWO boys were like north and south, winter and summer, as opposite as could be. David was the thinker, Andrew, the doer. But like macaroni and cheese, put them together and they made a delightful combination. David was a quintessential firstborn, ultra-cautious and a bit of an introverted soul. He wanted to follow the rules and do it right. He loved books and figuring out how things worked. He liked to scope out the situation and make a plan. Andrew, on the other hand, was happy with absolutely everything. He was his own little party in a box. He was an adventurer, a comic, unafraid of trying something new and totally comfortable chatting with anyone about anything. He was game.

Like every parent, I wondered how these two could possibly have come from the same gene pool. I also wondered if I was going to make it through the toddler and preschool years—maybe I had signed up for more than I could handle. My emotions changed regularly and, like a pendulum swinging back and forth, I vacillated between feeling one moment that I might go insane if I had to take one more minute of little boy antics, and the next moment wanting them to stay small forever, wishing the days would never end.

Andrew was in constant motion, only stopping if he was asleep. He and David were like the characters from *Toy Story*—Cowboy Woody and Buzz Lightyear—sometimes competing with one another for my attention, sometimes working together to solve a problem and always devoted to having the most fun possible. It was exhausting, being a mom to these two, and our worlds—the very different worlds of a mother and her rambunctious boys—didn't always mesh well. Just when I'd manage to get life pretty well put together, they could turn it upside-down, wiping out my agenda for the day. The more control I tried to have, the more frustrated I would get. I couldn't make my life look like I thought it should, and some days I went a little loopy trying. I hadn't been prepared for the many changes that two small children can bring, but the changes in my own life were not as worrisome as the changes I began to notice in Andrew.

From my day-to-day viewpoint, I thought I noticed his energy levels going down—but with Andrew, it was hard to tell. He was a bundle of constant motion; it was not like Andrew to quit playing or complain that he couldn't breathe or that he had chest pain. At his regular checkups that fall, the doctor noted his oxygen saturation levels falling, but the news was grim at his December cardiology appointment. An echo confirmed suspicions that scar tissue had accumulated on his pulmonary valve and built up until it was now nearly impossible for blood to get through to his pulmonary artery. His body wasn't getting the oxygen it needed because his blood couldn't flow freely to his lungs. Blood barely squirted through the pulmonary valve; the hole was the size of a needle. He needed surgery. Tom and I sat in the darkened echo room, frightened and disappointed. Devastated. It hadn't even been two years.

"While the surgery would be a definite correction, there is another possibility," our cardiologist said. "We could try an angioplasty, a balloon dilation. It might work, and it might not. The decision is yours."

We sat there for a minute, thinking. I bowed my head then looked at the ceiling and took a deep breath, feeling helpless. What should we do? This lack of direction or decision from the doctor was frustrating. *Just tell us what to do! You are the one who knows more about it—can't you even give us a hint? How are we supposed to know what's best for our child?*

"If there's a chance it will work, I think we should try," Tom said. "If it doesn't work, he'll have to have the surgery anyway, but if it does work then maybe we can put off the open heart for a while."

They scheduled the angioplasty for mid-January, right after Andrew's second birthday. We checked into the hospital early that morning. Everything went well. The dilation was successful, and his oxygen levels came back into the normal range. A couple of days in the hospital and he was ready to come home, once again full to the brim with energy, sporting rosy cheeks and his very silly personality. I was glad it was over and relieved that we could put off his next open-heart surgery for a while longer. But I came away from that experience with a nagging apprehension about his oxygen levels that would not go away.

I worried about the effects that low oxygen levels might have had on him in the months before it became a crisis. Somehow, we needed to be able to recognize when his levels were low before it manifested in blue lips, etc. It seemed to me that by the time he was actually turning blue or having shortness of breath or other symptoms, his oxygen levels would have been getting lower for some time and the damage might have already happened. I mentioned my concerns to the cardiologist, but nothing ever came of it, so I assumed they didn't think it was that big of a deal.

"I know I don't have proof, and I'm just going on my own instincts, but I think my instincts are pretty good. I think it's a legitimate problem, don't you?" I vented my frustrations to Tom one afternoon.

"Um, yeah, I agree with you," he replied.

"I'm not a cardiologist, but I *know* Andrew. I know his normal coloring, his breathing patterns, his tendencies. The doctor doesn't know Andrew the way I know him, and yet he doesn't take me seriously? What's wrong with this picture?"

As the parents, the ones who live with our child day in and day out and take care of him and know him intimately, aren't we the ones who could possibly provide insightful and valuable information? One would think that a parent's input would rank high. But this time, at least, I felt my input wasn't wanted, that the professionals felt I was ignorant and that they knew better. As frustrated as I was when they brushed aside my concerns, I had no choice but to work together with the doctor. I knew it was better for Andrew that we had a cooperative relationship with all the medical staff. I could have kept pushing the issue, but I decided to drop it. What was done was done, and there was no going back. It was like hitting a wall, and I didn't have the energy for a fight. I wish now that I had pursued the matter further, making sure he was getting what he needed. It haunts me that I didn't follow through. How could I have just let it go? What differences in his thinking and speech and even his physical development were a result of lower oxygen levels? I've wondered a million times why I didn't speak up and make sure all was well.

When Andrew reached school age, we had him tested by an independent doctor whose background included both the medical and educational fields. Andrew struggled with his fine motor skills as well as cognitively in some areas. This doctor felt that there *was* evidence suggesting a lack of oxygen during those months might have caused or contributed to the learning problems he was experiencing. It wasn't definitive, and it was impossible to know for sure, but this doctor felt it was probable.

"Don't look back and wonder, *what if…*Don't live your life with regrets," my friend Becky encouraged me. She said to stay true and stand firm as Andrew's advocate.

I promised myself I would keep pressing forward. I didn't want to look back and be sorry. Nobody wants to have regrets, but there are times when life happens, and there's just no controlling it. I asked myself, *What do I do when regret hangs around and nags at me even though I really don't want it to?*

I struggled with feelings of regret and guilt about my pregnancy with Andrew and his heart defect on a regular basis. Since Andrew's birth, I had pointed fingers back at myself, wondering about the whys and the what ifs. Now I felt apprehension about the oxygen levels issue, but my self-blame goes all the way back to the actual causes of his heart defect. Like a little devil on my shoulder, doubts and questions pop up and override my logical, objective understanding. *Was his heart defect caused because I decided to fertilize the yard one morning before I knew I was pregnant and I breathed in something unhealthy? Was it because I worked part-time in an office that was part of a warehouse where chemicals and toxins filled the air? Had the chemicals leaked into my office through the air filters? Was there something else I did or didn't do to cause it?*

I felt so unsure that my feelings could easily send me into a frenzy, and I'd blame myself for the entire situation. It wasn't healthy. I couldn't go back and change what had happened. All I could do was pray for

God's help in the future. At that time I wasn't sure my prayers were very effective , but what else could I do? Where could I turn? Emotionally I felt responsible even though I knew that was ridiculous. I wanted to let go of the guilt, ask God to erase my regret and move forward to accept the blessings that He had for us. I knew few people could comprehend why I kept wrestling with such a heavy burden, but for me, the letting go happened over time.

The Old Testament tells us the story of a young boy named Joseph being sold into slavery by his older brothers. Reading about the brothers' mistreatment of Joseph and their selling him into slavery, knowing he would be taken far from their homeland to Egypt, and then lying to their father about it all is appalling. It's hard to fathom that God would allow such a horrifying situation. But many years later Joseph was appointed second to the king, reunited with his family and given the opportunity to save them all from starvation. Joseph didn't become bitter, for he knew that God was with him. In fact, at the end of the story, Joseph tells his brothers, "You intended to harm me, but God intended it all for good. He brought me to this position, so I could save the lives of many people."

I want to be like Joseph. I can't see what will happen later in my life, but I can pray and know that even if I totally screw things up, God is big enough to turn it into something good. Letting go of my guilt and regrets, as well as my fears and hurts, is not something that happens all at once. It has been an ongoing process for me to push away the negative thoughts, accept what is and trust God with an unknown future. I am not going to be bitter because of my circumstances; I am going to be better.

Twelve

Let the morning bring me word of your unfailing love,
for I have put my trust in you. Show me the way I should go,
for to you I entrust my life.
– Psalm 143:8 NIV

We'll talk of sunshine and of song, and summer days,
when we were young;
Sweet childish days, that were as long as twenty days are now.
– William Wordsworth

I DON'T know if it was because of all the stories we read or because God has given children such wonderful imaginations, but not a day went by without the boys dramatizing some wild, make-believe tale. For Andrew, now two and a half, this absolutely *had* to include donning the appropriate clothing. He'd dress up in any kind of uniform or costume; helmets and capes, jackets, belts, boots, eye patches and magic hats were part of his everyday repertoire. The more authentic and true-to-life the attire, the better. It didn't hurt that his big brother was totally into it as well. The old blue metal trunk that I had used in college now overflowed with costumes. Oh, and I must say that we were *never* to call a costume an "outfit." Equally horrific would have been to refer to them as "dress-up clothes." That language was strictly for girls, and these were *boy costumes*.

Andrew was always on the lookout for something new to wear, some-body new to "become." One summer evening in July my sister, Cindy, brought her new boyfriend over to meet us. It was a big deal since I'm the older sister—of course, Tom and I had to vet the new guy. I could tell John was nervous. I offered him iced tea, and we all stepped out to the back deck for the usual talk about the weather and his job, and how he and Cindy had met. Tom and I (like any good sister and brother-in-law) needed to make sure John was who he said he was. We wanted to get to know him better before we gave our stamp of approval.

David and Andrew, however, never had a millisecond of doubt. As far as they were concerned, the minute John stepped into the house, he was "the man." The rest of us no longer existed. John was a real cowboy (cue the *Bonanza* soundtrack). He wore a leather belt with a shiny silver belt buckle, a black felt cowboy hat and well-worn cowboy boots. Cindy told us he rode bulls in the rodeo. Andrew and David were mightily impressed by this handsome man in his authentic cowboy garb. They both looked up at John with eyes as big and round as John's belt buckle. David was shy and hung back, but as soon as we'd settled on the back patio, Andrew stepped into the middle of the conversation and, point-ing up at John's midsection, demanded, "I want that belt on me!"

There was no question about exactly what he meant or whose belt he wanted. He'd voiced his request with the fierce conviction of a two year old. We chuckled under our breath, a bit embarrassed because we didn't even know this John guy yet.

"Andrew, we don't ask our guests to take off their belts," I instructed. "It's not polite."

But John was already on his feet. "No, no, that's okay. He's fine," John assured us with a smile as he began pulling his belt through the loops. "Here you go, Buddy," he said, kneeling to strap it around An-drew's waist. The metal-tipped end hung way down in front and, even though John put the notch all the way through to the last hole, the belt wouldn't stay up. He finally just pulled it tight around Andrew's waist and wrapped the belt around itself, securing the buckle in front. Andrew's day was made. He turned around with a grin as wide as a Western prairie sunset and we *oohhed* and *ahhhed* at how amazing it looked. I gave my sister a smile, nodding in John's direction and whispered, "He's a keeper."

One of Andrew's all-time favorite costumes was the "official" (note, *real* NFL) Cincinnati Bengals uniform he got for his third birthday from his Uncle Ken and Aunt Jeanne. Our families are Bronco fans all the way, so Jeanne had tried to find a Bronco uniform, but there were none to be had. Honestly, Andrew didn't care. He loved that uniform regardless of the team. When he put it on, he *became* a pro football player, a force to be reckoned with. He'd flex his muscles and growl that invincible football player growl as only a three year old can, and then he'd proceed to throw himself into tackling David or Tom or whoever was closest. It didn't matter that he had no idea who the Bengals were; he was looking sharp, and he knew it. That uniform became so critical to the execution of "the game," that whenever he and David played football together, they'd share the uniform. One would wear the helmet and pants while the other wore the shoulder pads and jersey. At "half-time," they'd switch. They'd play football in the backyard for hours on end.

The two of them may have been as different as is humanly possible, but in real life, Andrew and David were best friends and could go from being Robin Hood and Little John to Batman and Robin with just a quick change of clothes; sticks that started out as shotguns became swords, then baseball bats, then fishing poles, and then circus tent posts. It always intrigued me as I watched their imaginations take flight, and how they interacted with each other and the simplest of toys or props.

Another game they loved was "UPS Guy." Uncle Kevin, who worked for UPS, took the kids on a tour one day, showing them his truck and what he did at work. The boys thought they'd died and gone to heaven standing on the steps of Uncle Kevin's real UPS delivery truck as I took a picture. After that, the boys created a game where they'd put on their brown t-shirts and sweats and ring the doorbell with pretend packages to deliver. It was hilarious. They even had a clipboard and would make me sign it before giving me the "package." Then they'd go back to their truck (a cardboard box) and drive on to deliver a package to our dog, Cody.

David and I were running errands one day, just the two of us. We'd been driving for a while in silence when he interrupted my thoughts with, "Mom?"

"Yes."

"Mom, you and me...we like to be quiet."

"Hmm, yes, I guess we do."

Another pause and then very matter-of-factly, "Andrew...he likes to talk."

It was hard not to laugh. So, so true! That's the way David operated; even at five, he was a careful think-it-through kind of guy. Always cautious, exceedingly observant. Andrew did like to talk, and he talked all the time. Questions poured out of him, one after the other—questions I sometimes had no idea how to answer. He made funny comments and funny faces just to get us to laugh. He was the comedian of the family, with the rest of us serving as his willing audience. If he wasn't talking, he was acting or moving about in some way—jumping off this or climbing onto that. He was the prototype for action figures, and the action never stopped.

A perfect example of Andrew's exuberance happened one summer afternoon when we were visiting my grandparents. They lived across the street from the city park in Gunnison, a small mountain town. The park playground was a favorite place for the boys, then three and five years old. Tom had walked them across the street to play for just a few minutes. When it was time for lunch, Tom said, "One more minute, boys, then we have to go home." They were playing on the four-seat bouncy horse at the time, sitting across from each other, trying to bounce each other off (with a little help from Tom). Then Andrew started trying to walk back and forth on the large pole going from the center out to each little horse, while David sat on one of the horse seats and tried to bounce him off. They thought it was great fun. I'm pretty sure if I had been the one watching, Andrew wouldn't have been such a little daredevil, but with Dad, well, it was a bit more like, *Anything goes, and life is so much fun.*

"Okay, guys, it's time," Tom said. "Let's go get lunch." He turned to head home when he heard a heavy thud behind him. Whirling back around, Tom saw Andrew lying on the ground, flat on his back, spread eagle.

"Whoa, Dad!" David was excited. "Did you see that?" David hurried to get off his bouncy horse and ran over to him. "Wow, Andrew are you okay?" he asked, bending over to check. "That was cool!"

"What happened?" Tom asked, stooping down opposite David to help Andrew, who looked shaken, but was smiling.

"He just did a front flip off that thing. You shoulda' seen it, Dad!" David said, pointing to the middle hump between the four bouncy horses. His voice was wild with admiration. "That was so cool. Can you do it again?"

Before Andrew could answer, Tom interrupted. "I'm sure he *could* do it again, but he is *not going* to do it again, are you, Andrew?"

Andrew shook his head. It could have ended up much worse than it did. Tom was surprised, but nothing really shocked us anymore. Of course, Andrew had just done a flip off the big metal equipment. That's how he rolled. Tom helped him stand up and brushed off his backside. Squatting down to Andrew's level, he asked, "Are you okay, Buddy?"

"Yeah, I'm okay," Andrew said, whispering because he'd had the wind knocked out of him. Tom carried him home, rubbing the goose egg popping out on the back of his head. Such occurrences were just typical Andrew. Thank goodness God kept a close eye on him then and all through his life—I do believe his guardian angels really should get an overtime bonus.

Although we didn't realize it at the time, the coming year would be one of emotional highs and lows, spiritual questions, and devastating news along with a couple of miracles thrown into the mix. We were challenged to hold tight to our faith and to each other.

In February of the new year, when Andrew and David were three and five, we welcomed a sweet baby girl into our family. We felt God's grace and love in creating this precious new life, and we named her *Amy* which means "dearly loved." The boys were thrilled to have a new sister and not jealous in the least. They were helpful and gentle, taking turns holding her and giving her a bottle, helping me put fresh jammies on her after a bath, shaking a rattle for her. I'm not kidding when I say she was an absolute delight—she was a patient and easygoing baby who hardly ever cried, loved to be held and was completely and utterly captivated with her brothers. She was a gift from God.

My parents had a swimming pool in their backyard, and we spent many sweltering afternoons and evenings splashing and playing like dolphins in the cool, refreshing water the following summer. Very strict rules were laid out regarding Gramma and Grandad's backyard, and the boys were careful to obey because they knew the consequences would be harsh, and they loved that pool. They were never allowed outside without a lifejacket on, and they were not to be in the pool area without an adult to lifeguard. But despite the rules and our ever-watchful eyes, one evening that July, with the whole family close by, we experienced a near tragedy.

Our family had gathered for a birthday barbecue, and we'd spent the afternoon outside in the backyard congregated on the patio, playing in the pool, getting in and out of the hot tub. The aunts and uncles had come with all the cousins, grandparents and great-grandparents, great-aunts and uncles and even cousins of the cousins. We hadn't all been together in years, so there was much catching up to be done, as well as bets on who would win pool volleyball. The dads played an intense game of basketball in the pool, and the kids took turns jumping in cannonball style to see who could make the biggest splash. Although the kids all had lifejackets, we didn't dare take our eyes off them; lifeguarding was a job traded back and forth between the adults, and we took it seriously. There was never a moment when an adult was not sitting in a chair next to the pool with careful eyes on the children. Even if other adults were interacting with the kids, the lifeguard job was non-negotiable. Every fifteen minutes or so, we'd trade places.

Andrew had to use the bathroom, so he got out of the pool and ran over to me on the porch to unzip his wet lifejacket. "Hurry, hurry, Mom," he urged, doing a little dance as I worked to get him free. A minute later, while he was still in the bathroom, Grandma announced that it was time for birthday cake. I needed to feed Amy, so I headed into one of the spare bedrooms for a bit of quiet. I could hear the talking and laughing in the kitchen and then a somewhat off key, "Happy birthday to you, happy birthday to you..." before more laughter and clapping ensued as they blew out the candles and dished up cake and ice cream. Meanwhile, Andrew finished in the bathroom and couldn't wait to get back to playing in the pool. I heard his little feet running down the hallway, past the half open bedroom door. What I didn't hear was him opening the back door and running right past his lifejacket lying on the patio chair. In the midst of the birthday celebration, no one saw him run across the patio to the pool and jump in. No one heard even a small boy-sized splash.

At the very same time, Tom had come to the bedroom with a piece of cake and ice cream for me. "Ohhh, thanks," I said, then I immediately asked him where Andrew was.

"I imagine he's with your mom," he replied.

"Could you please check on him?" I had a funny feeling—I'll always wonder if I heard God's voice?

"Sure," he said, turning to leave. He peeked in the kitchen but didn't see Andrew, so he stepped outside onto the patio. At that very moment, Andrew was climbing up the ladder to get out of the pool.

"Andrew, what are you doing?" Tom was shocked and hurried over to pick him up. Not sure what had just happened, he looked around for a supervising adult and said, "What were you doing, Buddy?"

"Oh, I was just swimming."

"What? What do you mean, you were swimming? No one else is out here." Tom was dumbfounded. He grabbed a towel to wrap around our young son. By this time, the rest of the family had seen Tom and Andrew through the kitchen window and had gone outside to find out what the commotion was all about. Obviously, Andrew had been in the pool. What was not obvious was how he got out. The pool was four and a half feet deep all the way across with a small ladder on each end—there was no shallow or deep end. It was thirty-two feet long and fifteen feet across. Andrew could not swim by himself. We'd been working with him, helping him learn to hold his breath and put his head under water, and he was getting better. He could jump off the side to us, but we knew he couldn't swim on his own.

"You know you're not supposed to go swimming without your lifejacket and without an adult to supervise." Tom was still shaken and halfway between mad and terrified.

"I forgot."

"Can you tell me what happened?"

"I went to the bathroom, and then I came running out and jumped in the pool. I was going to put my lifejacket on, but I forgot."

"Where did you jump in?"

Andrew pointed to about half way down the side of the pool. "Right there."

"How did you get out?" Tom asked what everyone was wondering.

"Well, a man swam with me and helped me swim to the ladder."

"A man?"

"Uh-huh. He was an angel." Andrew was calm and matter of fact.

"An angel? How do you know?"

Andrew shrugged his shoulders, "I don't know. He was."

I heard this whole story related back to me *after* the fact—I'd been finishing up feeding Amy in the bedroom and then laid her down for her nap. I quietly closed the bedroom door only to be greeted by a wild fuss of frantic voices on the back patio, everyone talking and asking questions all at once. I hurried out to see what was going on. My mom was crying. Tom was holding Andrew like he'd never let him go.

"What's going on?" I asked.

"Well," Tom said, looking at me, "Andrew went for a swim without his lifejacket. No one else was out here." I could read the fear in his eyes.

"What?" I gasped. "Oh, Andrew!" I took Andrew from Tom's arms and hugged him tightly. "Are you okay?" I looked at him face to face. He nodded his head yes, and I squeezed him again. My heart was pounding against his wet body. "How could this have happened?" I looked at Tom, "We've always been so careful…" Tears started to well up in my eyes, but I looked away so no one would see.

"I know we have. I can't believe it happened either. But…he said a man helped him swim over to the ladder and get out…a man that was an angel."

"What? There was…an angel? Really?" I was stunned. I couldn't remember that we'd ever even talked about angels. How did Andrew know about angels? I looked right at him. "An angel helped you, Andrew?" I sat down on the patio chair, holding Andrew on my lap now. I asked him to tell me again what had happened, and he did, same story, same ending with the angel-man. He was very matter-of-fact about the whole thing, and I didn't want him to get the sense that we didn't believe him or that we thought he imagined it, so I tried to act as if it was the most normal thing in the world. I knew he had a great imagination, but clearly, this was not that. He was telling us the truth. He would never have made this up; how could he? After talking with him and getting the details, I was shaken but convinced there really was no other way he could have made it to the ladder and climbed out of the pool. An angel had been there to help him. It was a miracle, and the whole family had seen the results. I guess angels can swim. Who knew?

I don't think that Andrew had ever seen an angel before, and yet he specifically mentioned that it had been an angel that had helped him, he didn't just say it was a man. How did he know? Maybe he'd heard of angels from the Christmas story in the Bible. I couldn't really fathom it, but he never doubted; he knew. Later, when Tom and I talked about it together, we wondered why. We tossed around possible ideas—that perhaps because of Andrew's innocent faith, a door had opened, and he was able to see into the spiritual realm. We will never know, but it came down to realizing that God had more in store for Andrew. We knew it wasn't the first time that his life had been supernaturally spared, but we could not have known it wouldn't be the last.

Even before the incident with the pool happened, I believed in miracles. Some people do, and some don't; everyone must make up his own mind about the supernatural. I believe God does outright miracles today, and most of the time we don't even realize what has happened. I believe there is a whole spiritual dimension that we are not privy to—similar to the way there are colors of light we can't see with the naked eye and sounds our human ears can't hear. It's obvious to me that God and His angels are at work around us all the time. Just being able to recognize that something is a miracle is a miracle itself.

We can be skeptical when we hear about a supernatural happening from the friend of a friend. But when God intervenes and a miracle happens right before your eyes, it shakes up your world. We were all so rattled after Andrew's rescue from the pool that I had to keep reminding myself that it wasn't just a dream. God is much more powerful and astonishing than our feeble little brains can take in.

In the days following that experience, a part of me wanted to explain away the angel-man. If I could wrap it all into an earthly perspective, it might be easier to grasp. But the very idea of putting a human explanation to a supernatural act of God is ridiculous. I cannot explain God. I cannot begin to understand His thoughts or His plan or His reasons for miracles. He is God, and I am me, and I can't help but recognize the enormous chasm between us. This great divide seems especially evident when we are face to face with a miracle. If it's possible that the God of the universe has stepped in and altered the natural outcome of events in my little pocket of the world, I choose to be humbled and in awe. There is so much about God that I will never understand. I do believe He loves me, but I also know that He's not going to step in and make my life worry-free. Sometimes I wonder if I will be brave enough to bear the pain of this life until I make it to the next. I've been a Christian for years, and I want to work through my questions with Him, but just like everything else in my life, I want God to be predictable. And that is one thing He is not. This awareness of God's great power and judgment in contrast to my frail humanness and need are tough to fathom. Because He is God, I can trust Him, but He is not going to fit into my little imagination or act a certain way simply because I wish it.

In July of that same year, Tom's brother and his wife learned the devastating news that their youngest two children—their daughter Kendall, 7, and their son, Taylor, 3—had tested positive for a rare genetic disease called Fanconi's anemia. It is usually fatal before adulthood. Our lives stood still as we tried to make sense of this horrible diagnosis. I couldn't wrap my mind around it. The only cure for this disease would be a bone marrow transplant. Friends shifted into high gear to organize bone-marrow drives to try to locate a match for the kids. Tom and I wanted so badly to be a match, but neither of us was. We hurt deeply for our niece and nephew, and for our brother and sister-in-law and their older daughters. Our world—their world—had shattered, and I could see no way it would ever be right again.

Situations like this are beyond human understanding. We certainly have no answers for the whys because it's impossible to make sense of such pain. All we can do is bring our questions and pain and anger to God and ask for help. I realize I simply will not understand some things while I am here on earth, and this situation fit that category. The pain we felt seemed nearly unbearable, and we prayed for a miracle. We'd seen and experienced miracles, and we knew God could perform another one. We believed He is good and that He loves us. Whether He would heal Kendall and Taylor outright, through a bone-marrow transplant, or in some other way, we did not know yet; but we prayed every day that somehow God would save their lives.

Thirteen

The LORD protects those of childlike faith;
I was facing death, and he saved me.
– Psalm 116:6 NLT

Mercy is a command of God, yet it cannot simply be a response
to a demand. It must arise out of hearts made generous and
gracious by an understanding and experience of God's mercy.
– Timothy Keller

I T WAS in the fall, when the leaves let go in shades of crimson
and spice, that I began to notice small, subtle changes in Andrew. Usually, it took an act of God to slow down this three year old,
but I could tell that my ordinarily energetic little boy was at times now
a bit more subdued. His always sparkling, mischievous eyes became
a little less of a bubbling stream and a little more of a deep mountain
tarn. Naps could last all afternoon, play was a bit less rambunctious.
I tucked these thoughts deep inside, knowing that it was happening
but not wanting to acknowledge it outwardly. I told no one. Maybe if I
didn't say it out loud, it wouldn't be true.

"Come on, sweet girl," I said, lifting Amy into her stroller one afternoon and zipping Andrew's jacket. "David, did you brush your teeth?
Do you have your backpack ready to go?" Every day at 12:05 p.m. we
walked David to kindergarten three blocks away. We'd stand at the edge

of the playground, give good-bye hugs and then walk back home. I'd put Andrew and Amy down for a nap and throw in some laundry, pulling out the dry load to fold. Sometimes I'd fall asleep on the couch as the afternoon sun poured through our west window. Those naps were heavenly. Then, we'd do it all again at 3:15 when kindergarten was over. David would come running out the blue kindergarten door across the sandy play yard and throw his arms around my hips. He'd give Andrew and Amy a hug, and all the way home he'd fill us in on the events of his afternoon at school. I missed him being at home. I missed his company. All the same, it was good to have time with just the two little ones, and sometimes a bit of time to myself.

At the beginning of the school year, I could hardly keep up with the boys as I pushed the stroller up the hill to the school. Andrew and David would run ahead of me, and then run back saying, "Hurry, Mom, hurry." They skipped and raced each other, ran circles around the stroller and sang songs as we walked. They discovered rocks and sticks and roly polies along the way, and each treasure was carefully piled on top of the stroller to take back home for their "collections."

By October, though, Andrew was no longer running and skipping ahead with David. He would walk along beside me, and there were days when he begged to ride in the stroller with Amy. I'd situate him behind her with his legs poking out on either side. *Maybe he's just tired of this routine*, I thought. *Maybe he's tired of having to interrupt his own day to walk his brother to school.* But I knew that wasn't the case. The truth was that he didn't have the stamina to walk even three blocks.

I remember one afternoon on our way to pick up David, Andrew was riding in the stroller with Amy. He was quiet, still waking up from his earlier nap.

"Mom, look," he said, pointing to the overcast sky.

"Yep, it looks like it could rain. Or maybe it will even snow," I replied. Earlier I had noticed the low-hanging bubbly clouds that had moved in, covering the entire sky. Fall was in full swing and bringing with it chilly storms and sweater weather.

"No, Mom," he insisted, "look right there." He pointed to a small opening in the clouds where the blue sky shone through.

"Uh-huh, I see it," I acknowledged.

"What's up there?"

"That's just the sky behind the clouds."

"Is that heaven?"

"Umm…well, I don't know where heaven is, honey, but I do know that's part of the sky, and maybe heaven is behind the sky."

"Oh." He paused for a minute as we continued up the hill. "So, Mom, even though there's clouds up there, the sky is behind the clouds?" I could see his little wheels turning. "Right, Mom?"

"That's right, Andrew."

"So, it keeps on going and keeps on going, and there isn't any end to the sky?"

"That's right," I confirmed, but my thoughts did a *whoa, Nelly*. Now my wheels were turning. Was he going all scientific on me or what? Sometimes my kids can ask crazy questions. Did he actually want to know about the layers of the atmosphere? I sure hoped not.

After a pause, his little voice piped up again. "I wish I was a bird." Immediately I knew he wasn't looking for grandiose answers to scientific questions. My whole body ached for my sweet boy, normally so full of life and energy, longing to fly fast and high and endlessly free. He must have felt so frustrated. Trapped by a body that wasn't working right, he couldn't run and jump and play as he had before. He didn't understand why, but I did. He couldn't have verbalized it any better, and I knew exactly what he meant. I wished I could be a bird, too, to just let go and fly free.

"Me, too," I agreed, my eyes misting.

Right then, something inside of me clicked. I knew that if I was going to survive this journey emotionally, I needed to say good-bye to my silly notions of a well-planned and lookin'-good kind of life. That would never be me, no matter how hard I tried. And I realized I didn't want that life anyway. We all know that life is a valley and a mountaintop, a desert, a placid lake and a torrential river rapid. What I knew I wanted was to live in the moment I'd been given. I didn't want to put on a wannabe charade—pretending to live life as it "should" be or mimicking what looked good for someone else. I needed to accept and embrace each moment of my life for what it truly is and be real about it. Yes, I know, these lofty thoughts and philosophies roll easily off the tongue, but they are so much harder to live. But way back on the farthest burner in my mind, all the little seeds of thought I'd kept incubating were beginning to germinate.

The differences I saw in Andrew may not have been noticeable to most people, but I was aware of even the tiniest changes. Red flags began popping up, disrupting my internal flock of ducks, which had been flying in neat rows for several months now. That's the funny thing about Andrew's particular situation. The days and months go by like nothing is wrong, almost as if his illness was only a bad dream. Then there is that day when something happens and, like a punch in the gut, it becomes very, very real again.

At his December cardiology appointment, the echocardiogram showed that his pulmonary valve (the one put in during his first surgery in Boston) had disintegrated and was not working at all. The angioplasty he'd had eighteen months earlier had cleared some of the scar tissue away, but it had grown back again. There was no question this time. He needed a surgical repair and a replacement homograph. A homograph is like a transplant of a valve and artery. It's part of a human heart—in this case, the pulmonary valve—removed after a person has died. When he was in Boston, the replacement valve had been the aortic valve from a pig. At this point, the technology had improved so that they were able to use human pulmonary arteries and valves, which work much better. Andrew's surgery was scheduled for January, after his fourth birthday. All the thoughts and ponderings I'd kept tucked inside floated to the surface, and although I wasn't totally prepared, I wasn't entirely surprised either.

As soon as the holidays were over, his birthday took center stage. He got cowboy chaps and spurs and a hat. He proudly wore his new getup plus his blue plaid flannel cowboy shirt and helped me make his chocolate cowboy birthday cake. He wanted so badly to go to the National Western Stock Show and Rodeo held in Denver every January, but we couldn't risk him getting sick this close to surgery. We stayed home from everything that month.

Andrew's Uncle John (John and Cindy had gotten married at Christmas) promised to take Andrew to the rodeo later in July so he could see the bulls up close and watch the cowboys ride. In preparation, we threw a striped wool saddle blanket over a couple of suitcases to make a makeshift bull, and Andrew practiced his calf roping and bull riding skills all month long. He was determined to be ready to go to that summer rodeo with John. The day we checked into the hospital, he insisted on wearing his flannel cowboy shirt, his cowboy boots, new cowboy belt and black felt hat. True grit.

How could I possibly communicate what was going to happen without scaring him? What could I say, what *should* I say? We didn't talk a lot about his heart—we would if he asked questions, but it wasn't usually a part of our everyday conversation. It was just who he was, and neither Tom nor I made a big deal about it. We didn't treat him any differently than we treated David or Amy, and he was involved in all the same activities as his friends. I'm pretty sure he thought everybody went to a cardiologist and had echocardiograms and heart surgeries.

During January, however, we started talking more purposefully about his heart and how he needed the doctors to fix it like they had when he was a baby. We told him we'd be going to the hospital where he would get some medicine to help him sleep while the doctors made his heart better again. I showed him some of the non-graphic pictures from when he'd had surgery as a baby. We reassured him in every way we knew how that we would be there and that he was going to feel better when they fixed his heart. But I knew our efforts to ease his anxiety would never be enough. When the time came, he'd need the assurance that only God can give. We reminded him all the time that God would be with him to help him through it all.

Our faith—Tom's and mine—was solid and had been growing deeper and stronger over the years. We talked with the boys about God and read stories about Jesus. We bought an easy-to-understand children's Bible and read it out loud. We read about missionaries and men and women of faith. Even at four years old, Andrew's own faith was strong. He believed God's promises in the Bible, and he knew that God would be with him and protect him. In their four- and six-year-old ways, the boys understood that God loved them, and they trusted Him absolutely, as only a child can. In my experience, I've seen that a child can have a very deep faith in God, without pretense or a studied understanding, but deep nonetheless. In fact, I've come to believe that it's *because* of the simplicity of a child's faith that God draws near. There is an amazing connection between God and children. You would think if any age group were to deny the existence and overwhelming love of God, it would be the kids. After all, God is abstract, and children understand the concrete. They can't see Him, and He doesn't bring presents. He isn't something they can hold on to and touch. Still, kids get it.

_____

God's love, the love of a perfect Father, is not conditional. He loves us simply because we are His children, and not because of how clever or beautiful or athletic we are. His love is not based on us—He loves us because of who He is. As adults, we often stumble trying to figure this out. Sometimes our experiences tell us we're not deserving enough, we're not good enough, and we shouldn't expect to receive God's love. I think this is why Jesus said in Matthew 9:14, *"Allow the little children, and don't forbid them to come to me; for the Kingdom of Heaven belongs to ones like these."* Somehow, God meets the heart of a child and is known and understood. I could see this in my boys, and I knew when the time came, Andrew would be able to draw strength from Him.

Fourteen

The Sovereign Lord is my strength! He makes me as surefooted
as a deer, able to tread upon the heights...
– Habakkuk 3:19 NLT

It always helps to have people we love beside us
when we have to do difficult things in life.
– Fred Rogers

THE AFTERNOON before Andrew's surgery, I was determined to
be brave. Reassuring David and Amy, giving hugs and more
hugs, I dropped them at my sister's house for the day. Then Andrew and
I made our way through traffic to the hospital downtown. We found
In-Patient Registration and were escorted to his bed space. Instead of a
hospital room, it was more like the CICU in Boston—one huge room
with curtains cordoning off each bed. It was an exciting day for a four
year old, one he'd anticipated for over a month, and his senses were on
high alert. He asked me about every single thing he could think to ask.
I once read a study that found that four year olds ask more questions
than any other age group—averaging about four hundred questions in
one day. I could seriously vouch for that—I was living it.

Happily oblivious to the real reason we were there, Andrew wanted
to know about each instrument hanging on the wall and how it worked.
Why are there curtains hanging right here? Why are they attached to the

ceiling? Why do the nurses listen to your heart? What is this tube? The bed moves? Wow! Up and down and up and down, up and down ad nauseam. *What's under here? Why is the TV way up high? Who is that? When will Daddy be here? And there's a playroom just down the hall? And it has a TV!* This place was a kid's dream come true!

Andrew padded to the playroom in his hospital slipper-socks and oversized green gown, excited to check out the toys. We brought puzzles back to his bed to put together. We read stories and played Candyland, raced matchbox cars across vast blanket mountains on his bed, played tic-tac-toe and called Gram and Granddad at least twice on the phone. Ecstatic to be able to order his own dinner, he looked at the pictures on the menu with me, and I read the selections to him. He chose the macaroni and cheese and applesauce, cherry gelatin, vanilla pudding, apple pie with ice cream, and chocolate milk. I won't say he ate it all, but he put a good dent in it.

Andrew rather enjoyed himself that afternoon, and I was glad he didn't realize what the next day would bring. He knew heart surgery would help him to feel better, and he knew that it would happen in the hospital, but he wasn't quite sure what that meant. From his perspective, this first hospital experience hadn't been bad at all. Tom popped in after work, and we prayed with Andrew that evening. Tom went home to be with David and Amy, and I stayed the night, planning to sleep in a chair next to Andrew's bed.

I rocked him in the big wooden rocking chair next to the bed, and we talked about cowboys and horses and chaps and why some cowboy hats are black and some are white. Then, out of the blue, he turned to me and said, "Mom, how come David and Amy aren't having heart surgeries?"

So, there it was. A question for the ages. It caught me completely off guard, and I had no idea how to answer my four year old in a way that he could understand. I wasn't sure I understood it myself. Why did God allow this? Why Andrew and not David or Amy or the little boy next door? *Help me, Lord. Give me the right words.*

"Well, hmm," I muttered, pausing to collect my thoughts. "You know, Andrew, how when we lie outside at night and look at the stars, and some of the stars sparkle?"

"Yeah."

"Well, it's like this…Every star has its own special sparkle—we don't always see it, but it's there. God made those stars, and He knows what will make each one sparkle. He puts the sparkle in each star."

His forehead wrinkled in confusion, but I continued.

"God gave you a special heart, and it's kind of like your very own sparkle, and we need to get it fixed. David and Amy have different kinds of sparkles."

"Oh." I could tell he was thinking about all this. "So, when the doctor fixes my heart, then God puts the sparkles in?"

"Mm-hmm, something like that," I agreed, smiling. I hugged him, wrapping the blanket closer and humming quietly as he drifted off to sleep. The unit was busy that night, and I couldn't get comfortable in the recliner. I laid awake watching him sleep into the early hours, knowing that after his surgery tomorrow, and next week, and even the next few months would be an uphill battle to recover. I wondered what he would remember from the coming days.

Morning came quickly and with it my stomach began somersaulting as if preparing for the Olympic trials. Tom arrived moments before the cardiac nurse, Cathy, stuck her head around the curtain with a candy sucker sedative to help Andrew stay calm. He seemed pretty calm to me, but we gave him the sucker anyway, even though I was the one who probably should have eaten it!

One of the assistant pastors from our church appeared by the curtain. "Hi, are you Tom and Cathy?" We nodded. "And you must be Andrew," he said, pulling a chair around from behind the curtain. I recognized him, but we'd never met; we attended a very large church, so we'd seen him only occasionally. He introduced himself and then said, "I came down to pray with you before Andrew's surgery." He turned to Andrew, "I understand you are having an operation this morning, young man." Settling his rather large frame into the smallish plastic chair, he looked sympathetically at our son. "How are you feeling about all this?" Andrew had no idea who this man was or how to answer (who would, really?), so he shrugged his shoulders and sort of half-smiled.

We appreciated this pastor's thoughtfulness, but it felt slightly awkward since we barely knew him. It was very nice of him to come all the way down to the hospital at such an early hour, so we went with the flow. *It certainly can't hurt to have someone pray,* I thought. So we bowed our heads and he prayed…and prayed and prayed.

After that, we talked some, but the words were just a blur in my mind because I couldn't stop thinking about what was coming next. *What time is it? Will they be coming for Andrew soon?* I couldn't focus on anything else, and I just wanted this man—however nice and helpful he was—to give us some time alone with our son. *Okay, we've prayed, you did what you came to do, now it would be perfectly fine if you need to leave. It's okay.* And I thought he would, but he didn't. He kept talking. I dug deep for my best fake smile and pasted it on because what else do you do when a pastor is there and he's just trying to be nice? They would come to take Andrew any minute now. The conversation ran dry, and still this man waited with us, working hard to make small talk.

I suddenly realized he intended to stay with us until *after* Andrew went into surgery. Panic set in because those moments before a surgery are, for me, a thoughtful (and hopefully) peaceful time. I want to take it all in, to breathe and pray, smooth his hair and hold him tight and thank

God that I've had four years with my beautiful son. That's me, though. I'm sure there are people who would like their pastor to stay as long as possible. We didn't know this pastor, and although he had been so kind, I simply didn't want him there. It wasn't anything personal, but I didn't know how to politely say, "Please leave." I wanted to say something, anything, to let him know we needed time alone—he probably would have been happy to oblige. But I couldn't get the words out. My mouth was dry, and my tongue stuck to my lips, and I was just too scared of hurting his feelings. So I sat there silently, holding Andrew on my lap. A minute later, though, I was saved. The nurses came in and—thank you, God—they told the pastor it was time to leave. I poured myself a glass of ice water to celebrate.

"Okay, Tom, here's your bunny suit," Cathy teased, holding out some white linen-looking scrubs. Earlier, the cardiac team had asked Tom if he would like to go into the operating room with Andrew until he fell asleep. Of course he absolutely wanted to. No question about that. She handed Tom a set of disposable scrubs, including shoe covers and a hat. "I'm sure you'll find your new outfit to be in keeping with the latest fashion," she continued to joke, and we all laughed nervously. Once he was dressed, the all-white ensemble covered everything except Tom's face.

When I asked Andrew if he thought Daddy looked funny, he nodded his head, but he wasn't as perky as normal on account of the meds they'd given him. With Tom accompanying the team right on into surgery, saying good-bye was less traumatic. Andrew wasn't scared at all, held tightly in Daddy's arms. Honestly, it was easier on me, too. Tom told me later that he held Andrew's hand until he fell asleep.

Waiting for surgery updates felt like the definition of forever. The day was peppered with calls from the operating room every now and then, letting us know how the surgery was progressing and what was happening at that moment. The constant flow of information helped us get through the hours, but the surgery wasn't over until late afternoon. Although it had taken much longer than expected, everything had gone quite well. Still unconscious and in recovery, Andrew had been a trooper. We were finally given the go ahead to see him in the ICU.

Walking into Intensive Care, the smell almost knocked me over. I'd forgotten how strong that smell can be. And then when we saw him, I just wasn't prepared. I felt woozy and wondered what was wrong with me? After all, this wasn't my first rodeo. I began to wobble, and my vision faded to black, so I sat down in a chair really quick and put my head down. I almost passed out which was a complete shock because I'm not normally the woozy type. Tom was completely focused on Andrew and totally oblivious to my feeling faint. That was fine—even good, actually. I wanted to be the attentive mom, next to my son every step of the way, but I just could not get myself to the head of that little bed. I told Tom I had to find a bathroom.

I was angry at my own lack of hospital-parent savvy. How could I be so weak? Pointy fingers of guilt began poking at me as I splashed cool water on my face. Mothers of sick children do not faint. I do not faint. In fact, I was rather proud of the fact that I could count on one hand the number of times I had nearly fainted. And I had never truly fainted—I'd just come close…one time being when Andrew was three and having the stitches taken out of the finger that he'd almost cut off. That was pretty bad, but nothing compared to heart surgery. *Why, when I am needed most, do I wimp out?*

Angry that I was unable to will away my nausea and lightheadedness, I left the unit and walked around for a bit. It was much cooler in the hallway, I realized. When you live in Colorado, you learn to dress in layers. That's what I'd done this morning. Realizing this, I slipped off my jacket then raised my arms to pull off my sweater over my head. Next,

I removed my denim button-up shirt. I was left wearing a long-sleeved shirt. Don't laugh—that morning when it was still dark out and everybody else had been freezing cold, I was just fine, thank you very much. You never know about Colorado weather, and it was January, for Pete's sake. I was going to be prepared if I was anything. Of course, all those layers of clothing plus the fact that I had skipped breakfast and lunch waiting for a surgery update probably contributed greatly to my feeling faint.

Okay, okay, lesson learned. I stepped back into the ICU to find that Andrew was still unconscious. *Whew! That smell is still here.*

"Do you want to grab a bite to eat?" I asked Tom. He did. My mom and dad had arrived and were in the waiting room (only two visitors at a time were allowed in ICU), and they were happy to sit with Andrew while we popped down to the cafeteria.

At that time our Children's Hospital did not have a dedicated Cardiac Intensive Care Unit. Except for the isolation rooms, it was all one big pediatric ICU. Kids that had cancer, kids that had meningitis, and kids that had been in car accidents all shared one big room. There was no privacy at all. Nurses were swamped with caring for their patients. We all knew exactly what was going on with the patients and their families nearest to our own child's bed. There were so many beds, one next to another, that it sometimes felt as if Andrew was just the next one on the docket; I suppose everyone felt the same way.

One morning about two days post-op, I was sitting next to Andrew's bed when his nurse walked up and said, "I overheard the doctor saying he would take the chest tubes out during rounds this morning. So, if you want to leave, now's the time."

Want to leave? What does she mean? Why would I do that? I'm sure she thought she was doing me a favor, but I wanted to be with Andrew no matter what was happening.

"No thanks," I politely declined.

I noticed the doctors doing rounds a couple of rows away from us. I wasn't clear on how a chest tube removal worked since it was only Andrew's second surgery. I hadn't been around when they did it the first time in Boston because they made the parents leave before they removed chest tubes—which should have been my first clue. I didn't know if I should be asking questions about the chest tube procedure, or if I should just relax and keep quiet.

The nurse gave Andrew some Tylenol and went back to charting. Not five minutes passed before the doctors walked up. They talked for a minute, ignoring me, and then Andrew's surgeon looked at the nurse and asked, "Has he been given pain medication?"

"Yes, he has."

"Tylenol?"

"Yes."

And then before I knew what was happening, the doctor snipped the stitches holding the chest tubes in place, grabbed the tubes lodged in Andrew's chest and pulled them out. First one, then the other. No fanfare or warning pause—he just yanked, and they were out. Without saying anything to me or Andrew, he pulled off his bloodied gloves, one at a time, casually nodded in my direction and walked over to the next bed.

Andrew had been half dozing, but now he was wailing—not loudly, but a deep, sobbing cry that came from real pain. When I realized what had just happened, I stood up on the opposite side of Andrew's bed from where the nurse was mopping up the blood on Andrew's chest. I looked right at her, now holding pressure on the wounds, then taping a gauze bandage across the gaping holes.

"Why didn't you tell the doctor you'd only just *now* given Andrew the painkiller? It hasn't had a chance to take effect!"

"The doctor wanted to pull the tubes while he was on rounds." Her voice was flat and callous; she looked down at Andrew's chart, away from me.

Turning to Andrew, I said "I'm so sorry, Andrew," pushing his hair off his forehead. "I know that hurt."

Then I turned to the nurse again, "Why couldn't you have told the doctor?"

"I did."

"You could have given us a little warning, just so Andrew would know what was coming." She shrugged and walked away. She didn't even look at Andrew's face, crumpled in pain. I was livid. How could someone who claims to care, whose job it *is* to care for children, make a decision that seemed so uncaring? I had trusted her, and I felt betrayed. As if she didn't want to be bothered by Andrew and this was just another day on the job, she was not the least bit interested in how this little patient (or his mother) was feeling. She looked at me from the nurse's station a few feet away and remarked calmly, "It'll kick in in a couple minutes."

I narrowed my eyes and set my mouth. There was no denying how angry I was. If I'd been a dragon, you'd have seen fire explode into the room. I looked at her, unblinking, then turned my attention to Andrew. All I could do was cradle his head and tell him I was there. Pulling chest tubes is an intensely painful procedure, and he was barely four years old. He wasn't the least bit comforted by knowing the painkiller would start to take effect within a few minutes. I wanted to go home right then and take Andrew home with me. Forget this hospital. Forget these doctors and nurses who didn't care.

When Tom came by after work that day, I filled him in. He felt angry, too, but we didn't know what to do. Neither of us knew whether we had the right to confront the nurse or her supervisor about the situation, or if that would even be a good idea. We'd never heard about patient rights. We were afraid to rock the boat that was supposed to carry our little boy to healing and wellness.

I felt alone, defensive and angry at the staff, but also angry at myself. It was partially my fault because I didn't speak up when I had the chance. I should have stepped in before the doctor pulled the tubes, but I didn't know it would happen so fast. Why didn't I say, "Hey, wait a minute," and then take a second to ask about the pain. How bad could that have been?

I remembered the time in Boston when Andrew's eyes weren't focusing. I'd asked questions of the doctors, but I felt dumb for doing it. At times, I've felt that some doctors and nurses have acted as if my opinion was insignificant or that I didn't know anything. While probably not intentional, it has happened. And I tend to back off or cave in because of my own insecurities, which is ridiculous. My job as a parent is to be an effective advocate for my child. I want to be the kind of person who speaks up and asks questions and intervenes if I'm unsure—even if the medical staff is formidable. It's not right that patients or their families should feel intimidated by those who are supposed to be helping. It's not okay for a nurse or a doctor to be blind to the pain of another person, no matter how small that person is. We should be working as a team toward the healing of the patient. I promised myself I wouldn't let this happen again…that I could be—I must be— uncompromising in protecting my child, willing to confront an issue and still be kind and understanding toward those who are caring for him. Thankfully, we didn't have to deal with that nurse for the rest of Andrew's stay.

Andrew's recovery took a slow turn down Molasses Avenue. He struggled with an obstinate cough that kept him sicker and weaker than he should have been—he'd cough and cough and cough until he'd throw up. I held him and cleaned him up, gave him ice water, kept a cool cloth on his forehead. I couldn't imagine the pain that hard coughing must be causing considering he'd had his chest opened wide a couple of days earlier. He didn't complain, though. I think he was just too weak. After a coughing spell, he'd fall asleep exhausted, and then wake up later, coughing again.

Andrew missed Tom and David and Amy and our dog, Cody. Amy was still too little to come visit, but David's laugher and smiles cheered Andrew for hours each time Tom brought him to visit with games and toys from home. They took Andrew for wagon rides around the floor, or Tom would carry Andrew around for a little walk while I pushed the IV pole. In those days, many of Andrew's favorite stuffed animals had matching books. Oatmeal, his favorite teddy bear, always occupied the place of honor right next to Andrew on his bed. Oatmeal's book was called *Old Bear*; we must have read that story a hundred times. Spot the Dog and the Little Polar Bear and Dogger were also part of the entourage. We read lots of stories and watched re-runs of Andy Griffith and *Gilligan's Island* on TV. We rocked and rocked into the wee hours. But the cough was stubborn, and his little body was weak; his oxygen levels fell into the seventies.

The respiratory therapists began coming every four hours (instead of every six) to "pound" on his chest and back so that the fluids that wanted to settle there wouldn't get comfortable. He was switched to a stronger antibiotic, and the doctors increased his oxygen. The nurses checked his vitals every couple of hours. Most of the time he was just too weak to really do anything. Some days were better than others, but I guess that's true no matter where you are and what you're doing.

I stayed with Andrew all day every day, except once when I went home to shower while my mom stayed with Andrew. When you're staying at a hospital day after day with a critically ill loved one, time seems different than it does in the outside world. Like breathing, time passes without us consciously thinking about it. In the same way that we take breath after breath, second by second the hours fly by, then the days and nights and weeks. News from the "outside" world is rare, and usually we have no real desire to hear it anyway. All emotional energy is focused on helping our loved one get well. It's actually kind of a shock to the system when you do leave and re-enter the real world.

It was a long two weeks before Andrew was well enough to be discharged. I was anxious for us both to go home, but then I was scared to be home without the medical support he might need. It turned out we did fine. He came home on oxygen and needed it for about a month. We didn't go many places that month, but it was a cold, snowy February, so I was fine staying home. We didn't even go outside (except to the doctor's office) for that entire month. He'd had such a hard time getting well, and I didn't want him to catch another bug and end up right back in the hospital. It was just too risky. We were content to hunker down, giving him ample time to heal.

The first Sunday back at church, we happened to see Andrew's Sunday school teacher, Mrs. Lamb, in the hallway. Andrew told her he'd had his heart surgery, and she knelt right down in front of him and said, "Are you feeling better now?"

Andrew nodded his head. "Yes."

"Did the doctor open up your heart and make it all better?"

"Yes."

"When he opened up your heart, did he see Jesus inside?"

Andrew giggled and looked up at me. Grinning ear to ear, he looked back at Grace and nodded his head again. "Uh-huh."

Then she gave him a hug and said she was so glad he was better. Sometimes the simplest of conversations can mean the most. I'm sure Grace doesn't remember that exchange, but I'll never forget the grin on Andrew's face and the way I felt, bubbling over with happiness. Like

Jesus Himself when He was with children, Grace cared enough to bend down to Andrew's level and make him laugh.

Once we were home from the hospital, Andrew slowly but surely regained his strength and enthusiasm for life. We were thrilled with his progress and relieved, since he had been so sick. Then—in just one day—everything changed.

Thoughts from Andrew

MOST PEOPLE don't remember much from when they were three or four years old, but with something as big as a heart surgery, you'd think I'd remember a little bit. However, I don't really remember much at all. I'm pretty sure the strong medications account for a lot of that, and maybe that's good since heart surgeries are not exactly memories you want to look back on.

Of all my memories, my earliest is of watching football on TV with my dad when I was three. I remember our house and our backyard with the swing set and our gigantic sandbox where we spent hours playing. We'd drag the hose over to it and make lakes and puddles and roads everywhere.

When I had my heart surgery at age four, most of what I remember is being surrounded by people who loved me. I remember my parents and my brother David being there. My grandparents, aunts and uncles came sometimes. I remember teddy bears and other stuffed animals piled on my bed to keep me company.

I remember one day my grandfather and brother took me on a ride in a red wagon down the halls of the hospital. One time when my mom left my bedside, I remember being scared. The room I was in with all the beds and many nurses and doctors was huge and noisy.

I don't remember any of the pain, but when I look back at pictures,

I can see that I must have been miserable. I guess it's good that I don't remember. I do remember how good it felt to get home again. I had to be on oxygen when I came home, which meant I couldn't really do much of anything. That was hard for me because I wanted to do stuff. I helped my mom cook sometimes, but that wasn't as much fun as playing outside. I wanted to go outside in our backyard to play on the swing set and hit the tetherball, and there were tons of other things to do, too. Our backyard was one big hill that sloped down toward the house with a flat level section at the top and the bottom. David and I would push our bikes to the top of the hill and then go speeding down—we could really fly. David usually held my bike steady on the top of the hill so I could get on and get situated, and then I'd say, "One, two, three!" He'd give me a push to make me go faster. I loved going fast, but that was before my surgery.

Mom wouldn't let me go outside to play while I needed the oxygen. To me, it didn't seem fair.

Amy and I watched David play outside from the sliding glass door in the kitchen. He would do tricks on his bike and then come over to the door to see what I wanted him to do next. He was the entertainment, I guess. He always did whatever I told him to because he liked making me laugh.

When we got tired of watching David, we'd bring our toys out to the living room and ask Mom to pull out the big couch. As kids, we thought we had the best couch ever because it would unfold and, like magic, turn into a big bed. We'd set up our toys all over the bed and play for hours. Sometimes we got a flashlight and played pirates under the blankets. It was like a cave. Sometimes we made a fort on top of the bed. When we were tired of playing, we could just lie down on the bed and go to sleep. Cool.

I guess the takeaway from all this rambling is that, when a child is four or younger, the memories of heart surgery are probably very few thanks to all the medication. What mattered most to me, and what I do remember, was having my family close by to comfort and reassure me.

Fifteen

*What is the price of five sparrows—two copper coins? Yet God
does not forget a single one of them. And the very hairs on your
head are all numbered. So don't be afraid; you are more valuable
to God than a whole flock of sparrows.*
– Luke 12:6-7 NLT

Miracles are a retelling in small letters of the very same story
which is written across the whole world in letters too large
for some of us to see.
– C. S. Lewis

*A*BOUT A month had passed since Andrew's surgery. Recovery had been slow, but then it plateaued. He wasn't feeling terrible, but he wasn't great either. So, we'd been keeping our eye on him. One morning he woke up late, and I could tell he felt bad. He had "the look." David and Amy were already up playing when Andrew climbed into my lap for a morning hug and stayed there for an unusually long time. The rays of sunshine that warmed the end of the couch crept along the cushions and floor until they finally disappeared. He still sat in my lap and wouldn't eat breakfast. He didn't have a fever, and he said his throat and stomach felt fine. He just didn't feel good, and I noticed that he was pale. All morning he laid around, doing nothing except dozing off to sleep a couple of times. He firmly refused lunch—I couldn't even coax him to eat cookies or a granola bar. Andrew loved cookies—so much that we called him the cookie monster—so this was very abnormal. He didn't talk or play much that afternoon, and he was very compliant and lethargic. When I noticed that his breathing was labored, I decided to call the cardiologist. When I described Andrew's symptoms, the doctor said to bring him in right away.

I had a bad feeling in the pit of my stomach. I called Tom at work to tell him what was going on so he could pray. I quickly called my mom and sisters and several others to ask that they start a prayer chain. We left for Children's Hospital, which was a thirty-five- to forty-minute drive. I fully expected Andrew to be admitted. Call it mother's intuition, gut instinct, or a sixth sense—but I knew something was not right.

When we arrived at the hospital, Andrew seemed even worse than when we left the house. I carried him into the office. Our cardiologist called us into the examining room right away and lifted Andrew up onto the table. "What's going on here, buddy?" he said. Andrew shrugged his shoulders. I pulled his t-shirt up and over his head and noticed that his arms were limp. The doctor rubbed his stethoscope on his palm to warm it and then placed it on Andrew's chest.

"Let's take a listen to you." He must have listened for three minutes or more. It seemed like an eternity. Then he flipped Andrew around, legs up onto the table and laid him down flat and listened again. He probed Andrew's abdomen. He asked him questions about how he felt, and Andrew said he was tired. He asked if he would eat something, and he refused. The doctor asked if he would like to play with a toy and received another no.

"Okay, I'm going to go check on some of his previous test results, and I'll be right back," the doctor remarked as he left the room. Even though this particular doctor didn't let his feelings show, I could tell he was concerned.

I looked over at Andrew as he started to sit up from his prone position on the examining table. Suddenly, at that very moment, something changed—right as he was sitting up. I still remember that moment as clear as day. As he sat up and hung his feet over the edge of the table, his pale face suddenly became pinker and his dull eyes brightened. He stretched out his arms to his sides and remarked casually, "I feel better now."

The doctor came in the room and addressed Andrew. "I found some cookies in my office. Would you like one?" Andrew nodded his head yes. I was dumbfounded. Dr. T handed him the cookie and glanced at me with a half-questioning, half-smiling look. "What just happened?" he asked.

"I don't know," I said. "He was lying down, and then when he sat up, it seemed like something changed; but I don't know what."

"He looks different," he asserted, watching Andrew eat the cookie.

"I—I know. He does, he is," I agreed, faltering. I had tried to get him to eat all day to no avail. These cookies didn't even look that good.

The doctor looked at me and raised his eyebrows. "What did you do after I left?" he asked with a small, inquisitive smile.

"Nothing," I insisted, shaking my head. "He just sat up." I started to doubt myself—*Of course he feels better now—right when we get to the doctor's office. It figures.* But I stopped myself. *No, he had not looked good, and it wasn't my imagination. Even Dr. T had agreed with me.*

The doctor took out his stethoscope and listened again to the *lub-dubs.* "I'm not usually one to rush to conclusions, but whatever was wrong," he said, "is better."

Andrew and I waited in the examining room for about twenty more minutes before Dr. T came back in and checked his heart again before saying, "I have no idea what was going on, but whatever it was seems to be fine now." The doctor, although he didn't exactly admit it, was clearly baffled. "Keep watching him," he admonished, "and call right away if it happens again."

I knew people were praying. I believed God could heal, and I had prayed that He would. He did. What else could it have been? God healed Andrew right there in the doctor's office. He had done so without any fanfare or drum roll, just like we see recorded so many times in the Bible. When I told Dr. T that I thought God had healed Andrew, he just laughed and shook his head.

"Oh, I don't know about *that*," he demurred. But I knew. I could see no other explanation, nor did I need one.

I doubt I will ever get used to seeing a miracle as it is happening. Even seeing the results of a miracle or hearing about one usually brings me to tears. I've realized that my faith puts me in a small minority; not many people actually believe in miracles. Most people today don't believe that God acts and intervenes in our lives or that He would choose to do something outside the norm at times. Even some Christians shake their heads at the idea of an outright miracle, believing that God only performed miracles in Biblical times. Others explain it away logically by saying, "Well of course it happened that way because…" or, "There has to be a scientific explanation."

Even for me, with a solid belief in God's ability to do whatever He sees fit, when I hear the doubt and logical explanations from others, I sometimes start to waffle. My own skepticism can make me pause and wonder if I've missed something or if I need to understand the situation better. And when I'm absolutely sure that something miraculous has happened, I wonder if I should even tell people. Will anyone really believe me? Will they think I've gone loopy and try to explain it away? I do know if I go that route, I'd better be ready to deal with some major skepticism.

The thing is, when you do witness a miracle, you can't deny that it happened. We'd seen the miracle of the angel in the pool, so it wasn't hard at all to believe that this was God's hand as well. We knew what we had seen. The facts don't change simply because someone else doesn't believe them. Everyone has to make up his own mind about spiritual things like the Bible being God's Word and angels and miracles and such—and that's okay. But for me, when it's obvious God has done something very out of the ordinary, I don't just believe in His power—it takes my breath away.

The following month, as the snow began thawing and tiny yellow-green buds poked out of their winter hiding places, another odd mystery captured our attention.

"Who wants to go on a bike ride?" Tom asked one Saturday morning.

"I do, I do!" David and Andrew came running at the suggestion. Tom's bike had a child's seat mounted directly behind him for Andrew, and David had his own little bike. It was still a chilly March day, so they bundled up, helmets on top of knit hats and warm winter jackets zipped up to little chins. Andrew was fairly bursting with excitement because it was his first real adventure outside since he'd been home. No longer on the oxygen that had tethered him to the house, he was finally beginning to feel more like himself.

"See ya later!" he called to me, grinning as they headed out. Not far from our house, a creek and a bike path wound snake-like through trees and willow bushes. It was the perfect place for a morning ride. They had not been gone more than fifteen minutes when, through the front window, I saw them cruising back up the driveway. Why would they be back so soon? One look at Andrew, however, and I knew something wasn't right. His face looked funny.

I turned off the vacuum cleaner and went out to meet them to see what was going on. "What's wrong?" I asked. It looked like Andrew had been crying, and I assumed they were back because he'd gotten hurt somehow. I looked a little closer. "Oh! What is going on?"

"Huh? What do you mean?" Tom hadn't even known there was anything wrong. He had returned only because David had to go to the bathroom. Since Andrew sat directly behind him, Tom hadn't noticed his oddly swollen face. But now, as he dismounted, he turned and saw with horror what I was talking about. Andrew hadn't been crying at all, but his face was red and puffy like a little sumo wrestler. I'd never seen anything like it. His eyes were tiny slits behind those swollen crimson cheeks, and his nose was all out of proportion. I began unbuckling him from the child safety seat as fast as I could.

Tom and David hurried to put the bikes away while I carried Andrew inside. I remember praying the whole way, *Lord, show me what to do.* I took off his coat. His hands were swollen, too, like surgical gloves when you blow them up—they looked like little hand-shaped balloons. I stripped him down, checking all over for a bug bite or rash. His face and hands were all that were swollen, nothing else. It was the weirdest thing. "Andrew, do you hurt anywhere?"

"No." His lips were so swollen they looked kind of squished between nose and chin.

"Can you breathe okay?"

"Mmm-hmm."

"Is it itchy?"

"Yes."

"Okay, let's get you in the tub." I led him into the bathroom and turned on the bath water. *Hands and face. Hands and face. Nothing else swollen. What could this be?* It was bizarre. The rest of his body was normal. If it hadn't been so scary, it would have been hilarious.

David came into the bathroom. "Whoa! What happened to Andrew? Can I take a bath, too? I'm cold."

David was already peeling off his clothes. *Sure, why not,* I thought, *the bike ride is obviously over, so we might as well get baths over with, too.* I checked David's hands and feet as he got in the tub just in case he had some swollen body parts as well. I wondered if they could have eaten something poisonous, but David looked fine. I poured warm water over Andrew and held the washcloth on his forehead and cheeks. I had no idea what to do but came to the conclusion it must be some sort of bizarre allergic reaction due to the anesthesia he'd been on during surgery. Checking the dosage amount, I carefully poured a tablespoon of children's allergy medicine into a small medicine cup and gave it to Andrew.

"Yuck!" He was not thrilled.

Meanwhile, Tom was on the phone with the on-call pediatrician who suggested we take Andrew to the emergency room. "Okay, fine. Let's get you guys out of the tub, dried off, clothes back on."

By the time we arrived at the ER, the swelling was beginning to subside. Andrew didn't look nearly as scary. After a forty-five minute wait, his face was almost back to normal by the time the doctor had a chance to look at him. The doctor said he had no idea what had caused the swelling or why, but felt like we had done the right thing (they always say that), and that it probably was an allergic reaction to something (even we could figure that out). He sent us home with instructions to keep an eye on Andrew and come back if it happened again. Tom and I looked at each other, thinking, *We came all the way to the ER to hear that?*

On our way home, I knew Tom was not happy. "I guess we hadn't wasted enough time or money this week," he said sarcastically. "Well, we don't have to worry about that now." To say we were frustrated would be putting it mildly. We'd incurred an expensive ER bill and still didn't know what was wrong with Andrew—and of course we wondered if it would happen again.

The next day, Tom's brother agreed to meet us at his office with Andrew. We explained everything that had happened. He thought for a minute then got an ice cube and held it on Andrew's arm. After a few seconds, the cold spot didn't just turn red like it normally would have. It swelled up with a red welt the exact size and shape of the ice cube. Ken looked at us as he remarked, "Just what I thought."

"What?" Tom and I asked simultaneously. It was crazy, seeing that swollen ice-cube shaped spot on Andrew's arm.

"It's called *cold urticaria*—it basically means he's allergic to the cold. Yesterday when you were on the bike ride, everywhere that was exposed to the cold air swelled up with hives in an allergic reaction. He's lucky that his windpipe, mouth and throat didn't swell shut. Was he having any trouble breathing?"

"His lips and mouth *were* swollen," Tom said, "but we didn't check inside his mouth."

"It can be very serious." Ken was thoughtful. "As swollen as he was, it's a miracle he could still breathe. My guess is you came in out of the cold just in time."

"Why did it happen?" Tom asked.

"I don't know. No one really knows why this happens or when it might happen again. Sometimes it's a freaky one-time incident, or it can be chronic. But you need to keep your eye on him in the future," Ken said. "And for now, young man," he started laughing and tickling Andrew, "just don't get cold." Andrew dissolved into giggles then, wrestling with and tickling his Uncle. Tom and I shook our heads, astounded by yet another baffling incident. Had God stepped in and protected Andrew's life once again?

Becoming aware of the miraculous, life-changing ways that God sometimes intervenes opened my eyes to His presence and power in my everyday life. I experienced a paradigm shift. Instead of calling a situation an amazing circumstance or quite a coincidence, I now saw God's hand at work. I know some will say that's ridiculous and that I'm looking at things through my miracle glasses. I'm okay with that. People can think what they want…I know what I experienced. I saw it firsthand, and I am thankful for that.

Whenever I do see God at work, it's an extra blessing. During trials and trauma, I may not see Him or feel His presence. Similarly, when my life is rolling along dandy-like, I may not notice or recognize His presence because I'm so busy enjoying the good times—but through good times or bad, whether I notice His presence or not, I believe He is always with me.

We kept Andrew out of the colder weather after that, and soon it was spring and then summer and fall. Luckily for Andrew, the cold allergy was a one-time incident; we never saw any evidence of it again. Even so, we were not taking it lightly. We can't prove that God brought a quick end to the bike ride to prevent Andrew from experiencing a life-threatening event, or that God prevented the swelling from blocking his airway. But it doesn't really matter, either way. We just felt that if God had intervened in this, we were humbled. We realize that most people are not aware of even one miraculous event in their lives. How blessed we are to have seen several.

Sixteen

I waited patiently for the LORD; he turned to me and heard my cry. He lifted me out of the slimy pit, out of the mud and mire; he set my feet on a rock and gave me a firm place to stand. He put a new song in my mouth, a hymn of praise to our God.
– Psalm 40:1-3 NIV

No matter what storm you face, you need to know that God loves you. He has not abandoned you.
– Franklin Graham

"Mom, do dogs go to school?"

"Hmm, maybe on special days, like if they have a pet show, but not every day," I answered, smiling at Andrew as he snuggled with our dog Cody on the kitchen floor.

"I wish Cody could come to school with me. Does Miss Furlong have a dog?"

"Yes, I think so."

"What is his name?"

"I don't know."

"How come some people don't have any dogs or cats?"

"Well, not everybody likes having a dog or a cat for a pet. Some people have birds or fish or no pet at all." I turned to grab the milk out of the refrigerator.

"Does everybody eat lunch at school?"

"Well, the older kids stay for lunch, but you will come home and eat lunch with us."

"Oh, good. Because, well…do you think they have the same kind of milk that we have, 'cuz I don't like the other kinds of milk."

"You don't need to worry about the milk at school. Your lunch will be right here at home, just like always."

"How come there are different kinds of milk?" Then he quickly inserted, "Can I have chocolate milk for lunch?" I paused and looked over at him again. He was grinning like he'd won the lottery jackpot. He knew perfectly well that chocolate milk was for special occasions. He thought he was being sneaky trying to slip that in while he thought I wasn't paying attention. His covert attempt to trick me made me laugh, and looking at his adorable, silly smile I suddenly felt like his partner in crime. Maybe we'd both have chocolate milk for lunch.

Andrew talked incessantly about anything and everything, and it seemed like we were living in a non-stop quiz show. But as the end of August drew near, his questions focused mainly on one thing—starting kindergarten. The week before school started, Andrew fell and bumped his forehead, resulting in two black eyes. Those shiners were swollen, too, and I wondered if he'd be able to see well enough in class. They didn't seem to bother Andrew, though; he was as rambunctious as ever and kept reminding me that he was ready for big kid fun stuff. We'd been up to the school to explore the playground and stopped in for a quick meeting with Miss Furlong, his wonderful teacher-to-be.

Andrew was excited to experience school for himself instead of merely watching from the sidelines. He spent a long time deciding what pencils and notebooks he wanted to use and which backpack would be just right; his top choice that year was the red Rescuers Down Under backpack with Miss Bianca and Bernard on the front.

Carolyn Furlong, his teacher, was the quintessential kindergarten teacher. Nothing rattled her—she'd pretty much seen it all. She was unbelievably patient, quick with a hug and a multitasker extraordinaire. She and I had become good friends when David had been in her class two years earlier, and I was confident that Andrew would have a great year.

David, now starting second grade, considered himself officially a big kid and (like any firstborn will attest) was absolutely confident that he knew the ins and outs of the whole school thing; he readily dished out advice to his younger brother about how to survive in kindergarten. For instance, I heard him tell Andrew that when everyone lined up at the water fountain after recess, he shouldn't rush to be first in line. In fact, he advised him to be the very last person so he could have as much water as he wanted since nobody was behind him. Andrew took it all very seriously.

That first morning before school, I helped Andrew get his shirt buttoned straight and his hair combed, and I made orange juice and oatmeal for breakfast. Andrew was fairly bursting with excitement and spending twice as much time talking as he was eating. I made him take five bites before the four of us left the house at 8:15 in the pouring rain, with huge sunshiny smiles, tummies all aflutter with a hundred butterflies and little backpacks full of promise. A new chapter was upon us, bringing a whole new set of adventures, new friends and brand-new shoes, now soaking wet due to the irresistible combination of little boys and puddles.

By the time the first round of parent-teacher conferences arrived in late fall, kindergarten was not looking as good as it had back in August. Andrew had missed quite a bit of school due to illness. His bronchitis turned into pneumonia in October and, as soon as he was well and back at school, he came down with a bad cold and cough that lasted through Christmas. His immune system just wasn't up to the challenge of a whole classroom full of germs. It was hard on him physically, but he also struggled with some of the more academic areas of kindergarten. He had a hard time sitting still, and after his last surgery, he'd developed a tremor in his right hand, so writing his name was a challenge, and forget about trying to cut a straight line or any of the other fine motor skills he needed to develop. Looking on the bright side (as he always did), he loved his teacher, excelled socially and, according to Andrew, was the fastest in his whole class to climb to the top of the jungle gym!

When Field Day rolled around that spring, however, I knew something needed to change drastically. Andrew had been too sick too often during that kindergarten year. He needed time to get and stay well. He had missed so many days that I wondered if he needed to repeat kindergarten. My college background was in elementary education—I knew I could work with him at home when he felt up to it. However, homeschooling wasn't very common yet, so I wasn't sure how to begin. I heard about a homeschooling meeting for families considering it, so we attended and listened to the pros and cons from families who had tried it. It sounded doable, so we decided to try it for one year so that Andrew could really get healthy. It was an easy decision, really—we'd do what we needed to do for Andrew. And it was only one year. Staying home for school sounded great to David, and I knew it would be more fun with both of them together so they could keep each other company.

We met and talked with friends who homeschooled their children, and then we purchased the books and supplies we'd need and dove right in that fall. The teaching part was challenging for me, but I enjoyed the freedom it gave us as a family, not being tied down to the school district schedule. At first it seemed odd to have the boys with me all the time, but being together soon became the norm. I wasn't super strict, but we did have a schedule. We also made an effort to be involved in activities outside our home: swimming lessons, Cub Scouts, basketball, baseball, soccer, and choir. I could tell that the boys were learning and, even better, they were excited about learning. It wasn't that we didn't have our bad days; many times I'd say to Tom after a long day, "Remind me why I thought this was a good idea?"

I considered homeschooling to be my job. It was a non-negotiable just like any job; I didn't take phone calls, do household chores or run errands during school time. It worked for us, and now we look back on those days as some of our favorite memories. Best of all, David, Andrew and Amy learned to appreciate each other. Over the years they became close friends.

When David was eleven, Andrew nine and Amy six, after fifteen years of working for the same company, Tom lost his job in March due to company downsizing. I chalked it up to a bad year for the economy. *It's got to get better from here,* I thought. Little did I know what was coming. We used our retirement money to get through the six months Tom spent looking for work. We tried to stay positive, but our beloved fourteen-year-old golden retriever, Cody, died in April. It was traumatic for Tom to have lost his job, but losing his "best friend" was devastating.

In May, I noticed David seemed a little thinner than normal—he just had a different look about him. One day at baseball practice, he needed four bathroom breaks. Then I overheard one of his friends joking about how much water David was drinking. I put it all together and realized he must have a urinary tract infection, so the next day we took him to Uncle Ken for a checkup—but it turned out it wasn't an infection. One simple test showed that he had Type I diabetes. We never saw that one coming. No one in our family has diabetes. We were in shock and denial at the same time, both angry at God and clinging to God, hoping that He'd get us through the next day, or the next hour—sometimes wishing He'd just leave us alone.

We were sent to the hospital for a crash course in diabetes. We had no idea how to draw up the insulin, how to give a shot, how to identify warning signs of blood sugar highs or lows. In fact, I never wanted to be a nurse and had no interest in learning how to give a shot. But, of course, I had to hide all these thoughts and feelings from David. *If this can happen to David, what's next?*

Not one thing in my life felt secure, and everything seemed to be a balancing act with me standing on the high wire juggling the china plates. I had never realized just how complicated and life-threatening diabetes is, and it scared me. It fell on my shoulders now to know all this information. I was scared because I didn't know what he could or couldn't eat. All the routines, finger pokes and monitoring were daunting. Even the simplest questions became huge.

The answer to "What can I have for a snack, Mom?" would normally have been easy. "How about an apple?" Now it meant I had to look at the apple, decide whether it was a small or medium apple, remember how many carbs are in an apple, do a finger poke to determine his blood sugar and find out what else he had eaten recently. And we had to do this for every single bite he ate. I was tired of trying so hard to keep my own spirits up along with everyone else's, but to be honest, I was tired of trusting God when things seemed so out of control. However, I realized there was no one else to trust.

One night I took a long soak in the tub. As I sat there alone in the bathroom, I cried out, "No, God! Not David, not *my* David!" But I knew this was not going away. My only option was to plead, "God, if You are there, please, help us get through this." David still battles this insidious disease, and even now we pray for God's help and mercy and the strength to get through.

It was a rotten year...it just was. It's difficult to coach your spouse through a layoff and then job hunting, which gets to be so discouraging.

I was never quite sure if I should be sympathetic and caring or show some tough love by not letting him feel sorry for himself. It was definitely a fine line to walk. About the time I began to wonder if I needed to panic, he landed a job. The bad news? It was two hundred and fifty miles away. I did not want to move. This city was home. Everything and everyone we knew and loved were right here. After the year we'd had, moving to the other side of the state seemed like it might be the final blow. Our family and marriage were already suffering from the stress of the past few months. Would we survive a move to no-man's land? I really wasn't sure, but what else could we do?

I packed box after box through my tears and, early one September morning, with everything we owned loaded into the back of a U-Haul, we headed west over the Rocky Mountains to a new city and a new life. I couldn't hold back my apprehension and incredible sadness. Over the next few hours, I watched the beautiful snow-capped peaks of the Front Range disappear. We drove through breathtaking fall leaves, aspens just turning golden in spots against the hills of dark green Ponderosa Pine and Blue Spruce. For five hours we drove west until the mountains lay behind us and the horizon ahead showed only flat-topped mesas and dry, dirt cliffs.

Tom said our new home was in a "high desert." I returned under my breath that it should be called something else entirely, and I had no intention of liking it. It didn't help that we knew no one in our dusty new community, or that he was taking a tremendous pay cut, or especially that our new home was, well, less than what I'd hoped. It had been the only house we could afford—a fixer-upper that was barely habitable. I insisted the entire house be fumigated, painted and have new flooring and carpet before we arrived. I hoped that would at least get rid of the critters and that it would at least *smell* clean when we walked in.

It's a good thing I didn't know about the previous owners' refusal to vacate and the large family reunion taking place on the property as we drove over those mountains—complete with excessive amounts of alcohol and loaded guns, pit fires raging, tempers flaring and neighbors calling the police. I just remember thinking at that point in my life, *Oh, Lord, what have we gotten ourselves into?*

Seventeen

"When I am afraid, I will put my trust in You."
– Psalm 56:3 WEB

Every experience God gives us, every person He puts in our lives
is the perfect preparation for the future that only He can see.
– Corrie ten Boom

I F I'D been pressed to find something positive about the dreadful house in the miserable new town, it would have been that it was a bit outside of town in the middle of farming and orchard country. I did like the seclusion and peace that came along with that, but I wasn't necessarily jumping up and down with joy. I promised Tom I'd give it the good old college try, hoping the kids would be game for country life and we could all make a fresh start. I was in the middle of, well, Nothingville, and I wasn't really seeing any way of escape. So, with a smile plastered all over my reservations, I dove head first into our country life. Surprisingly, a few months into this new lifestyle, I found I loved it—in fact, we all did. We met our neighbors and joined 4-H and Boy Scouts and Little League. We found a church we liked and made even more friends. It seemed right for us, and we became accustomed to the slower, peaceful pace that comes with life in a small town.

The house didn't have much going for it though. I'm just being honest. It was way more fixer-upper than we knew what to do with. Little by little, we tackled one project and then another. We pulled out all the stops and dug deep to find our inner small-town DIY moxie. With help from friends, we put on a brand-new roof. We replaced the picture window that had a bullet hole in it. We pulled down the disgusting light fixtures and began a remodel on the bathroom. We had no idea what we were doing, but we learned as we went. There was no room for perfectionism in those days. Our family's working motto was, "I think this will be *just* fine," followed by a rousing, "Mmm-hmm," from the helpers.

Whatever we sacrificed in the house, however, we more than made up for with the view. The mountains stretched to the north and east of us, with a wide beautiful valley between us and them. Nestled between peach orchards, cherry orchards and cattle-filled fields, I began to see potential in this funny little house with its huge grassy front yard and five giant cottonwood trees that extended miles into the sky. A menagerie of pets and farm animals kept us busy and entertained.

A year in our new home flew by. That spring, we again watched the birth of baby goats—three this time—and we once again were milking the mama goats every morning and night. Milking the goats was the main chore each day, as well as feeding and watering the other animals and making sure they were cared for and healthy. All told we had a horse, three goats (plus babies), a couple of 4-H lambs, bunnies, an outdoor cat and two dogs. I was planning on adding chickens when we got a coop built. Oh, and inside we had a tank full of fish. Most days I milked and fed the goats while Tom and the kids took care of the other animals.

Rising earlier than usual one morning, I figured I'd tackle all the chores and let my family sleep. Heading back to the mudroom, I gulped down my last swig of coffee, tied on my apron, shoved my feet into work boots and collected the stainless steel milking buckets from the shelf. The screen door's *swish, swish, clank* behind me alerted the animals that I was on my way.

Some would say a barnyard smells disgusting, but I totally disagree. I think that pungent aroma lets you know exactly where you are and that someone in the world is alive besides you. I love the sounds of the horses snuffling and the goats and sheep all bleating and baaing for their breakfast. Pushing back the sliding barn door, a sliver of sunshine caught me in the eye as it slipped through the wooden slats, dancing across the dusty floor and up the opposite wall.

I dug into the grain bin and set a tin of sweet grain on the front of the stanchion. Then I walked out to get Gracie, our oldest (and most stubborn) mama goat. Tom came hustling out the front door, briefcase and tie in hand, and met me halfway across the yard. "I'll see you later," he promised, "I'm running late." He leaned forward for a quick kiss then turned back toward the car.

"Bye," I called. "Have a good day." A few seconds later he was pulling out of the driveway, and it was just Gracie and me again. I've always been a city girl, so milking a goat was still a bit of a novelty. I'd wanted to try something different and new, and this was certainly that. I'd met a new friend, Linda, who was teaching me the ins and outs of raising goats. I like the symbiotic relationships we have with our animals—we take care of them and they, in turn, provide for our family. I cleaned Gracie's underside and gave her a few pats so her milk would let down, then I sat down on the milking stool and got a good rhythm going. The warm milk streamed out in creamy ribbons, splattering noisily against the bottom of the bucket. Every now and then, I'd give the cats a squirt.

About halfway through the milking, I heard the back door and noticed Andrew sauntering slowly over to me. "Morning, buddy," I called out to him as he walked up. He still looked sleepy as I surveyed his tousled blonde curls and an adorably crooked grin above his inside-out tee shirt, rumpled jeans and bare feet.

"Hi, Mom," he returned. He stood there watching me milk for a minute or so, and then he remarked with studied calm, "Mom, I fainted."

"Hmmm?" I looked up at him, wrinkled my forehead and kept on milking. I had heard what he said, but the words skipped across my brain like a rock on a lake.

"I fainted. Inside, on the couch."

I stopped milking and looked right at him. "What do you mean, you fainted?" Gracie looked back at me to see what the hold-up was. No one in our family had ever fainted. We don't faint. He was only eleven. How did he even know what fainting was?

"Well," he continued calmly, "I got dressed, and then I went into the living room. Then I got this weird blackness in my head, kind of in my eyes, and then I woke up on the couch—and so I thought that was fainting."

I turned back to Gracie. *Okay, well*, I mentally agreed, *that does sound like fainting*. My hands moved to finish the milking, but my thoughts jumped ahead, trying to collect themselves in a neat and orderly fashion, the way my thoughts try to do. Immediately, I was flipping through my mental files for anything I could think of regarding fainting.

"Okay, hmmm. Well, umm…" I was stalling, but I came up with nothing. *What do I say? What do I do?* I remember telling myself to stay calm. I stopped again and looked at him. "Why don't you go back in, Andrew, and I'll be right there and we can talk about it." All kinds of thoughts were crowding my mind. "Wait a second," I said as he turned to go, "take this with you." I lifted the bucket of foamy milk off the stanchion. He grabbed the handle and turned toward the house.

I watched him walking all lopsided with that heavy bucket in his right hand, but my mind was still racing. I sprayed Gracie's teats with sanitizer and led her back to her pen, wondering all the while what his fainting might mean. I didn't even need to lead our other mama goat to the barn—as soon as the gate was open, she waddled over comically, with her huge, full udder, and climbed on the stanchion all by herself. Goats can be so funny. I grabbed a pan of grain for her and called out to Andrew as he neared the house, "Please ask David if he'll come out and milk this goat for me!" My brain was running full speed ahead now. So much for my plans for the day!

With three active kids, I was not one to panic over something little. Blood I can deal with; broken arms, dislocated fingers, sprained ankles…no problem. Stitches…piece of cake. But I'd never encountered fainting, and I really didn't know what to make of it. How big of a deal could it be? Andrew looked okay; nothing seemed suspicious. He said he felt fine. He'd not been sick, and he didn't have a fever. And he'd never, ever fainted before. Could this have been just a freak thing? I wasn't sure, but I had a gut feeling that I'd better call the pediatrician and see what he had to say. I figured he'd want me to keep an eye on Andrew, at the very least, and maybe bring him in if it happened again. I had the number on speed dial. The nurse put me on hold and took the message back to the doctor.

A couple of minutes later I heard her ask, "Are you still there?"

"Yes," I answered.

"The doctor wants to see him. Can you come in this morning? We'll fit you in," she said. "He just wants to be sure…"

I finished her sentence in my mind…*just wants to be sure it's not* "*Something serious.*" My stomach thrust its way into my throat and a tiny, sickening thought wedged into my consciousness. In the span of about three seconds, I got it and my brain jolted into overdrive. *He thinks it could be serious?* No, I countered, *it's nothing. But…he wants to see Andrew.* Somewhere deep down in my heart, I knew what was coming, and I raced to quiet those thoughts before fear consumed me. They bubbled up to the surface anyway. *It can't be time for another surgery already, Lord! No, no, no. Today? I'm not ready! I've got so much to do today! No, Lord, not today...*

I think my brain took off in two opposite directions at that moment. One part was way out there trying to handle the questions and fear I was feeling, and the other part was able to remain present and respond perfectly normally to the nurse on the other end of the phone. I overheard my own voice saying, "Yes, absolutely. We can be there in half an hour."

I said good-bye and immediately jumped back into the real world as my adrenaline kicked in. I needed to get organized. I didn't really know how long this appointment would take—maybe not that long, but maybe quite a while. My mind and body were racing around each other, trying to get in sync. David could stay with Amy at home while I took Andrew in. I called my friend, Robin, to let her know that I was sorry, but I wouldn't be able to watch her kids that afternoon; then I called our baseball carpool to say we needed to switch driving with someone. *Oh, yeah, I forgot about Amy's drama class.* I called the drama teacher. *No, I told the kids, I don't know if we'll be doing baseball today, or drama, or Home Depot, or any of the things any of us had planned.* In the back of my mind, I saved room for a little hope that I might still have time to plant the flowers later on that afternoon. I pulled on some clean jeans and a fresh t-shirt, called Andrew to get in the car and we were on our way.

Andrew and I waited to be "fit in" while cranky, sick kids and worried moms and dads waltzed in and out at the pediatrician's office. I had brought a couple of Andrew's school books and his writing journal. It was a school day, so at least he could do some reading. I know, it sounds ridiculous now—but at the time, I was trying to keep everything normal...for Andrew as well as for me. Besides, I had no idea how long we'd be at the doctor. But we were both distracted and nervous and not a stich of schoolwork got done. Finally, a quick opening in the schedule sent us to the examination room. The doctor listened to Andrew's heart, asked a lot of questions, and then sent us across the street to the hospital for an x-ray and an EKG. We walked the large manila envelope of results back to the pediatrician's office. He called our cardiologist in Denver and sent over the results. Then it was back to the hospital for an echocardiogram. It was lunchtime when we walked back to the office again with more test results. We continued to wait while discussions took place and decisions were made. I absentmindedly thumbed through old magazines, trying to ignore the sick feeling in my stomach. Andrew wandered around the waiting room, bored, looking in the fish tank for a while, then plopping down in a chair and swinging his legs back and forth.

Our whole summer was about to change if he needed surgery. All the fun adventures we were looking forward to, and all Andrew had planned as well, would go straight down the drain. We had never held Andrew back from the physical activities he wanted to do. He had mountain biked, swam, hiked, skied and played basketball and baseball from the time he was five. He begged us to let him play. His favorite was baseball, and he was a good little player. I made Andrew and David wear heart-guard chest protectors (which they hated), but those balls come at you fast even in Little League. Any mom in my position would have done the same. Andrew usually played second base, but he wanted to try it all, so his coaches rotated him through most every position, including pitcher and catcher. His favorite position, though, was second—and it was even better when he and David were on the same team and David played short. A ground ball hit in their direction almost never got by those two; they practiced together at home all the time and could anticipate each other's moves. I wondered if the doctor would let Andrew play through the rest of the season.

I thought about how to help Andrew through this next hurdle. If he did need surgery, I wondered how in the world I could prepare him? Would he be angry, sad, scared? The last time we'd been down this road, he was only four years old. His worries and needs at four had been totally different than they would be now. I had been there to hold him, to help him feel safe and comfortable. Back then, I could explain to him in very concrete terms what surgery was and how it would help him grow strong and run fast. It wasn't easy then, but it was simpler.

At eleven, he would need us in a different way. He needed more facts, but not too many; he needed us to help him understand what was about to happen, why it was happening, and that no matter what, we would be there for him. I wanted to reassure him that God was with him and help him find comfort in his relationship with God. The Holy Spirit would be his best friend in the hard days ahead.

Finally, the doctors agreed that we had better head to Denver for more evaluation and possibly another surgery. Our cardiologist there wanted us to come as quickly as possible. As in *today*…no waiting until tomorrow.

With an event like this, everything else in life stops. Just about the time I thought I had it all under control, I realized I never really did. Everything being under control was simply an illusion I made up. Such a realization feels like having the rug suddenly jerked out from underneath you. It reintroduces the need to be flexible and always ready for changes. It reminds you that you must trust God for each step. It affects the family as a whole, but since our children were still fairly young, it taught us that we were all in this together—as a family, there are times when the needs of one person override our individual activities, and we must be the ones to sacrifice. With a chronically ill child, planning any activity becomes more akin to shooting from the hip, you *hope* you can do something. You even plan on doing it, but you don't dare get your heart set on it. Even several years after a child's last procedure or surgery, your personal adrenaline supply is always at-the-ready just in case the bottom drops out.

Thoughts from Andrew

BASEBALL. OH, how I love that word. I was born loving all sports, but baseball is my favorite. I wish I could play it every day of my life. Maybe if things had been different, who knows? Maybe I could have made it in high school and college ball...I think almost every little boy dreams of playing in the big leagues, and that was definitely a dream of mine. I love learning about the history of the game, and I love listening to games on the radio. One of my all-time favorite movies is *The Sandlot*. When I was younger, I could relate to the kids in that movie because baseball was as important to me as it was to them. Even now, softball is my top choice to play and baseball to watch.

As a kid, I always looked forward to spring when Little League would start. I could not wait to get to practice. Yes, I am that guy who even loved baseball *practice*. My brother and I spent hours playing catch in the yard. We even made up our own game to improve our skills. We simply called it "the game." I was always on great Little League teams. The worst my team ever finished was second. It wouldn't have really mattered to me if I'd been on a bad team though, because I just love playing.

When I was eleven, I was on the Braves—and it looked like my team was going to be unstoppable. We had talent everywhere. I was very excited and felt like this was going to be a great season. But one crazy summer day turned out to be the end of all those dreams.

It was pretty early still when I woke up and went out to the living room couch for a minute. Then I decided to go see where Mom was. As

I was standing up, I fainted. Thankfully I just fell back onto the couch. I don't think I was out for very long, but I don't really know. When I came to, I somehow knew that something was off. My mom was outside doing chores, so I walked out to the barn and told her about what had just happened.

She thought we had better make sure everything was okay, so we went to the doctor's office. It turned out that we spent the whole day at the hospital and doctor's office and ended up driving over the mountains to Denver that night. I was going to need my third heart surgery.

All I could think of was, "Darn, I guess I won't be playing ball this summer." It was a crushing blow, and at eleven years old, it was a very hard thing for me to accept. I'd been so excited, and I was really looking forward to being part of a great team and having a great season, and now all of that was gone. Just like that, my entire world changed. I was going to have to endure my third open heart surgery and miss a season of baseball, too.

Eighteen

Because of the LORD's great love we are not consumed,
for his compassions never fail.
– Lamentations 3:22 NIV

Compassion is expressed in gentleness. When I think
of the persons I know who model for me the depths
of the spiritual life, I am struck by their gentleness…
– John Biersdorf

OUR ENTIRE family arrived at the hospital in Denver about eleven o'clock that night and had to enter through the emergency room night entrance. They were expecting us, and we followed an orderly up to Andrew's room. What is by day a busy, bustling hospital is still and quiet late at night. The newly buffed floors shone like a river in the moonlight down the long, long corridors.

So tired from the drive and the stressful day, David and Amy both fell asleep right away in two of the overstuffed vinyl chairs while Tom and I tried to get comfortable in the plastic chairs next to Andrew's bed. I wished for an unending night of sleep instead of the unending parade of medical personnel. We answered a labyrinth of questions as we told and re-told the story about his fainting episode, relayed the pediatrician's words, and handed over the x-rays and notes. The nurses took Andrew's vital signs. Our cardiologist listened to his pulsing, murmuring heart, checking what he heard against the test results in his brown folder.

I kept wondering why we were doing all this in the middle of the night. Could this not wait until morning? Andrew was hooked up for another EKG—and the doctor wanted to do a heart catheterization right away. I was flabbergasted. *Now, at midnight?* Yes, the cardiologist wanted to double check the echo results. Tom and I sat on the couch in the surgical waiting area, alone in the quiet darkness while Andrew had the catheterization. I was reminded that hospitals and airports never sleep. On the positive side, at 12:30 a.m. there's no waiting—not one person was scheduled ahead of Andrew. Tom and I dozed on the couches until the cardiologist returned, results in hand. The cath showed that Andrew's pulmonary valve had calcified, leaving an opening the size of a thread for blood to squirt through on its way to his lungs. It was more serious than the doctor originally suspected. He wanted Andrew to have surgery that morning, in just a few hours.

Back in the room about 2:30 a.m., we moved David and Amy to sleeping bags I had spread out on the carpeted area of the room, leaving their chairs for Tom and me. We settled in the best we could. Even though I was exhausted, I didn't know if I'd be able to sleep at all. Andrew was having surgery in the morning! *I'll just close my eyes and...* I was suddenly aware of a bright stream of sunlight peeking through the crack between the curtains and settling across my face. I stirred, vaguely aware of a nervousness in my gut, and then squinting, opened my eyes. *Oh, yeah, today is the day.*

The room looked different in the daylight. The walls were covered with a faded aqua wallpaper, peeling a bit at the seams. Heavy floral curtains hung from ceiling-height windows, looking like they might have been recycled from *The Sound of Music*. My eyes quickly scanned the rest of the room to find a small white sink and mirror, a bathroom door, huge corner windows and dusty ceiling tiles surrounding the fluorescent lights. Obviously, this was not one of the newly updated rooms the receptionist mentioned when we checked in. It was a private room, but the small, odd shape of the room barely provided enough space for our family to maneuver.

Though it was early, I knew the hospital would be bustling soon enough. I woke the kids. Amy rolled over and moaned, "I don't feel good, Mom."

I took a good look at her flushed cheeks and could tell—she *was* sick. Bending down, I felt her forehead. She was burning up. Her temperature must have been about 101°. I sighed. *This can't be happening. Amy is supposed to stay with her friend Allegra for a few days. But now… Oh, Lord, what am I going to do with a sick daughter and a recuperating boy?* For the moment I let Amy sleep while I packed away our hodgepodge of belongings, straightened my hair and clothing, brushed my teeth in the little sink and tried to figure out what to with my little daughter.

Yesterday I had called Allegra's mom, Melody, hoping Amy could go over there to play during the surgery. Melody said she'd be delighted to have Amy and even asked if Amy could stay overnight with them for a couple of days. I had breathed a sigh of relief. That would be perfect. So, that had been the plan.

Now, with Amy being sick, that was out of the question. I called Melody to let her know. "I'm afraid Amy can't come this morning after all—she's sick," I confessed.

"Oh, I'm so sorry. That's terrible," Melody commiserated. "But, do you think she'd come over anyway? I can still come get her, if she'll come." Her voice was caring on the phone. "Amy can sleep in a real bed and get better over here."

"Oh, I couldn't ask you…" I began, but Melody interrupted me.

———

"No, Cathy, it's fine, really, she'll be fine. Can I be there in about an hour? I'll meet you out in front."

"Well, okay. Yes, that would be wonderful. I'm so sorry she's sick, though." I still wasn't quite sure I should let Amy go. It is a rare friend who will take your sick child, and Melody was not only a rare friend and wonderful mother with three young daughters but also a busy woman who worked part-time as well. She was—and is still—one of the loveliest, most elegant and gracious women I have ever met.

Amy had already thrown up once, and it's not easy taking care of a sick child. But Melody became Mother Teresa for my daughter that week, and oh, how I appreciated her loving kindness. It was hard for me to let someone else step in and help this way, but I knew Amy needed mothering. It was supposed to be my job, though, and I worried that Amy would think I was passing her off to some other mother, that I had abandoned her in her time of need. She was only eight years old, so I wondered if she would understand…if she would know that I wanted to be the one to hold her and take care of her, to reassure her that everything would be okay. Regardless, I had to let it go. I couldn't do both—I had to focus on Andrew and, as much as I wanted to be with Amy, we just could not have a sick sibling in his room.

That week Melody stood in for me as a mom, taking such tender care of my daughter and giving me the ability to concentrate my energy on Andrew. Her graciousness was an incredible blessing to me (and to Amy), and it really made me think about the limitations I often put on myself in the area of serving others. I might not be a rocket scientist, and I'm barely fluent in my own language—much less a second one, but I know how to hold a child. I know how to rock a baby and give a bottle and change a diaper. I can clean up after someone when they've been sick. I can do laundry and wash dishes. So many people all around me and around the world have needs that I can meet. I need to remember that God can and will use me just as I am. I simply must be willing. I don't have to wait until I'm "good" at something special. If I just open myself to Him, He will use me in ways I might not ever expect. I want to be an example of His tender care and love for others, like Melody was for Amy.

Two hours prior to surgery, nurses and doctors started appearing every few minutes in our small hospital room, checking vitals and discussing anesthesia and what to expect in recovery. Although his surgery was scheduled for eight that morning, they said they'd come for him by seven. My stomach was upset, but I didn't say anything. I put on my fake smile, we prayed with Andrew as a family and then, when they came to get him, we all accompanied him to the doors leading into the pre-surgical area. Melody took Amy, David went to the waiting room and Tom and I went into the pre-surgery area to wait with Andrew.

Maybe my feelings were heightened that morning because of what had happened right before the last surgery when the pastor wouldn't leave. I'm possessive of those minutes right before a surgery takes place. This time, I wanted to be one hundred percent present. I wanted to grab hold of and savor each moment because they melt away so quickly, one into the next. There wasn't much to say, really, so we just sat quietly for a while. The realization that this could be the last time I saw Andrew alive was making its way to the forefront of my mind. I try not to think about that possibility, but it's always there. We wanted to be positive and composed for Andrew's sake, but my stomach was in knots. I desperately wanted to hold him and finger through his tousled blonde hair and breathe in his smell, but of course he was eleven years old—and much too grown up for all that fuss.

Andrew was calm that morning. He'd shown me an index card he'd brought from home. I unfolded the card and saw he had written out a Bible verse in crayon, *When I am afraid, I will trust in Thee.*

———

"I'll hold onto this for you while you're in surgery," I told him as I gave him a hug. *How can I possibly send my son down that hallway into the care of people who don't even know him? They don't know his sweet, sunny disposition and how he loves making people laugh and how he is crazy about baseball and how he innocently trusts God to be there when he's afraid. Is this just a job to them? Is he more to them than a name on the board, the eight o'clock Truncus repair? These people don't know Andrew, and yet we are trusting them to save his life.*

Right then it sounded a little crazy to send him into the operating room, but what else could we do? I remembered that God knew Andrew and that he was loved and treasured, even created by this very same God. I prayed for protection and healing and care.

Minutes sped by like seconds. We signed the papers giving permission for surgery. Nurses checked and double-checked Andrew's wrist band. A surgical nurse came to get him, we gave a last kiss and hug, and then he was waving and smiling as they wheeled the gurney backwards down the hallway. I watched his smile, his legs, his toes disappear around the corner before the long day of waiting began.

It was still early, so Tom and I settled in on the "good" chairs in the corner of the waiting area. David was already there, earbuds in place, reading and listening to his music. I looked for a decent magazine but there weren't any, so I sat and stared, watching the other families arrive and assemble for their own private vigils. It was crowded, and I wished I could be alone. How interesting, I thought, that gathered here in this one space, all kinds of families wait while their children and loved ones undergo surgery. A hernia repair, a tonsillectomy, open-heart surgery, ear tubes put in…we're all feeling the same love and fear, sitting on the edges of our chairs, watching for the familiar face of our doctor to come through those doors. Some of us stay longer than others.

It felt different this time—this third time around. We knew what was coming, but that didn't help. I think the knowing may have made it worse. We would have given anything for Andrew not to have to endure what we knew was coming. I was sad, and I hurt for him. Everyone who's been through multiple surgeries with their child knows that, although the steps and processes are somewhat familiar, the nervousness and fear are as fresh and new as the very first time.

Our extended family and good friends came and went throughout the day; even cousins, aunts and uncles were there supporting us, praying for Andrew and the doctors. We found a small, private room right next to the waiting area that we sort of claimed as our own. After all, we were going to be there a long time. Everyone was eager to do whatever they could to help, so since the doctors had suggested directed blood donations, we all took turns heading down to the blood center to give blood for Andrew.

Around 9:30 that morning, the surgical nurse came out to let us know that Andrew was on bypass and the doctors were beginning the repair. "Everything is going smoothly," she reassured us, "there haven't been any surprises. He is doing very well." We breathed a sigh of pure relief at such good, good news. She said she'd keep us posted.

We got more excellent news at noon when she came out and said the repair was completed. Everything was still proceeding exactly as expected. His vital signs were stable, and it would only be a short time until he came off of bypass. We were ecstatic. All of the other families that had been waiting throughout the morning were gone, and new families waiting for afternoon surgeries had settled in. I felt like we and our family members were hospital groupies, hanging out in the wings till the last possible minute, ready to go backstage to meet the star.

My inability to focus during surgeries had not improved over the years. I love to read, but I could never read a book to pass the time because it required too much concentration. A magazine was the best I could manage. I could knit if it was a mindless pattern. Tom fell asleep right on cue. I was always surprised how easily he could fall asleep. I can barely fall asleep in my own bed in a quiet, dark room. Although our family was with us and I appreciated them being there, I couldn't bring myself to do much chitchatting. I'm not a big talker when I'm stressed; I'm a prayer and a thinker. I internalize. I get restless, but I don't talk.

The nurse came back in the early afternoon to let us know they had run into some trouble with bleeding and that it was possible Andrew was showing some very early signs of graft versus host disease. We had no idea what graft versus host was or why it would be happening to Andrew, but I could tell it wasn't good. Tom's brother, Ken, had been waiting with us, so he explained what it meant. The complete name is Transfusion Associated Graft Versus Host Disease (TA-GVHD). It's rare, but it happens because of complications with transfused blood. Andrew's body (the host) begins to reject and attack the grafted in (transfused) blood. This can happen for a variety of reasons, but one factor that increases the risk is blood donations from immediate relatives, which we had done. It is a very serious situation—in fact, it is fatal about ninety percent of the time.

Suddenly my adrenaline kicked in, and I needed to walk and pray. I took off down the main walkway, down the escalator, around the lobby and back up the escalator on the other end. Again and again I circled, down and up, around and back. Anywhere to get away from people. I couldn't talk…or think. My stomach was in my throat. "Please, God, help Andrew," was about all I could muster. I couldn't believe this was happening. Was I really here at the hospital? Yesterday morning I was milking goats, and today I am begging God for my son's life? It was surreal.

A couple of hours later, we were startled to see Andrew's surgeon and the cardiologist walk through the doors. Of course, your heart starts pounding when you see the doctors walking toward you, still in their surgical scrubs, somber looks on their faces. The surgeon started, "Well, he's doing better than expected. Not out of the woods, but we've got him stabilized for now. He's a fighter." He explained further the graft versus host situation and then continued, "We feel like his bleeding is under control, but it has been touch and go. We'll have to wait and see on the graft versus host, but from now on he needs to be transfused with blood other than family directed donations." He paused and then continued, "He cannot receive family blood again because his system won't accept it. He *must* have blood from unrelated donors."

Then it was the cardiologist's turn. "We were considering putting in a pacemaker but decided against it. My thought is to go ahead and put the wires in place so that if we decide to put in a pacemaker later, it will be much easier. How does that sound to you?"

Tom and I looked at each other. We agreed with their recommendations. "That sounds good," Tom said, and I nodded my head in agreement.

"Absolutely, do what you think is best," I replied.

"Okay then. We'll see you in the ICU after surgery." They turned, punched the button on the wall and disappeared back through those heavy, gray doors.

The afternoon dragged on, and we kept expecting to hear something any minute. By five o'clock, I was beginning to feel just a pinch of panic. It was taking too long. We wondered what was happening. We hadn't heard a report from the operating room in over two hours, and I desperately needed to know that Andrew was still fighting, still breathing.

Nineteen

Ah, Sovereign Lord, *you have made the heavens*
and the earth by your great power and outstretched arm.
Nothing is too hard for you.
– Jeremiah 32:17 NIV

Heartache forces us to embrace God out of desperate, urgent
need. God is never closer than when your heart is aching.
– Joni Eareckson Tada

ONE REASON why I prefer not to have a multitude of people around during surgery is because I feel as though I must be brave for everyone. I don't want someone else to panic simply because I am panicking. I don't want to have to carry on a conversation when my mind is somewhere else. Our family and one or two good friends was as much as I could handle. I had managed to hold it together so far, but with each minute that ticked by without any word of Andrew's progress, I felt closer to that narrow edge.

My good friend, Yvette, was waiting with us during this go-around, and she must have sensed my fears growing out of control. I leaned on the second-story railing overlooking the main lobby with tears pooling in my eyes as I blinked to keep them at bay. I couldn't cry now—I might not ever stop. Yvette put her arm around me and simply hugged me. She didn't say a word—she was just there at my side. At that moment, I felt as though an angel's arm had surrounded me. *Thank You, God, for good friends.*

Finally, a phone call from the operating room to the waiting room receptionist about six o'clock let us know Andrew was out of surgery and headed for the ICU. He'd been in surgery for over ten hours. I don't know how much of that time he was on the heart-lung machine, but I know it was a long time. We were told we could head to the ICU by seven. By now I knew to prepare myself for the smells. I do eventually get used to it, but it can almost knock me out at first. I make sure I've had something to eat, then I hold my breath and walk right in.

Eleven years old doesn't look so grown up lying on a big hospital bed after a day of open-heart surgery. Andrew's body was puffy and bloated, and very pale; his skin looked like shiny cream-colored vellum. Wires and tubes and IV lines ran everywhere, as if someone had spilled a bowl of spaghetti on his tummy. His eyes were closed and swollen, goopy with ointment to keep them moist. The bloody tape running the length of his chest was the ultimate scar of his battle. Four blood-filled drainage tubes resembled strings of red licorice poking out of his chest. My son looked both horrifying and beautiful all at the same time. Dried blood was caked on his neck and arm and side. I really didn't care, though. I bent down and kissed his forehead, stroked his hair and started talking to him—just like when he was a baby…just like when he was four. The only thing that mattered to me was that he was alive.

When Andrew opened his eyes later that night, he immediately tried to say something to Tom who stood next to the bed. Since he was intubated, he couldn't talk, and try as we might, we could not understand what he wanted. The nurse came over, and it was like playing a game of charades. Do you have to go to the bathroom? Are you in pain? Are you thirsty? Sounds like…rhymes with…I was beginning to worry. What could possibly be wrong? He was so insistent on communicating that we finally found a piece of paper and put a pencil in his hand. Over all the IV lines, tubes and ventilator, he managed to scribble, "Who won the game?"

Who won the game? What game? Are you kidding me? He'd just spent the entire day with his chest open, surgeons scrambling to keep him alive, and he was worried about a *game*? I looked at Tom because I had no idea what Andrew was talking about. Tom informed me that the NBA championship game had been that evening, and Andrew had been disappointed to miss it. Tom spent the next few minutes filling Andrew in on the outcome of the different sporting events that had happened that day as his eyes fluttered open and closed and he tried to smile under the ventilator tubing. Later, we got a good laugh out of the whole situation—so relieved that it wasn't something terrible. I finally took a deep breath, glad to know that nothing had changed. My son was going to be fine.

Andrew never complained about the pain, and I'm not making that up. He really never did. He was such a trooper and so eager to get well that he'd push through physical therapy or a walk around the hallway with the stamina of a Sherpa on Mt. Everest. He'd always had a very high pain tolerance coupled with a wildly adventurous love of life. It was a delightful combination because he did everything with complete abandon; he was a physical kid. He would throw himself at you for a hug, he loved to cuddle and sit close—practically on top of you—and he never missed a wrestling match with Dad.

The downside to his exuberance was that he would jump and bump and fall and hurt himself all the time. His physical intensity was caused partly by his personality, but also partly because of what the doctors called sensory integration issues. He'd had sensory integration therapy when he was three and four years old to help him learn to process what his senses were telling him. One consequence of his sensory integration problems was a lack of actually feeling or processing pain. Andrew's sensory intake button was set on low, so being overtly physical was his attempt to get the sensory input he so desperately wanted. It was an "invisible disability," and I always had to pay particular attention to his actions and reactions in order to identify when he was sick—because he didn't hurt or feel sick, and he rarely complained. Consequently, when he did say something was hurting, you knew he was *really* hurting. That's why I got steaming mad a couple of days post-op.

One of the ICU nurses was very impatient and just did not want to deal with Andrew. I can only assume that she either didn't like us, or else she wanted to impress the student nurse who was training with her. Andrew was in tremendous pain the third and fourth days after surgery. The medical staff had tried to get him up and going sooner than his body was ready. The nurse did not want him in bed, and she insisted he sit up in a chair to eat his lunch. Well, he was sitting up, but he was in so much pain that he couldn't talk or even hardly move. He looked like a statue—he wasn't moving his head or engaging with us. I was trying to feed him tiny bites of the hamburger they had brought for lunch, but he was in survival mode, silent tears welling up in his eyes and spilling down his cheeks. Just then, the nurse(s) stopped by and saw that Andrew hadn't eaten—and this particular nurse must have taken it personally. She scolded threateningly, "I'll have none of this! You need to stop your crying right now and sit up and eat your lunch. Crying is for babies."

I looked up at her from my seat next to Andrew, too shocked to say anything. I never before (or since) have heard a nurse make such a demeaning and demoralizing remark. Stop his crying? We had asked for an increase in pain meds and had been denied. He was three days out of surgery and his pain was over the top. I was doing my best to comfort him, and she had the nerve to tell him to stop crying? But she didn't stop there...she continued with, "Don't you want to go home?

You can't go home if you don't eat." Then, looking at me, she asserted sharply, "He'll eat when he's hungry enough. He's just trying to get some attention." Then she turned and walked out of the room.

Stunned into silence by my anger, I opened my mouth to say something, but nothing came out. I looked in the direction she had gone. *You've got to be kidding me! How could she treat him—and me—like that?* I knew that Andrew was doing the absolute best he possibly could; he was not trying to manipulate or get attention. That simply wasn't Andrew's way. This was one of my worst fears coming true—that my child, in such a vulnerable and totally dependent state, would be at the mercy of an abusive nurse or doctor. I was livid, but the whole exchange also really upset Andrew; he was crying hard. He'd reached his breaking point. Instead of leaving to confront the nurse, I turned my attention where it was most needed.

"Andrew, it's okay," I assured him over his crying. I scooted over next to him instead of in front of him and held him as best I could without hurting him or dislodging IVs, etc. "It's okay; you can cry. You can cry all you want, and you don't have to eat that hamburger." His crying soon quieted because it hurt him so much to cry. "It's going to be alright. She's gone, and I'm here, and I say we get you into bed." He nodded into my shoulder and then lifted up his head and looked at me in the eyes. He didn't say a word—he just looked at me. I saw great pain reflected in his eyes, and I knew he was pleading for help. I could hardly stand it. My eyes filled with tears as I spoke. "Oh, honey, I promise I won't let that happen again. I'm so, so sorry." I held him close another minute then wheeled his chair and the IV pole close to the bed and carefully helped him back under the soft covers and adjusted the pillow under his head. He slept, and I didn't leave his side again.

My stomach was in knots. Once again, I'd failed as a mother by not standing up for him. I'd have given anything to go back and change the way I handled that situation—or better yet, prevent it from happening in the first place. How could I have let that nurse charge in and say such awful things? Why didn't I do or say something? It was unfair for her to treat him that way. The chest tube incident from the previous surgery popped into my head, and I hated myself for walking right back into the same trap. How I wished I had silenced her judgmental words before they sliced so deep. I tend to be cautious about leaving Andrew alone in the hospital, and this event made me even more so.

As Andrew slept, my mind was spinning. *I've always protected my children—or at least I thought I did. Maybe what I imagined myself to be is not the reality of who I actually am. I thought I was the kind of mom who was brave and unafraid to face an army of enemies to defend her child. Ha! I'm obviously not even able to stand up to a bossy nurse; I wilt straightaway like a dead daylily. What is wrong with me?* The incident was a rude awakening that made me think more deeply about myself. *What kind of example am I setting for my kids? What will it take for me to learn my lesson? I am going to have to step out of my safe little world and take some risks if I'm really going to be the person I envision. Why did his nurse snap at him like that,* I wondered. I was angry with her, but I decided not to react in anger or retaliation, but to try to understand her. Perhaps she was having a bad week, or maybe she'd dealt with one too many complaining adults or whiny kids and she was having none of it. Maybe she was hardened to the pain because she saw so much. Maybe she lacked compassion because she'd never experienced what it was like to hurt. Or, if she had experienced hurt, maybe she didn't hear a gentle voice or feel strong arms around her to give understanding and encouragement. It could have been a combination of all these things, but the biggest possibility is that she had never experienced the compassion that comes from God.

It matters that Jesus experienced every single bit of the pain that we do when He lived here on earth, that God is omnipotent and merciful, and that the Holy Spirit is a comforter. These spiritual issues matter because, when Andrew is hurting physically or when I am in the pitch black pit of despair, we can pray and know that our pain is felt. We are not crying out to an empty sky. God is there and hears us and loves us in the midst of it all. It is only because He loves me and shows compassion to me that I can then be compassionate toward others.

Jesus was not only compassionate, but He also stood up for what was right. He defended the children when the disciples wanted to shoo them away. He stood up to the spiritual brainiacs of His day, the Pharisees, and wasn't afraid to speak the truth. He confronted wrong behavior without condemning the person caught in it. I knew that He could give me the right words to say, and that I need not fear standing firm in the face of opposition.

When people go through trials of their own, they often develop a deeper level of compassion. Even though he was only eleven, I witnessed a deepening in Andrew's character through this surgery and recovery. He was still the same funny comic, still lived and breathed sports, and still loved spending time with friends; but he was old enough now that his experiences affected his perspective. I watched a subtle sensitivity toward others developing just under the surface. He was determined and sure of what he wanted. Maybe he was more tuned in spiritually, or maybe it was an emotional thing. In fact, I could see changes in all three of my kids because of this experience. David and Amy became very aware of people who were hurting or less fortunate.

After a week, Andrew was moved out of ICU onto the cardiac floor where the nurses quickly realized his pain levels were out of control. He couldn't eat and could barely move. They immediately put him back on morphine and finally got his pain levels under control. These nurses were opposite of the one in ICU. They were compassionate, caring and professional. When Andrew said his pain was an eight or nine, they believed him and attempted to alleviate his suffering. The relationship between pain and healing has been proven to be a primary agent in a patient's health and recovery from surgery. Because they work closely with their patients, nurses have a unique perspective and can communicate the patient needs with the doctors. These nurses would have made Florence Nightingale proud; they truly cared about Andrew's need to getting well, pushing him just a little, and understanding when he'd had too much. Even so, Andrew spent three extra days in the hospital because his pain had not been managed well early on in the ICU.

Before we had left our home in such a rush that evening almost two weeks ago, I had stopped by to see my around-the-corner neighbor, Robin. "We have to go to Denver for a check on Andrew's heart; he might possibly need surgery."

"Oh, no," she replied, "I'm sorry to hear that."

"Is there any way you could help me with the animals?"

"Of course, and don't worry about a thing," she replied. "I am happy to do whatever I can to help out. Do you want me to milk the goats?"

Oh, Lord, thank You for Robin!

"Well, if you want to you can. Otherwise, I was thinking I'd just dry them out."

"I don't mind at all. You just drive safely and get Andrew well. We will take care of everything here." She gave me a hug. I appreciated Robin and her husband, Mark, and their kids. It's an extra special friend who will milk your goats!

She told me later that when she came by the following morning, she was completely surprised to see all kinds of people at our house. People were planting the flowers I had not gotten to, watering and mowing the lawn, folding the laundry left in the dryer, vacuuming the carpets, and performing any other household task they could find. She talked with everyone and found out these were our friends from church wanting to help in any way they could. A group of men even finished our bathroom remodel! Their love and generosity meant the world to us and spoke volumes to all our neighbors. Robin and her family were so impressed that they decided to come to our church!

Our next-door neighbor, Mary, an elderly widow, also came over to see what all the activity was about—it's always good to have neighbors watching out for you. She wasn't the type to look the other way when something fishy was going on. She knew we were out of town and had been ready to call the police, not knowing why all these strange people had descended upon our house. Everyone happily explained to Mary that they were just helping out, doing what they could. Mary told us later that so many people were coming and going that she thought a wild party was going on, but she was pleasantly surprised by the reality.

Mary wasn't the only one who was surprised. We were shocked when we got home. Our neighbors and church friends didn't *have* to do anything at all; we knew they all had busy lives and other things to do. But they made time to help us, and we will never forget their outpouring of kindness. Over time I noticed a common thread of people helping people and realized how much we enjoy reaching out to help others in need. It makes us feel connected and reminds us that we are important to each other. Whether it is caring for a sick child, praying for a hurting friend, planting a bed of flowers or milking a goat, what we do for other people out of love is one way that we share God's love with others.

———

Thoughts from Andrew

I CAME out of this one with an even bigger scar. I guess the third time around the scar gets wider, spreads out a little. And then there are the chest tube scars. I've got eight of those, but they're small and fade pretty fast. It doesn't really bother me. I cannot remember a time that I was ever embarrassed about my scars. I guess when you have a huge scar running down the length of your chest for as long as you can remember, at some point you get over it and learn to embrace it. So, for the most part, that's what I've done.

A friend of my mom's gave me a shirt that said, "Chicks Dig Scars." Man, I loved that shirt. I wore it so much that one day it literally fell into three pieces as I was very gingerly taking it off. It was old, holey and had lived a great life, but it had to be retired. I need to find another shirt like that!

I think my scars are cool. In a way, they kind of help define who I am. They tell a story, my story, and I am proud of it. My body is full of scars not just from surgery, but from grabbing life by the horns and holding on. I think that my scars are a testament to who I am—one rugged, resilient hombre. I'd be crazy to let all my health problems stop me from getting my elbows bruised and my knees scraped—what kind of boring life would that be? I love having scars. I think of them as God's tattoos. They remind me of what God has brought me through and how He has shaped me and proven to me time and time again that He's with me all the way.

ABOUT A month after that third surgery, I was super-excited that we were going to go visit my cousins and Aunt Cindy and Uncle John up at their ranch north of Denver. We had decided to go to the Greeley Stampede over the Fourth of July. It's a huge rodeo not too far from where they lived with a fair and midway and concerts at night. I couldn't wait.

Finally, the day came and when we got to the midway, one of the first booths we saw was the mechanical bull. It looked like so much fun! All my cousins and my brother and sister got to ride it, and they all got bucked off and had a great time; but I wasn't allowed to ride. My mom and dad didn't want me falling off (onto the ultra-padded floor) and hurting myself. That was a low blow. I couldn't believe it. I begged. I promised I wouldn't fall off. They still said no. The rest of the day was fun, but I kept thinking about that bull ride.

The next day, my dad and Uncle John decided to take all of us kids on a bike ride. Okay, I can do this, I assured my parents. *Puh-leeease! I'm not three years old anymore, I've ridden a bike for years, and besides, I am good at bike riding.* I used my best persuasive techniques, and they let me go. I was pumped. Finally, I was going to do something that was actually fun. We headed out to the foothills and found some great trails.

At the top of one of the trails, we all paused to survey the next steep, downhill portion. It didn't look too tough. We'd ridden down similar hills before. My brother went first, standing up on his pedals for balance. He pulled up his front tire and hung in the air for a second, and then he flew. The bumpy, dusty trail disappeared in a blur of brown bravado. He skidded to a stop at the bottom, whirled around and straddled his bike, then looked back up at us with a cocky grin. He was the bravest person I'd ever known.

I was next in line. I pushed off and my stomach dropped like it did on the first dip of a roller coaster, but I got some great speed under me. A split second later, I was flying, too—right over the front of my handlebars, up through the air, tossed like a rag doll. I landed with a thud on the hard dirt. On my chest. That kind of hurt. I knew they'd all be wondering if I was okay and that I'd probably be banned from doing any more fun things, so I rolled over, looked up the hill and managed to yell, "I'm okay." But it came out a little weak because I'd knocked all the wind out. My dad was already running down to make sure I was unhurt. I laid there a minute to catch my breath and realized that it had been a blast, completely and totally exhilarating. All the same, we decided it might be better not to tell Mom.

Twenty

Hope deferred makes the heart sick,
but a dream fulfilled is a tree of life.
– Proverbs 13:12 NLT

It's not the strength of the body that counts,
but the strength of the spirit.
– J. R. R. Tolkien

I T TOOK five long years, but he did it. Andrew convinced his cardiologist to say yes to football. This had been Andrew's dream for as long as I could remember. He loved football. I always felt helpless at his check-ups when the cardiologist would say no to the one sport Andrew truly wanted to play. But as we sat in the examining room the summer he was sixteen, everything checked out well and the doctor said yes. You'd have thought the entire world came to life that very moment. He already had a plan. He'd be playing on the team of one of the local private high schools, which meant eight-man football in our small town, but Andrew didn't care; he just wanted to play. His good friend, Skaff, also made the team so, as far as Andrew was concerned, life was sunshine in a bowl.

I treasure the moments when Andrew's health issues settle to the bottom for a while, not exactly out of the picture, but enough on the periphery that they're not the focus. It feels like getting a glimpse of what life might have been like without a heart defect. During those times, Andrew was able to forget about his heart and just do what he loved. He never missed a practice or a game and, even though the team was outmatched and outsized in almost every game, it may as well have been the NFL to Andrew. Those were Andrew's "glory days," full of high school activity, all kinds of sports, friends galore and not so many worries about his heart.

He told his coaches about his heart and his asthma, so they knew. I'm sure he gave them the briefest of details, so they couldn't have really *known*. All they cared about was that he had a doctor's clearance to play. I wanted to stand up during the games and shout, "Does anyone realize what a big deal this is? He's living his dream!" One time I thought maybe I'd go talk to the coaches after a game and tell them how far Andrew had come to be able to do this…how it almost didn't happen for him. But Andrew begged me not to say anything, so I didn't.

Thoughts from Andrew

"You are cleared to do just about anything you want."

"Can I play football?"

"Well, no, that's the one thing you can't do."

This was how the conversation went between my cardiologist and me every year when I had my annual check-up. Baseball is my favorite sport, but more than anything I wanted to play football. I think it was because I wanted to go out and run and score a ton of touchdowns. I knew I could do it. I just had to get medical clearance. Every year I begged my doctor to let me play football, but every year he gave the same answer. NO.

Every year, that is, until I the summer I was headed into my junior year of high school. I finally wore him down! He said yes! So, for my last two years of high school, I played eight-man football. I was the starting defensive end and the starting tight end. Eight-man football is more of a running offense than passing, so I was a blocking tight end, which was boring. I did my dirty work on the defensive side of the ball.

I still remember the first time I entered a game. It was late in the second quarter when Coach told me to get ready—I was going in for the next play. This was it—my dream was coming true. I had to make it count. The quarterback snapped the ball, and I came in unblocked, my eyes dead set on blasting the quarterback. I hit him so hard he dropped the ball, and I was able to fall right onto it. One play, one sack, and one forced fumble—not too shabby.

Unfortunately, that was the highlight of my football career. Our team stunk. We won two games in two years. I had two catches as a tight end, and it's not like I dropped all the balls that came my way. I was thrown to only three times, and the one that got away from me was ten feet over my head. But I did get a few more sacks, and I had a one-handed interception (despite a very badly dislocated finger). Even though the team was terrible, I wouldn't trade that experience for the world. And I will always have that first play. I may not have been a four-star college recruit going to a powerhouse college team, but I had accomplished something that no one ever thought I would.

———

Early in September of his senior year in high school, Andrew had some intermittent chest pain, so we made an appointment with his cardiologist. He had an echo, and everything checked out fine. The doctor chalked it up to Andrew's new exercise regimen, and so he was allowed to continue. After seventeen years of dealing with heart stuff, you'd think I'd have flags flying. In that moment, though, I was so happy that it wasn't something serious showing up that I was more than eager to accept the findings without question. The doctor was not concerned in the least, and we practically danced our way out of his office that afternoon. We should have listened more carefully to Andrew's complaint; we should have insisted that it not be dismissed so easily.

What we did know was this—it mattered more to Andrew to be able to play for that little eight-man team than anyone could have known. I couldn't have explained it, and I don't think his coaches ever really got it. To them, a kid wants to play football, so he plays football. No big deal. With a heart defect, it's never that simple. The signs of Andrew's struggles were hidden under his jersey. Most people were shocked to find out that he'd had heart surgeries. The battles he's faced and won don't announce themselves to the world, and we never made a big deal out of explaining it. Sometimes we don't say anything because, like a typical teenager, Andrew wants to blend in, not be labeled or thought of as different. Sometimes we don't say anything because explaining means re-living some of that pain, and we just don't want to go there.

Any pain we'd already been through, however, could not begin to compare to the grief that our extended family was about to face. Our niece Kendall's health had deteriorated due to the Fanconi's anemia that she and Taylor had, and she now needed a bone marrow transplant. In the absence of a perfect match, she would have to go with a near match— and the outcomes for that procedure had not proven very successful to that point. Tom's brother, Ken, and his wife, Jeanne, and their kids all traveled to the University of Minnesota for Kendall's transplant, hoping and praying for a miracle. She was so strong. However, on a miserable day in March four weeks after her transplant, we got the devastating news that Kendall had passed away. She was only twenty years old.

We adored Kendall—she had a devoted spirit with a little bit of rebel thrown in. She loved children and was so sweet with Amy, spending hours painting fingernails and fixing hair together. Kendall had struggled with the effects of her medications and, even though she had been so sick, she dreamed of getting well so she could make a difference in this world. She made an incalculable difference in ours. I will always be thankful for the twenty years I got to be "Aunt Cathy," for the cherished memories of laughing together as I listened to her recount stories of one adventure after another. It is impossible to describe the depth of the pain her loss caused—both our own grief as well as the sadness we felt for Tom's brother and his wife and kids.

After Kendall died, my emotions were so mixed up that I struggled to find a balance I could live with. One moment I would be overjoyed for Andrew, finally experiencing freedom from the black cloud of his heart issues as I watched him love life and achieve more than anyone had ever expected. And then, within the very same moment, I'd be crying because of Kendall. How does one live with two contrasting feelings side by side? In his book, *A Grief Disguised*, Jerry Sittser wrote the following:

"What we consider opposites—east and west, night and light, sorrow and joy, weakness and strength, anger and love, despair and hope, death and life—are no more mutually exclusive than winter and sunlight. The soul has the capacity to experience these opposites, even at the same time."

Confusing as that concept seemed, I totally understood.

All of us had been so relieved after Andrew's last echocardiogram that showed everything was fine. None of us could see what was right in front of our faces—or perhaps we couldn't see the forest for the trees, I guess. However, we got the message loud and clear later that summer. Andrew and Amy had gotten up quietly in the pitch black of a cool summer morning, and I didn't even hear the door close when they left. They'd made plans to meet friends at the base of a beautiful fourteen-thousand-foot mountain. Climbing fourteener's is kind of a thing here in Colorado, and you'd best get an early start. Storms come up with a fierce regularity, especially in the afternoons. They'd been looking forward to this for weeks and were excited to enjoy a day of hiking and sunshine, and the chance to cross Mt. Sherman off the list of been-there-done-that accomplishments. The weather was supposed to be perfect.

All day I prayed for them, never imagining that there would be any problems. As the sun set, I expected they were on their way home. Wondering how far out they were, I called Andrew's cell. No answer. *They must be out of range,* I thought. I called again a half hour later. Still no answer. *I really thought they would be back by now.* I called my friend Diann whose husband and kids had gone on the trek. She hadn't heard from them either. *Be patient* I told myself, t*hey're fine. So they're not on schedule, but they'll be here soon.*

Another hour ticked by, and I became officially concerned—a step below worried, two steps below freaking out. I was just about to do something (though I had no idea what) when Diann called me back. Her husband had called to let her know that they had taken it slowly and were about a half hour away. I breathed a huge sigh of relief, glad everything was okay. But when Andrew and Amy walked in the door, I could tell immediately that everything was *not* okay.

"Don't ask me anything. I don't want to talk about it," was the first thing out of Andrew's mouth. He headed toward his room as I shot a questioning frown toward Amy.

"Do you want something to eat?" I asked her.

"Yes, I'm starved." She sat down at the kitchen table and, although she was exhausted, filled me in on the day. Andrew had barely made it up the trail, and he'd had a terrible time coming down. She didn't know why. Our friend Vern, one of the dads who had gone on the trip, had helped Andrew the whole way. Step by step he had walked next to Andrew, up and over the initial bump, through the narrows and then along the ridge crest, finally reaching the summit. After a rest up top, Vern stayed behind again as Andrew struggled back down. This news both worried and surprised me. I was, of course, grateful to Vern, but what did this mean? Andrew was in great shape; he'd been on many, many mountain hikes—why had this climb been so difficult?

I find it very frustrating when my teenagers are upset and don't want to talk. I know I need to give them space, but... well, I really don't know how other Moms do that. It makes me crazy. This was the me that wanted to know who, what, where, when and why as soon as possible so we could get whatever it was fixed and back to normal. About to burst into his room, I heard a little voice inside my head. *Slow down. Don't take it quite so fast. God has Andrew in His hands. You are in His Hands, too. You don't need to go in there. You can wait till he's ready. You need to respect Andrew's desire for privacy and his choices, especially since he's eighteen now. He's almost on his own.*

When your kids are little, eighteen seems very grown up. I remember that when my kids were still three and four and five years old, I felt a bit intimidated talking to older teens. Now I know better. Ask any mom of an eighteen year old, and she'll tell you that eighteen is still young. They're still in need of gentle guidance and definitely encouragement and praise. So, I gave him five minutes... and *then* I went into his room to hear the whole story. No, I'm just kidding—it was more like ten minutes.

"Andrew?" I called softly, knocking on the half-open door and walking in gingerly to find him lying face down in bed. "Andrew, what happened?"

"Just get Amy to tell you." His voice was muffled; he was still lying face down in the covers. I thought he might have been crying.

"I want to hear it from you," I said gently. "Please, tell me what happened…"

Thoughts from Andrew

I'LL NEVER forget that awful day. I had just finished high school. My heart was healthy, and I felt great. I'd played football, volleyball and basketball for two years in a row. I was in amazing shape and determined to keep it that way. One hundred and sixty-five pounds of pure muscle. That summer I was in a great workout routine—I don't think I took even one day off. I could do about 150 push-ups and sit-ups. I was playing on three different softball teams, mountain biking and running at a pretty good clip for at least a half hour every day. I felt great.

Then, just barely, ever so gradually, I'd have a day here and there that seemed a bit off. At first, I thought maybe I had a cold or it was just a rough day.

One weekend Amy and I were invited to climb a fourteener with some friends. Great idea! I was a Colorado native, and I'd never climbed a fourteener before. That just seemed wrong, so we went. I figured it would be fun and a nice little challenge. I didn't think it would be hard considering how much I had been working out. But it turned out that, for me, it was almost impossible.

During the hike, I put a good face on it, but I knew something wasn't right. My inhaler didn't help at all. I felt embarrassed because here I was hiking with my friends and my little sister and all her friends, and they were leaving me in the dust. I was just barely putting one foot in front of the other. I didn't even know if I could make it. I felt so humiliated because it wasn't like you could see anything wrong. It just looked like I was totally wimpy or completely out of shape.

I'll never forget how my friend Nikki's dad stayed behind with me and basically coached me to the top. He'd count ten steps, and then we'd rest. Then another ten and rest. He did that over and over until we made it up together. Gasping for air, I collapsed at the top and laid there for what seemed like an eternity. I had a really hard time catching my breath. Everyone else seemed fine and had plenty of energy left. They were all bounding around on the rocks at the summit while all I could do was lie there.

I chalked it up to the altitude and my asthma. I just needed to make it down the mountain and I'd be fine, I told myself. Going down should be way easier, right? But going down was almost more than I could handle. Every step was hard. I couldn't breathe. Nikki's dad stayed behind with me again while everybody else practically skipped down. Somehow, I made it down, but I felt worse than horrible. I was embarrassed that I had held up the entire group, confused about why and a little bit scared. I couldn't tell anyone how I really felt, so I just stayed quiet.

The next week I was all set to get back into my workout routine, but suddenly I felt like I was running through molasses. I was breathing heavily, and I kept having to stop and catch my breath. I had no idea what was going on, but something just was not right. I went from being able to easily run for half an hour to barely being able to get to five minutes.

We made an appointment to see my cardiologist, and I told him what was going on. After doing a stress echo, we found out that my pulmonary valve was bad again—I needed another heart surgery. I realized I had just climbed a fourteener with a heart that could barely get blood to my lungs. No wonder all my energy was zapped. I wasn't really thrilled about it, but I decided to have the surgery during Christmas break. I was thinking I'd have better luck climbing a mountain the next year, but I guess God had other plans.

Twenty-one

We can rejoice, too, when we run into problems and trials,
for we know that they help us develop endurance.
And endurance develops strength of character, and character
strengthens our confident hope of salvation.
– Romans 5:3-4 NLT

Through affliction He teaches us many precious lessons that
otherwise we would never learn. By affliction He shows us our
emptiness and weakness, draws us to the throne of grace,
purifies our affections, weans us from the world,
and makes us long for heaven.
– J. C. Ryle

WE SCHEDULED Andrew's surgery around his school
break, our insurance coverage and Christmas plans. It
would mean a trip to Denver where he'd probably be in the hospital for
four to five days, and then we'd be on our way home. He'd be feeling so
much better by his birthday on New Year's Day. If he wasn't up to celebrating Christmas, we'd just postpone it a few days. Everything would
be fine.

"Okay, I'll see you in a couple hours; drive safely. Bye." I was relieved
that Sheri and her kids were on their way. I smiled at Tom who glanced
up from an old issue of *Outdoor Life*. "They'll be here by dinnertime."

Picking up my knitting, I settled in. Hats were my latest knitting craze… fun, soft chemo hats in honor of my niece, Kendall. I could finish one in a couple of hours now. Knowing that Sheri could come to be with us for Andrew's surgery was a huge relief. Usually I preferred my space and didn't want people (other than family) to hang out with us. It's my way of coping, I guess. I can retreat inside and not have to worry about anyone else. But this time, I'd had a change of heart. I wanted Sheri to be with us. She's a nurse with a lifetime of experience, she's strong and true, and I needed her. I think it was God's quiet voice in my heart that prompted me to ask her to come. He knew what I didn't know—that in the days to follow, her presence with us would prove critical.

It was still pitch-black outside the next morning when a nurse stepped into our room, pushing a wheelchair. "Okay, Andrew, it's time to go to the pre-surgical area," she said quietly. We'd been awake for a while, anticipating this moment. I took a deep breath as Andrew slipped out of bed and into the wheelchair and, with the IV pole in one hand, the nurse pushed him down the hall while Tom and I walked on either side. We went through some swinging doors to a small curtained area with a few chairs. Everything was yellow and white—curtains, sheets, walls, floor…everything. I thought about how some hospital interior designer had probably imagined that the bright colors would lift our spirits. They could try those tactics, but it didn't work on me. I was nervous, and my mood didn't lift, yellow or no yellow. I have no idea why I was even thinking about interior designers and paint colors. It was ridiculous that I even cared about the colors in the room—maybe my brain went there because it didn't want to face the reality of what we were doing in this room. However, I was as scared as every parent whose child is going into surgery, and no amount of yellow was going to change that.

I always take pictures at the hospital. I'm kind of funny like that, and yes, over the years, some people have wondered why, thinking it was weird because Andrew was so sick. For me, the pictures help me remember the miracles and blessings God has given us, and they help me process what we've experienced in a slower, more removed kind of way. For Andrew, because of all the meds he's on, he doesn't remember anything, so it's also a way to document his experience.

The nurses brought warmed blankets and slipper socks for Andrew since he was shivering—we all were. It's always so cold in pre-op and the operating room area. After a while, it felt as if Andrew was a movie star and the hospital staff was the paparazzi. Everybody and their next-door neighbor stopped by our little cubicle to make sure Andrew was all set. Did he have the right wristband with the right date of birth and blood type? They checked every allergy and sensitivity he'd ever had, made sure we had the right records with the right kid and that they were going to perform surgery on the right body part. We spoke with the anesthesiologist, the surgical nurse, the surgeon, the recovery nurse, the cardiologist, the cardiac nurse and the ICU nurses. There could have been more; I really don't remember, but the stream in and out, in and out was steady.

We knew our surgeon a little, but not well. Of course, we'd met with him to discuss the surgery, but that's about all a patient generally sees of the surgeon. We definitely hadn't seen him long enough to feel like we had any kind of real connection with him. He was very experienced and good at what he did, but he was a keep-a-professional-face-on-at-all-times type. As we talked with him, he indicated that this would be a fairly routine surgery. They would replace the worn-out homograph and valve with a new one. He'd done it many times before and expected it to take six to six-and-a-half hours. Pausing, he glanced through the notes from Andrew's last surgery. "I'm not quite sure why his last surgery took so long..." he wondered out loud.

"Well, he had the trouble with bleeding and the graft vs. host," I explained.

He nodded but didn't look up, "Uh-huh." He was in his fifties, relaxed and confident, as if he'd just won a round of golf with his buddies. So, we tried to act relaxed, too, for Andrew's sake. Part of me was glad that the doctor thought it was going to be rather "routine," but another part of me questioned why he would be so blasé about performing open-heart surgery on my son. How could even the easiest open-heart surgery be routine? It certainly wasn't routine to me. I chalked it up to his laid-back personality and didn't think about it again.

Suddenly, it was already 7:00 a.m., and I felt that familiar sickening knot gripping my stomach muscles as we said our goodbyes.

"We won't stop praying for you, Andrew. We'll see you when you wake up." I held his hand and hugged him. This time he was mature—almost a man—but when I looked at him on the gurney, I experienced a moment like Steve Martin in the movie *Father of the Bride* when he looked at his adult daughter and flashed back to when she was ages four and eight and eleven. Even at eighteen, Andrew looked vulnerable and scared lying on that bed. He was still my little boy.

Tom and I watched as they wheeled the bed with the warm, white blankets and our almost grown-up son through the operating room doors. Tom put his arm around me, and we headed back to the waiting room. That was it. It happened so fast, and I wasn't ready. *How many times will I have to do this? No, how many times will he have to do this?* In some ways it gets harder each time because we *do* know what's coming, and we know it isn't easy. My eyes welled up—hot tears on cold cheeks. I took a deep breath, put on my fake face, brushed away the dampness, and walked into the waiting room. Instead of a room, it was actually more like a large waiting area with a walkway in between, with chairs and couches scattered around in little groups on either side.

I could smell the coffee. Starbucks it wasn't, but it was free and plentiful and would be comforting in my cold hands. The waiting area was buzzing with anxious families. Kids played at the vending machines, hoping for the accidental fall of a candy bar, intermittently running off to ask their parents for money. Adults stared at TVs tuned in to the morning news stations and flipped randomly through old magazines. The scene is familiar to me—in fact, it is the same in every hospital we've ever waited in. I wondered if there were any other parents waiting as their child had open-heart surgery.

I'd experienced similar feelings with Andrew's other surgeries, but just as his third surgery had felt different, something was different this time too. Seven years had come and gone since we had waited in these same tweed-gray overstuffed chairs—slightly more threadbare these days. My feelings of hope and fear were the same, but other things had changed. My kids now had their friends, phones, games and movies to keep them entertained during the wait. They could get a bite to eat in the cafeteria or just walk around without my needing to monitor their every move.

Mom, Dad and Sheri had claimed the chairs in the far corner. I grabbed a cup of coffee and made my way over to them, settling in for what I knew would be a long day. My sister and brother-in-law soon showed up and joined us for the wait. The *click-click-clicking* of my knitting needles kept a steady rhythm as we visited mindlessly about absolutely nothing. I was too nervous to think. Tom made it to page eleven of *Fly Fishing for Dummies* before his eyes closed completely. Same as always.

Around eight o'clock, the surgical nurse, Julie, came out. Tom woke up quickly, and we listened to the update. "Everything is going very well. He is intubated, prepped and under the general anesthesia, and they are getting ready to begin opening his chest." Julie was calm and confident, and she assured us that Andrew's vital signs were stable. "I'll come out every hour or so to give you an update." Smiling, she turned and headed back in.

I took a deep breath. *Good. Everything is good.* Back to knitting and talking and waiting and praying. *He is doing fine; it's going very well.* I repeated this mantra over and over, working hard to convince myself that it was okay to relax.

I had made some good progress on my scarf when I suddenly heard above the murmur of the waiting families a firm, no-nonsense voice, "Atkinson? Is anyone here the family of Andrew Atkinson?" I stopped knitting and looked up to discover this authoritative voice belonged to the elderly woman who had been sitting guard over the waiting-room phone. Her tone was so crisp and sharp that I almost felt obliged to stand and salute. I studied her as I waded through the crowded sitting area. Her petite frame stood about four and a half feet tall. Her face was deeply wrinkled, and I'm pretty sure they'd never been called smile lines. This woman was serious. Gray bangs pushed to either side divided her forehead into halves, and if she'd ever had a curl anywhere, it had long since been scolded straight. Her volunteer badge, pinned proudly on her purple vest, said "Hi, I'm HELEN." Without question, she had control of this waiting area. She handed the phone to me without a word.

"Hello?"

"Hi, Mrs. Atkinson, this is Julie calling from the operating room. I just wanted to let you know what's going on back here and why I haven't been able to come out and give you an update in a while."

"Okaaaay," I said slowly, waiting for her to go on, sensing something was amiss.

"Well, they are still trying to get the cannula tubing into Andrew's left femoral artery, but they have had some trouble, so they may need to do a cut down on his right chest area to get to a usable artery." Sheri got up and walked over and stood next to me. I tipped the phone so she could hear the nurse as well. Julie went on to say that it was going to take some time and something else that came out muffled about all the scar tissue. She mentioned that his vascular system was quite small for someone of his size, and that they were still working on figuring it out. She may have said some other things, but I couldn't remember. It was all I could do to piece together the parts I understood.

I could tell she was in a hurry to get off the phone, so I didn't ask any questions. She promised to keep us informed, and we said good-bye. I slowly walked back to the group. Everybody in our family circled around me for an update. I relayed it to them as best I could then sat down, numb. I am pretty sure I stared at the TV for the next hour or so. I couldn't even think.

At ten o'clock, I spotted Julie through the little square windows on the heavy doors that led to the operating suite. She hurried out and we—Sheri, Tom and I—walked over to meet her near the doors. She said the team was still working to get Andrew onto bypass. She seemed more rushed this time—even concerned. But it was hard to tell because I just couldn't read her very well. "He's had some bleeding and has been given some blood. His vital signs are stable. We could not get the artery in his leg to work, so we did make an incision in his upper chest area. Do you have any questions?"

So much information thrown at us. My mind whirled. *I don't know if I have any questions. How would I know what to ask? I suppose if I had a medical background, if I happened to be a nurse or a doctor, I might know the right questions.* Then I remembered Sheri was standing next to me. Thank you, God. She knew the questions to ask and could interpret the answers as well. I felt better knowing it wasn't all on me. Julie seemed in a rush to get back, so I managed to say, "Umm…okay, well, I guess just keep us posted." My stomach was doing its usual gymnastics. "Thanks for letting us know what's happening."

"I'll come out again in an hour," she promised as she turned to leave. "We should have him on the pump by then." The heart-lung machine, or cardiopulmonary bypass pump, is an amazing piece of medical technology that acts like a heart and lungs for a patient. It really is what makes open-heart-surgery possible. It maintains the circulation of oxygenated blood through the patient's body while the real heart is stopped so that surgery can be performed. A patient has gone "onto bypass" when he is hooked up with tubing to and from the machine so that his blood flows through the machine instead of his own heart and lungs.

I wanted to know more. I wanted a detailed painting of the operating room and surgery as it progressed when all I had been handed was a rough sketch. *Is he okay and do the doctors have everything under control now?* What was happening wasn't normal—I knew that, and what she didn't say spoke volumes. I thought back to his other heart surgeries and couldn't remember ever hearing that there were problems getting onto the heart-lung machine.

Wouldn't it be great if we could all be hooked up to a *spiritual* heart-lung machine where our life-blood would flow into the machine and God would breathe His life into it before it flowed back into our veins? We could be completely filled with Him in every cell of our body. In a way, that is sort of what having a relationship with Him is like. We pour ourselves out to Him, and He pours Himself back into us. In simple terms, God replaces our unhealthy blood with His Breath-of-Life blood, and we are restored to spiritual health.

Tom, Sheri and I walked back to our corner and shared everything with the family. No one knew what to say—we all just sat or stood there. We knew things were not going well but had no idea how bad it really was. I kept picturing Andrew lying on the table bleeding and the doctors and nurses rushing around, trying to get this tube and that cannula into place. Instead of talking, we prayed. I guess we knew God would understand if we didn't say anything at all. My dad led us in prayer, but I just prayed quietly to myself because the words wouldn't come. After that, I tried to knit but found it was easier to pray if I walked, so I walked the length of the waiting area and back again. And again, and again. And again.

Twenty-two

He will cover you with his feathers. He will shelter you with his
wings. His faithful promises are your armor and protection.
– Psalm 91:1-4 NLT

When a train goes through a tunnel and it gets dark,
you don't throw away the ticket and jump off.
You sit still and trust the engineer.
– Corrie ten Boom

W E WAITED. One excruciating hour then another crawled by before Julie came hurrying out again through the "Authorized-Personnel-Only" doors. She apologized for not making it out at eleven o'clock as she had intended, then she took a deep breath. Her hands were shaking, and I heard a quiver in her voice. "I want to start with the good stuff." *Uh-oh,* I thought, *that means there's bad stuff.* I took another deep breath as she began with, "He's now on bypass. It was rough, but they *finally* got him on. There were some really tense moments because, when the doctor was opening him up, he put a little tear into the pulmonary artery."

He what? A little tear? My mouth dropped open. Standing there, our throats tight with fear, we were hardly able to speak, anxious for every scrap of information but not sure we could bear to hear it. We tried, though. We tried desperately to comprehend the details as she explained what had transpired over the previous hours in the operating room. Thank goodness Sheri was there. She understood and translated the medical jargon for us, asking the questions we would never have known to ask. Teetering on the precipice of real panic, I stood as still as the eye of a hurricane and took it all in.

"His surgery started off well," Julie continued. "It was going exactly as planned. The surgeon made an incision over the top of Andrew's previous chest scars, cutting down to the bone. Then he removed the wires that had been wrapped around Andrew's sternum—that were put there after the last surgery to hold his chest closed." Then she told us that the doctor had asked for the saw, cut through the sternum and opened up the rib cage. Julie was shaking now as she talked, and I reached out and touched her arm. She kept describing the scene for us. "As the surgeon began dissecting through the tissues underneath, he ran into a great deal of scar tissue." This was expected because patients who have had previous surgeries develop areas of scarring, and it can be extremely difficult to remove those scarred heart parts away from the sternum.

"And that's when it happened," she continued. "He punctured a hole in the pulmonary artery...a big hole." What she proceeded to describe made it seem as though the operating room had suddenly become the setting of our worst nightmare. As we all know, life and death are truly only seconds apart. This operation had gone from being routine to a full-blown emergency with one misplaced swipe of the surgeon's scalpel. A torn pulmonary artery can be an immediate death sentence; a patient will easily bleed to death within thirty seconds. The surgeon and a resident immediately stuck their fingers into the hole (which they told us later was "very good sized") to stop the bleeding.

"Get him onto bypass *now!*" the surgeon shouted as blood spurted everywhere, covering the sterile drapes and the surgeon's gown, the floor under the table and everyone's shoe coverings. Andrew was about to bleed to death on the table, and they all realized that this was a full-scale disaster. The only thing that could save Andrew's life was to get him onto the pump (the heart-lung machine) so that the hole could be repaired.

In order to get him onto the pump, however, they needed to get the cannulas—the tubes through which his blood would flow to and from the pump—in place. Not an easy thing to do under normal circumstances, but in a panic situation, even harder. Usually the surgeon would place a cannula in the right atrium, the vena cava, or the femoral vein to withdraw unoxygenated blood from the body. The heart-lung machine then puts oxygen into the blood and sends it back to the body via the ascending aorta, or the femoral artery.

Seconds ticked away as they attempted time after time to insert the cannula into Andrew's left femoral artery. Over and over they tried to make it work but could not access the blood supply. So, they pulled it out and tried to cannulate at a different site—the right auxiliary artery (his upper chest area). Hands shaking, voices rising in alarm, they cut open the area but could see immediately that the artery was too small to use. The next option was to cannulate straight into his aorta. It was a long shot, but it was the *only* shot at that point. Finding a place on the aorta that would work was difficult. The area was hard to reach, and the surgeon's fingers were still plugging the pulmonary hole.

Finally, the team found a small spot and successfully twisted the cannula into place. Then, they put the venous cannula into his right femoral vein. They could see that it wasn't flowing exceptionally well, but at least it was usable. Everyone breathed a tentative sigh of relief. The first hurdle cleared, Andrew could now go onto the heart-lung machine. Anxiously, the team watched as the machine took over for Andrew's heart, pumping and oxygenating his blood. After Andrew's own heart was no longer pumping, the surgeon gingerly removed his fingers from the hole and stitched it closed.

It was at that point that Julie had come out to talk to us. This news was shocking and caught us off guard. When a loved one is in the hospital, the doctor might try to prepare the family for the possibility of a bad outcome, but you never expect something to actually go wrong; you're always hopeful, always waiting for the "excellent news"—the smiling doctor strolling through the doors, removing his gloves and telling everyone how perfectly wonderful it went, just like on TV. We have that Doctors-Equal-Superheroes mentality, and I admit that I have been one of the worst. I must constantly remind myself that doctors are not akin to God; they are human beings and can (and do) make mistakes, and life doesn't always end up the way we hope or predict it will. At least that's what I *try* to remember.

"Andrew is doing much better now, and the operation is proceeding," Julie finished. She said we should try to relax (was she kidding?), and that she was sure everything would go well from here on out. Oh, I hoped so. We took a collective deep breath and sat down again to wait. But relaxing? That would be impossible.

Several long hours of waiting and praying later, we found out what happened next. The next part of the surgery was progressing as expected, the surgeon retracted the chest to expose the pericardium, the sac surrounding the heart. He dissected out the heart, the inferior vena cava and right arterial junction. Then he located and removed the old calcified pulmonary homograft. A new homograft was being set into place when they noticed that, below the chest incision, Andrew's abdomen had become tight and tense and was filling rapidly with blood. A vascular surgeon was called to come immediately to assess and repair whatever was causing the internal bleeding. As it happened, the vascular surgeon was in the middle of a surgery at the hospital across the street, but he would rush over as soon as he could.

Andrew continued to bleed internally, but the doctors still did not know why or where the bleed was originating. What they *did* know was that the heart surgery, the homograph replacement they had started, must be finished before anything else. Staying focused on the heart must have been difficult when they could see that another life-threatening situation was unfolding before their eyes, but they had no choice. Finally, the cardiac surgeon finished stitching the new homograph in place. Pacemaker leads that had been put in during Andrew's last surgery were removed. Four chest tubes were sewn in place, and Andrew's chest was left open for quick access in case something unexpected happened—which soon proved to be a wise decision.

The unexpected was already happening and getting worse by the second. Andrew's internal bleeding was severe. His abdomen, now filled with blood, continued to become more and more distended and taut. Obviously, it wasn't going to be possible to wait for the vascular surgeon. Something must be done immediately. They decided to explore the femoral artery area where they had unsuccessfully inserted the cannula. Just as they were about to cut into his leg, the vascular surgeon arrived, which brought a change of plans. They decided on a complete mid-line incision that would open Andrew up from just below his sternum all the way down to his pubic bone (he was already open from neck to sternum). They wanted to allow the surgical team access to his entire abdominal cavity so they could locate the source of the bleed.

Because of the intense pressure building inside his abdomen, when the incision was made, Andrew's intestines and abdominal organs eviscerated—which means they burst out of his body. Blood spurted everywhere and was now pouring from his abdomen. Everyone scrambled to stop the blood flow, mop up the blood, call for more blood and put new blood into his body. In his report, the surgeon noted that "a substantial amount of clotted and non-clotted blood was beneath the bowels." That's "surgeon-ese" for "He lost a huge amount of blood!"

At that moment, Andrew's cardiologist just happened to stop by the operating room to check on the progress. Under normal circumstances, a cardiologist is not a part of the surgical team. Cardiologists diagnose and evaluate heart issues, but do not take part in the actual surgery. He walked through the doors completely unaware of the unfolding disaster. It took only a second, though, to comprehend that the situation was grave. The operating room was in a complete state of panic. The cardiologist put on a gown and hurried to help. He immediately started working with the anesthesiologist feeding blood into Andrew as fast as he could.

"Blood pressure's dropping," the anesthesiologist called out, trying not to overreact. His job had suddenly gone from challenging to overwhelming as he tried to keep up with the loss of blood and Andrew's other vital signs. "Still dropping."

"We're losing him!" Someone grabbed the crash cart.

For three hours the anesthesiologist and the cardiologist worked to pump blood into Andrew, but he was losing blood as fast as they could give it to him. A friend at the blood bank told us later that they were racing all over the city trying to locate enough blood for Andrew. The hospital records show that he received forty-five units of packed red blood cells, twenty units of fresh frozen plasma, and fifteen units of platelets. Sixty-nine units of blood products! A person only has about ten pints, or units, of blood in his body. Normally during heart surgery, a patient might receive one to four units of blood. This amount of blood loss was practically unheard of, and it was questionable whether someone could survive it. In the midst of this chaotic, unfolding horror, the vascular surgeon discovered Andrew's femoral artery had been completely torn and was floating unattached in his abdomen, so he put in a six-inch patch to repair the artery and slow down the bleeding.

In the waiting area, I was knitting again, and Tom was flipping through *Field and Stream*. We had no idea about the drama playing out in the operating room. It was an excruciating three-and-a-half hours before we heard anything new. At two forty-five, Julie and the cardiologist came out together to talk to us. Julie was obviously upset; she looked terribly distressed. As soon as I saw her, I knew something was wrong. My brain started taking quick little snapshots. Her eyes were bloodshot and puffy; she'd obviously been crying. Blood covered her shoes. She could not keep her hands or her voice from shaking. She looked frightened. It didn't take long to realize they were emerging from a battle zone.

The cardiologist began first, "Well, there were some additional complications." He looked down then back at us. "Andrew experienced quite a bit of bleeding—he lost and received several units of blood back there." His words came out fast and jittery even though he was attempting to sound calm.

"How much blood has he been given?" Sheri asked.

"I would say probably about ten units," he answered.

Julie spoke up, "Umm…try more like… greater than twenty units."

"Okay, yeah, that's probably right," the cardiologist hesitantly agreed and went on to explain more of what had happened. The heart graft was performing well. However, the massive bleeding had caused a whole new set of issues.

"There were a few times when things were really close, and we nearly lost him," Julie admitted, her voice almost breaking, her eyes filling with tears. "It was so close. At one point, his pressures dropped off completely, and we had to grab the crash cart." She took a wobbly breath, "But then he would bounce back."

My hands instinctively covered my mouth, then I grabbed Tom's arm and clung to him, squeezing with all my might. I thought I might throw up. What does a parent do when handed this information? Deep breath. *Oh, God.* Deep breath. *Oh, God. He is still alive. He is alive. I never expected this.*

The cardiologist assured us the situation was back under control. He said that the vascular surgeon had finished up and was gone, and the cardiac surgeon and his team were finishing up the last of the stitching. He said the surgeon would be out to talk with us soon and that he and Julie needed to get back. Then in a blink, they were gone again.

I tried to calm myself. Sitting down, I put my head in my hands as if that might help me think straight. *I really don't need to panic,* I thought. *They know what is going on now. The bad part is over. Everything is getting back to more of a normal status. Andrew is out of danger.*

I started praying. The whole of me—everything—was focused on reaching out to God, begging for His mercy. I remembered how all those years ago back in Boston, God reminded me that I do not own Andrew—he is God's, and God's alone, and his life is in God's hands and for God's glory. In spite of knowing that, I begged God to let him live. I didn't think I could let him go. It was hard to loosen my grasp and give him back to God. Maybe even impossible.

The cardiologist had indicated the surgery was all but over and that Andrew was out of the woods, but he was so, so wrong.

Twenty-three

Who shall separate us from the love of Christ? Shall trouble or hardship or persecution or famine or nakedness or danger or sword?…For I am convinced that neither death nor life, neither angels nor demons, neither the present nor the future, nor any powers, neither height nor depth, nor anything else in all creation, will be able to separate us from the love of God that is in Christ Jesus our Lord.
– Romans 8:35-39 NIV

The good that may come out of the loss does not erase its badness or excuse the wrong done. Nothing can do that.
– Gerald L. Sittser

I T WAS partly true, what Julie and the cardiologist had said. The surgical team *was* nearly done. They only had to finish up the stitches, close the incisions and clean up. Things could have—should have—been almost over. But just as the surgeon turned to leave, as the nurses lifted the drapes that had covered Andrew's lower extremities during the surgery, a gasp from Julie stopped everything. What they saw horrified them all. Andrew's feet and legs were swollen tight, like inflated balloons. Not only were they swollen, but both lower legs and feet were almost black. Someone let loose with a stream of expletives. Everyone else was deathly silent. The entire room of medical personnel from the surgeon and cardiologist to the nurses to the surgical techs became sickeningly aware that during the surgery no one had been checking to make sure that Andrew had a pulse and blood flow to his legs. Even the vascular surgeon who had repaired the femoral artery (and was now gone) had never actually looked at Andrew's legs to see if blood flow had been reestablished. They were all so occupied with keeping him alive that this vital piece of the puzzle was neglected in the chaos.

Another emergency call from Andrew's operating room was made to the vascular surgeon. Luckily, he had not yet left the hospital. He rushed back in as the others were measuring the internal pressures of Andrew's lower legs. They hardly needed to look—they knew the numbers were way too high. It would now be a race to see if Andrew's legs could be saved.

The story unfolded like this: when the doctors realized Andrew's femoral artery had been severed so that blood had been pouring into his abdomen, all the attention had been focused on finding the bleed and patching up the arteries. His intestines, stomach and spleen all spilled out along with the massive blood loss after his abdomen had been opened. It was imperative that the organs not be injured further, urgent that the source of the bleeding be found. So the main focus centered on his upper body. No one even looked at his legs. But no blood to his legs meant hours of injury as the muscles and tissues were deprived of the oxygen and nutrients they needed. For at least six hours, he lay there covered up with no blood flow at all to his left leg and very little to his right. The lack of blood to his legs caused the muscles and tissues to be damaged and to swell to dangerous levels; the internal pressure numbers were off the charts. As a result, Andrew developed what is known as compartment syndrome in his lower left leg for sure and possibly in both legs.

As if he hadn't already experienced enough serious situations during this surgery, compartment syndrome ranks right up there among the worst as both serious and complex. Our body's muscles, tissue, nerves and blood vessels are grouped into compartments and held together by layers of tissue called the fascia. Muscles and tissues swell when injured, but the fascia does not expand and that causes pressure to build in the compartment. If the pressure is high enough, the blood flow will be blocked and that will lead to permanent injury to the muscle and nerves. The pressure has to be relieved quickly or the muscles and tissue will die. So, to help relieve the pressure, the doctor made an incision down the length of his lower leg (the compartment), cutting into the fascia so that circulation could be restored. We later learned this procedure is called a *fasciotomy*.

I don't even remember who came out of the operating room to tell us about all this—but it was probably a nurse. I do remember being very confused about what compartment syndrome was and why it involved his leg. I thought they were talking about the compartments in his heart. We hadn't heard the entire story yet and were having trouble comprehending this new complication. I just kept on nodding like I knew what they meant, but I had no clue what they were talking about. Could I take in anything more? My dry tongue stuck inside my mouth. I remember putting up my hand to cover my mouth—it probably looked like I was shocked, but in reality, I was nauseous.

Whoever came out told us that they had had no choice but to perform a fasciotomy on Andrew's left calf—one incision on the inside of his leg and another incision along the outside. Honestly, after we first heard about it, we kind of shrugged it off. I thought to myself, *Okay, so they had to make a cut down the side of his leg, big deal. How bad could that possibly be? Isn't it just a cut on his leg?* We had no idea that the fasciotomy would turn out to be an extremely major deterrent to his recovery. We continued to be mostly concerned about the internal bleeding, his arteries, his new homograph and whatever compartments in his heart they kept talking about. At that point, though, we didn't see the tsunami coming. We simply focused on the fact that he was still alive.

About six o'clock that evening, the vascular surgeon and a different nurse emerged, looking spent and concerned. Peeling off his surgical gloves, the doctor said they wanted to keep an eye on the pressures in Andrew's left leg and wait a while longer before making a decision about doing a fasciotomy on his right leg. He said he thought they would know fairly soon, but his brow was wrinkled in a worried kind of way and his voice seemed tired. He said it might not be long now before Andrew was moved to ICU. He must have said more, but I really don't remember. I just heard him say Andrew would be going to the ICU.

Once we know Andrew's close to heading to recovery or ICU, the anticipation builds quickly. We anxiously await the phone call saying ¬we can head down the hall to see him. It's a double–edged sword, though. One part of me can hardly wait to see him, while another part of me is scared to death because of what I might see. No matter how many times we've been through this, I am always nervous. Just before it's time, I make sure I've eaten something. I try not to breathe too deeply when I first go in, because the smell of the anesthesia still bothers me, though it doesn't bother Tom so much. I make sure to remind myself that he is going to look very pale and bloated, that his skin will be almost translucent. That's from all the fluids and meds, and it's normal. I take a deep breath and go for it, like diving into cold water. I focus on the fact that I am actually looking at my child, and he's alive. Pretty soon I'm okay with the sights and smells, and it's just good to be with my son.

This time, instead of a call, the surgeon and cardiologist came out and walked us back to ICU. I wanted to run down the hall ahead of them and through the doors to Andrew's bedside, but I had to walk normally with the doctors. We walked up to the very first bed space, and the area around his bed was bustling with people—white-coated doctors talking to other white coats with clipboards, nurses with yellow gowns and stethoscopes and charts. Approaching the area, we were practically invisible as the doctors and nurses swarmed around Andrew's bed. That was fine with me; I wanted to blend into the wall and not cause a stir. I wanted to see Andrew, but I didn't want anyone to see me. My gut was uneasy and nervous about his current critical status. Obviously, the doctors were still extremely anxious. I pasted on my fake half-smile and pushed the fear back down, afraid if I started to cry they might make me leave his room.

Since there was barely enough room for Tom and me, it took a minute or so before one of the nurses actually noticed us plastered against the wall. Without an open spot near the bed, I ended up standing on the left side of the room. I was behind the doctors, so I wasn't in their way, but I could see Andrew's face as I peeked through the layers of long white coats. From my vantage point, I had a pretty good view. I stared at him lying on that bed; I couldn't take my eyes off him, in fact, as I prayed my heart out. My chest hurt like I wanted to cry but couldn't. I got a good long look, and he looked as if he'd been through a war. He was as pale as a person can be but with a grayish pallor to his skin. Swollen and bloated, his poor body had been cut from top to bottom, left to right and back again. He was covered with white bandages; dried blood caked here and there betrayed the horror he had been through. The length of his body was crisscrossed with wires and IV tubing. A ventilator taped across his mouth moved his chest up and down with each even puff of breath. Blood pressure cuffs were wrapped around his left upper arm and right calf, pulse-ox monitors were clipped to his finger and toes, heart monitor leads were taped to his chest and the ICU nurse on his left was trying to get a pic line inserted in his left arm. His entire left leg was bandaged, but I noticed that his foot sticking out from under the layers and layers of gauze was a charcoal gray.

For an instant, a part of you wants to cry out in shock, horror and anger. You wonder why it has to be this way. The pain goes beyond heartache; it hurts in your fingers and in your gut. You feel like you might not survive watching your child suffer through it all.

"Why don't you move up closer?" one of the nurses suggested, interrupting my thoughts. She motioned toward the side of Andrew's bed, and I stepped closer. I found myself in a place I'd been so many times before—leaning on the hospital bed near Andrew's head. I started stroking his hair and forehead, talking to him softly, letting him know we were there with him. I told him how brave and strong he had been and how much we loved him.

The doctors were talking among themselves, and one of them would say something very doctor-ish to us occasionally, like they thought they needed to talk about the situation or something. "You can see that his left leg is wrapped because of the fasciotomy we talked about," the vascular surgeon commented as he walked around the end of the bed. We nodded. He was examining Andrew's foot. Were we supposed to say something? He continued his conversation with the other doctors around the bed, but the words were all a blur to me. Tom stood opposite me, and we were both overwhelmed with emotion without really knowing what emotion it was that we felt. It was hardly fathomable that our son could have survived what he did that day. We could tell by looking at him that his life was still in very immediate danger. We knew bits and pieces of what had happened, but we really had no idea at that point how terrible the situation had been. Andrew had come so very, very close to death, and he was by no means out of the woods. He was alive, but in an oh-so-fragile state—hovering close to heaven, but not quite ready to leave us.

"He still has significant bleeding, so we may need to take him back in to find out where and why," the cardiac surgeon explained. We could see that Andrew was bleeding because blood was passing through the tubing in his chest and incisions, collecting in bags that hung on the side of his bed.

"You mean back into the operating room?" I managed to ask, my voice sounding strange to my own ears.

"Yes. We haven't decided if we will need to yet, but it is a possibility. We'll make that decision within a couple of hours. We need to see how his bleeding continues. If it slows down, we won't have to go back in."

Tom and I glanced at each other, our eyes communicating our mutual fear. Nurses were busy measuring vital signs, checking the monitors and emptying blood from the collection bags. Doctors moved in and out of the room, strolling around with their arms crossed, stroking their chins as if to extract some wisdom from the stubble. After agreeing to meet back in Andrew's room to discuss his condition in twenty minutes, they scattered to care for other patients. I did notice that none of the doctors strayed too far because they all kept checking in on Andrew. The tension was real. The nurses never left his side. He was bleeding profusely from his chest tubes. His urine bag was full of blood, and blood was oozing from every place where there was a bandage.

His left leg was bleeding through the gauze wraps and dripping blood onto the sheet, so the nurse re-wrapped it with a fresh dressing. When she took off the dressing, I could see all the way down to the muscles in his calf as they bulged out of the skin where his fasciotomy incisions were. It looked like little footballs had been cut in half and stuck on the inside and outside of his calves. What I was seeing was truly amazing in a scientific way, and I was intrigued on an intellectual level. I thought, *How many moms get to see the muscles inside their son's leg?* The muscles looked kind of striped, exactly like those in anatomy books, but I'd never realized until that moment that it was such an accurate depiction of what muscle actually looked like.

The doctors and nurses kept looking at me to see if I was handling everything okay. I half-joked with them that I'd done all this before and it was nothing I couldn't handle…but the truth was that I wasn't handling it very well—it was overwhelming and incredible and surreal, and more than I had bargained for. I was sick to my stomach, but there was no way I was going to leave Andrew's side. *I couldn't care less how graphic it is. This is my son. I will deal with all of it—whatever happens, I'm not budging. I am not about to leave over some bleeding, bulging muscles and a dressing change. What kind of wimpy mother couldn't take that?*

About the time I finished that thought, a strange blackness started shooting in behind my eyes and that little bit of nausea turned into full on wooziness. "I feel like…like…I…um…don't feel real good," I said quietly as my head started swimming.

Sarah, Andrew's nurse, had kept her eyes on me, anticipating this very response. She quickly grabbed a chair and pushed it underneath me just as my knees started to fold.

"I think I should sit down," I commented, grabbing the bedside rail as I stated the obvious.

"I think you're right. You're white as a sheet," the nurse replied. "You sit for a while. Can I get you some crackers and juice?"

Just then Sheri came into the ICU from the waiting room. She had traded places with Tom since only two were allowed in the ICU at a time. I was glad to see her. She was calm and reassuring, and right then I needed her more than ever. She laughed at my peaked face and teased me about how I liked to brag about never fainting. Sarah immediately sent her to get me some food. Sheri was exactly the help we needed, asking in-depth questions of the doctors and nurses and interpreting medical terminology that we didn't understand. It was Sheri who overheard the nurses talking that evening about Andrew being in DIC. "Did I hear you say he is in DIC?" she asked.

"Yes, he is" Sarah answered. "He's lost so much blood."

Sheri turned to me with a frightened look in her eyes. "That's not good," she whispered quietly. "Really, really not good."

"Why? What's DIC?" I asked, this new concern registering in my brain-file.

"Well," Sheri looked at me, "it stands for Disseminated Intravascular Coagulation. It means that he received so much new blood that his body isn't able to process it like he should. It's serious." I could see in her eyes what she wasn't saying out loud, what she couldn't bring herself to say.

Sheri and I prayed together for Andrew, and I'm fairly sure that Sarah was praying in the background as she worked. *Oh, Andrew,* I thought, *keep fighting. You are so brave. Please, please, don't give up.* As if I were balancing on the bow of a ship, lost in the ocean, I felt helplessly overwhelmed. A foggy darkness hovered on the edges of my mind and kept trying to descend; I repeatedly brushed it away and tried to sort out my thoughts. For a while I'd simply go through the motions, unable to focus or connect with what was happening around me. Then I'd force myself back into reality, knowing I had to understand what was happening because I was the parent, and this was my responsibility. I would fight to be present, but then it would feel like it was too much, and I'd slip back into my own thoughts. In and out and in and out of the storm I went. I tried so hard to keep my grip, but sometimes reality is just too much to bear all at once.

Twenty-four

The Lord is my rock, my fortress, and my savior;
my God is my rock, in whom I find protection. He is my shield,
the power that saves me, and my place of safety.
– Psalm 18:2 NLT

There is no circumstance, no trouble, no testing, that can ever touch me until, first of all, it has gone past God and past Christ, right through to me. If it has come that far, it has come with a great purpose, which I may not understand at the moment. But I refuse to become panicky, as I lift up my eyes to Him and accept it as coming from the throne of God for some great purpose of blessing to my own heart.
– Alan Redpath

THAT NIGHT, tension draped itself over all of us like a heavy fog, creeping into conversations and dampening our spirits. It was both palpable and frightening. Doctors whisked in and out, conferring with each other in low voices, lingering at the bedside, making notes in the chart, checking monitors. Every so often they'd say something to Tom and me, but it most often seemed that we were invisible to them. By midnight, my eyelids were propped open by sheer will alone—that, and fear. Every minute that Andrew was alive was a gift, and we knew it. I could hardly let go of his limp, swollen hand, regardless of the wires and tubes sticking out helter-skelter. *God,* I prayed silently, *please stop this bleeding. Help him not to have to go back into surgery.* But the bleeding continued. *God, are You hearing our prayers? Are You even there?* In the end, I had to believe God and trust Him because I knew He was all there was to trust—but I cried because of my fear.

By two in the morning, the consensus was to take Andrew back to surgery to try to determine the source of the bleeding. When they rolled his bed out of ICU and back into the operating room, we were fully aware of the huge possibility that he wouldn't come back out of those doors alive. Three doctors and four nurses walked alongside and behind us as we followed Andrew's gurney through the hallway. Andrew was still unconscious, but I walked beside him and held his hand as his bed was rolled through the ICU doors and into the back hall.

The vascular surgeon said to the cardiac surgeon as we walked along, "I've never seen someone lose as much blood as Andrew and survive—even when I was in combat—and I saw a lot of men who'd lost a lot of blood. I've also never seen anyone fight so hard to live." He shook his head. "Andrew is an amazing young man." My eyes met Tom's across the bed as we continued walking down that lonely hallway. We already knew that.

The operating room doors swung open, and a burst of cold air poured out into the hallway. They stopped rolling the bed so we could say goodbye. I leaned over and kissed Andrew's head and hand. We both told him how much we loved him and that we'd be waiting for him when he woke up (just in case he could somehow hear us), and then we turned to go. I thought I might throw up. One of the nurses stuck her head back out the operating room doors and asked if we would please wait in the regular waiting area instead of in the ICU. It was going to be a perilous, wintry night; a battle for Andrew's life lay directly ahead of us.

The whole waiting area was empty and dark except for a motion-sensor light that kept turning off and then on again every time someone walked through the area. But almost no one walked through at this time of night. Tom and I were so scared and probably still in shock at all that had transpired that day. We cried, we prayed. Reaching up in the dark, we begged God to spare Andrew's life. We both got on our knees and prayed like we'd never prayed before. I sobbed into the seat of the chair. *He is yours, God; please give him life.* It felt very much like a spiritual battle was taking place in the operating room where both life and death were fighting for the victory. We bowed our heads to God, pleading with Him to bring Andrew back from that battlefield alive.

The scope of the devastation done to his body that day was immense. As the doctors conferenced among themselves that night before they went back into surgery, they wondered if he could recover from the damage, wondered if it had gone on for too long and had pushed him beyond the limits of recovery. We were in shock as we listened to their conversation, but of course we didn't show any emotion. Somewhere inside, I knew that Andrew may have been pushed past his own limits, but he was not beyond God's. We couldn't do anything to help him except pray. We could pray.

I called Sheri who was asleep at the hotel to let her know what was happening. She called my mom and dad, but my mom was already awake and praying. Even though it was two o'clock in the morning, Sheri called friends back in our hometown and alerted them to the gravity of Andrew's situation. They all began praying. Friends of Andrew's had stayed together overnight at one of their homes so that if there was any developing news, they could all hear it at once and pray—which they did. It was not clear to anyone if he would live or die, but there was absolutely no doubt that hearts cried out, prayers were offered and angels were called to intervene in this battle for Andrew's life.

The hours inched by with no word. I laid my head on the armrest of the chair and dozed on and off. Each time I woke, I would pray. It was the worst night of our lives. Four hours later, at six in the morning, we were still sitting in the waiting area when families began arriving and checking in for morning surgeries. I must have looked awful—puffy eyes, wrinkled clothes, tousled hair. None of it mattered. The sun had just begun to peek through windows when Andrew's doctors finally came out looking utterly spent. They took off surgical caps and masks as they walked toward us. "He's hanging in there, he's…well, he is stable at the moment. He tolerated the surgery and is headed back to ICU, so you'll be able to see him soon." The surgeon sounded so tired. He pushed a weary hand through his normally immaculate gray hair.

"So, has his bleeding slowed down? Did you find the source?" Tom asked.

"Well, yes, his bleeding has slowed. When we got in there, we couldn't find any new site where the bleeding was originating, but we were able to stabilize him. We did everything we could, and now it's up to him to keep fighting. The next twenty-four to forty-eight hours will be critical."

A few minutes later, we were allowed to go back to his bedside. Again dried blood was everywhere, his poor body ravaged from top to bottom. I was so exhausted, my tears poured out noiselessly. I laid my forehead on the edge of the bed next to Andrew's arm and closed my eyes.

Walking closely with someone through a major illness or surgery is so completely life-changing that a person will never go back to being who they were before the experience. It is demanding and exhausting and in addition to tending to the needs of the loved one, the caregiver must deal with their own grief and loss along the way. Nobody's loss is exactly like another's. Sometimes a loss is sudden, jarring and totally unexpected. It can throw a person completely out of sync with the life they've been living. It can be like standing in front of a fire hose. Suddenly, you can be hit by a blast so strong and unforeseen that you find yourself yanked up, carried along, tossed and thrown by an avalanche of shocking (and often confusing) emotion.

At other times, though, loss is a long, lonely passage through the darkest night of nights. It's the slow drip, drip, dripping of pain over a period of time. It constantly erodes, peeling back layer after layer of hope and faith, nipping at the rawest of nerve endings until it seems impossible to bear any longer.

In either case, loss can awaken fear and loneliness. It can overwhelm even the most deeply rooted person. Although I was not experiencing the loss of losing a loved one, I was going through the loss of hopes and dreams. My grief was based in the trauma of watching Andrew suffer. When those moments of devastating grief and the waves of loss threatened to capture every hope I ever had, the most comforting thing I could do was to cling to God. He really is a Rock, and He can be counted on to remain the same from one moment to the next. Through the lowest valleys and the most tumultuous storm, God doesn't change. I don't know what will happen in the next day or hour or minute, but I know He will be there. Sometimes I don't even have the strength to *want* to get through the storm. All I can do is hold my Bible in my arms and know that He knows. Sometimes I can't read my Bible or even pray out loud, but I know God is there, loving me and He knows my every pain.

As I stood beside my son's bed through that dark night, I thought, *I refuse to lose my faith in the midst of this storm. I am going to hold on, and I want to have even more faith when it's over. I don't know how that will happen, and the end seems so distant right now that I would even say that's nearly impossible. But I want to be the kind of woman who is strong enough to hold onto You for dear life, and teachable enough to let You change me.*

Twenty-five

For though the fig tree doesn't flourish, nor fruit be in the vines;
the labor of the olive fails, the fields yield no food...yet I will
rejoice in the LORD. *I will be joyful in the God of my salvation!*
– Habakkuk 3:17-19 NLT

My trust in God flows out of the experience of his loving me,
day in and day out, whether the day is stormy or fair, whether
I'm sick or in good health, whether I'm in a state of grace or
disgrace. He comes to me where I live and loves me as I am.
– Brennan Manning

SEVEN WEEKS, then eight dragged by, icy cold and gray, and we still called the hospital home. It would have been intolerably dull if not for the few moments of pure, heart-gripping terror. Three days out from surgery, we had one of those moments in the ICU.

I was sitting next to Andrew's bedside reading a magazine as his nurse, Angie, decided to give him an additional dose of a very strong painkiller. He'd already had the maximum dosage of his other pain meds, but they hadn't touched the pain, so she decided to increase his dosage of fentanyl. She gave him the shot in his central line and left to help someone else. Almost immediately I could tell he was in distress. He started thrashing, and I could see the shock and fear in his eyes. He put his hands around his neck in a choking motion and mouthed the words, "I can't breathe!" Then his eyes rolled back, and he went limp. I panicked more than at any other time in my life. I ran to the foot of the bed and yelled, "Help, someone help! He's stopped breathing!"

About five nurses and every doctor who was in the ICU at that moment came rushing toward us. Angie had been a few beds away, and she ran past everyone and grabbed a blue bag from the wall behind Andrew's bed and thrust it toward the male nurse across the bed from her. "Here, bag him *now*," she commanded as she worked to inject something into Andrew's IV.

The nurse standing opposite her secured the mask and began squeezing air into Andrew's lungs at regular intervals use the soft plastic inflatable bag that could be hand-squeezed to deliver air to a patient when there is no other option for respiration. Someone else brought in the crash cart in case Andrew went from respiratory arrest to cardiac arrest. I watched for a minute longer before realizing I'd better get Tom and tell the others to pray.

I ran down the hallway that led out to the waiting area, pushed open the doors and told everyone to pray like crazy because Andrew had stopped breathing. Then, Tom and I ran back down the hall to his bedside. By the time we got back, probably only a minute had passed, but things had calmed down. Only Angie and the doctor stood by Andrew's bed talking quietly. No longer struggling, Andrew was breathing on his own—but I was still catching my breath though.

"Is he okay?" I asked. "What happened?"

Andrew opened his eyes at the sound of my voice, but he was very drowsy and almost immediately closed them again. I picked up his hand, "I'm here, Andrew. Dad and I are here."

"He had an adverse reaction to the pain medicine. Sometimes that happens with fentanyl," the doctor explained.

"So, is he allergic to fentanyl?" Tom asked.

"Well, this means he has a *sensitivity* to it. We increased his dosage, and it turned out to be too much fentanyl for his system. That caused him to stop breathing, so we gave him medication to stimulate his respiratory system so he would start breathing again. We bagged him the whole time, so he was never without oxygen. But we do need to keep our eyes on him this afternoon. Due to his sensitivity to the fentanyl, his body is having a hard time remembering to breathe."

I later did some reading and learned that fentanyl is a super-strong painkiller, but also a type of drug that depresses the respiratory system. It makes the whole body feel so drowsy that breathing is just too much work. Or, like in Andrew's case, it can paralyze the respiratory system so that you can't take a breath. One of the side effects is that people go into respiratory arrest and stop breathing altogether.

As we watched Andrew closely throughout the afternoon, I began to think my adrenaline levels would never come back down to normal. I was restless and antsy for hours. I watched Andrew's chest move up and down with each breath he took. I couldn't take my eyes off him. I was terrified he'd fall asleep and not ever breathe again. He'd be breathing fine and then just not take a breath. If I wasn't watching his chest, I was listening for the monitor that let us know the time between breaths. I'd wait and wait and count the seconds— twelve, thirteen, fourteen—until, finally, when the monitor said fifteen and he hadn't taken a breath, I'd shake him and say, "Breathe, Andrew," or "Take another breath, Andrew." And he would.

Sometimes I had to shake him fairly hard to make him breathe, and that was scary. Angie hovered nearby during those hours, keeping close tabs on him as well. I was so horrified as I thought about what might have happened had I not been standing right there. It reminded me of that time in Boston when the little girl next to Andrew stopped breathing, and the doctors all rushed over from the ICU. I was so scared

I couldn't look to see what had happened. I made Tom go check to see what was going on. I had been such a baby, but I had been petrified.

On day eight of Andrew's hospital stay, he had his first surgery on his leg and was "promoted" out of ICU and up to the ninth floor. The dead tissue within the muscles of Andrew's calf had started to die and smell bad, so they performed a debridement, which means they removed all the dead tissue so that the healthy part could heal more quickly. Before this surgery, if we got a whiff of his leg when they changed the wound dressing, believe me, it was not pleasant. The doctors were also very concerned about infection; we'd been visited by the infectious diseases doctor several times.

This leg surgery was performed by a plastic surgeon. During surgery, he not only debrided the wound, but he also closed the fasciotomy incision with a skin graft. A thin layer of skin about ten inches long by six inches wide was cut from Andrew's upper thigh then sent through a machine to stretch it out even more. It had a mesh-like appearance after being stretched. Up until that point, I knew nothing about skin grafts. I'd never seen one or known anyone who had one. I assumed it would just be like laying another piece of skin on top of the wound that would heal and look like a patch on a quilt. But the diamond-shaped mesh pattern that was left in the fragile tissue after it was stretched remained as the graft healed. It left a somewhat convex-looking scar within the edges of the original scar, looking more like the grill of a fancy car than a patchwork quilt. It was better than not having a leg, but I had thought it would look more like regular skin once healed. I didn't expect it to look like it did.

It's funny how doctors act like everything is just common knowledge we should already know, but we don't know and really have no idea what to expect. I wish doctors would tell us more about what is going to happen, and what we can realistically expect. You take what you can get, though, and some doctors are just better at explaining than others. Andrew never complained about it. I don't think he cared much at that point what the graft looked like.

We asked repeatedly to see copies of Andrew's records because we were curious about what exactly had happened in the operating room, but everyone kept putting us off. We didn't have a patient advocate, and, in the midst of this huge hospital and all these medical professionals, we felt very alone.

The following week brought bad news about Andrew's leg—it was infected, and not just a little bit. The plastic surgeons and infectious diseases doctors descended on our room.

"We'll need to re-open his leg, find the infection and cut it out. It is serious, and we hope the infection hasn't gone into the bone. We'll also be testing Andrew for necrotizing fasciitis."

My mind spun. *What? I've heard of that before. Isn't that the horrible infection that usually costs patients limbs or their life?* I didn't know what this surgery would mean for Andrew, and I was extremely nervous as we waited to get the lab results back.

I researched necrotizing fasciitis on Tom's laptop and learned that it is a serious, rare, aggressive infection that spreads quickly. It can be fatal if not treated promptly. It causes tissue death at the infection site, and that's why it's often described as a "flesh-eating bacteria." It can be caused by staph bacteria, including MRSA, but that's not always the cause. Methicillin-resistant staphylococcus aureus (MRSA) is one strain of staph that is harder to treat than most because it is resistant to antibiotics.

The physicians upped Andrew's dosages of Vanco and Clindamycin and stopped the penicillin. The lab results came back negative for the flesh-eating bacteria—*Praise God*—but Andrew did have MRSA deep in the tissues—a very aggressive staph infection that is extremely difficult to get under control.

Andrew was moved to the tenth floor where we had a much bigger and more comfortable room for our family, and we were thankful for things like bigger rooms. One of us stayed overnight in the extra bed next to Andrew's bed every night. During the day we pulled our chairs up to tables or near Andrew's bed. Living in such close quarters was stressful, with people coming in and out and in and out at all hours of the day and night. On the upside, I wasn't responsible for any cleaning or cooking! Tom tried to continue working while he was there—he had started his own business working from home before we had come to the hospital with Andrew. As a result, he was able to work on his computer and make phone calls from Andrew's hospital room most of the time. David was attending CU in Boulder, so it was an easy drive down to see us after classes on many days, and then he would stay with us on the weekends. For Amy, now in tenth grade, she read books and kept up in her textbooks, and she wrote in a journal. Her language arts teacher suggested she make a vocabulary list of all the words she was learning. We tried our best to make it work.

As it turned out, my sister-in-law, Jeanne, was still in New York City with Taylor who'd undergone a bone marrow transplant the previous June. Their family was trying to make it work as well. Ken and the older girls would fly out from Denver to New York as often as they could. Even when Taylor was not an inpatient, he needed to be near the hospital. They stayed at the Ronald McDonald House in New York City at the same time we stayed at the Ronald McDonald House in Denver. Life was crazy for all of us.

On January fifth, just two weeks after he was checked in, Andrew had his fourth surgery. The doctors re-opened the incision on his leg to debride the wound again, but instead of closing it, they left it open and used a medical device called a wound vac to help speed the healing process. The difficult thing about Andrew's wound was that it was so deep and so big that it was basically an infection waiting to happen. The wound vac was supposed to keep the whole thing closed and suction excess fluid from the inside. Hopefully, that would help.

Andrew began having his wound dressing changed every third day. Those dressing changes were like living through your worst nightmare over and over again—and it was almost as excruciating for those of us watching as it was for him. Two nurses who specialize in wound care, Marie and Anna, came to change the dressing, and his regular nurse stood next to him so she could inject Dilaudid—a fast-acting, potent painkiller—directly into his line. The Dilaudid barely even touched the pain. He became so practiced at knowing when the procedure was going to hurt the worst that he could tell the nurse exactly when and how much Dilaudid to inject. Andrew would squeeze rubber balls or hold our hands—*crush* might be a more accurate description—to help him endure the pain. The wound care nurses' unenviable charge was to clean out the packing gauze that went deep into the wound, locate and debride any dead or infected tissue, repack the wound with more gauze, rewrap the leg, then set up the wound vac again.

One day, during a particularly difficult dressing change, a doctor we knew only slightly came in and stood at the foot of the bed. Our whole family was gathered around the bed to encourage Andrew since it was so horrifically painful. Apparently oblivious to what was going on, the doctor started talking to us about Andrew's leg and the lab results. I was trying to listen, but I was so focused on helping Andrew get through the procedure that I barely heard what the doctor was saying…right up until he said the word *amputation*.

Shock flooded my system. I don't think the doctor even noticed how upset we were because he just kept right on talking. Andrew started crying, which is something he had not done thus far. Then I started crying and, before long, our whole family was crying, even David and

Tom. Marie and Anna, the wound care nurses, stopped what they were doing and looked at the doctor, who finally stopped talking. He looked at all of us wiping our tears, holding Andrew's hands, and asked, "Are you just now hearing that amputation is a possibility?"

As we all nodded through our tears, Tom found his voice.

"Amputation? That's a possibility?"

"You mean to tell me that no one has mentioned this to you before now?" The doctor was more than slightly agitated.

"No," I responded. "We had no idea. This is the first we've heard of it." Anna handed me a box of tissues. We were distraught and discouraged. *Why has no one said anything to us?* I passed around the tissues as my mind continued to spin. *Why did the doctor decide to discuss this with us now?*

The doctor excused himself rather quickly. He was obviously fuming, but we didn't know why. He never said he was sorry or tried to help us understand—he just left us standing there to process his shocking news. Marie and Anna were sympathetic, and they tried to soothe our fears and sadness. They agreed that the doctor should have been more sensitive, and that he never should have brought up something like amputation in the middle of a dressing change. Andrew was still crying, but they had to finish the dressing change anyway. All in all, it was a very rough day.

A new doctor came in the next afternoon, and he actually sat down and talked with us. I felt like he really listened and then explained things so that we could understand. He introduced himself as the limb preservationist—and I immediately thought, *And there's another one to add to the list.* We had no idea what was going on—first, one doctor said Andrew might need an amputation and, the next day, the limb preservationist stopped by. It was crazy! We finally just decided there must have been a miscommunication between the doctors, and that we were supposed to have heard about the amputation before we actually did.

Of course, I didn't know the whole story exactly, so I tried to piece it together from the veiled information we got. Anyway, we were assigned a new "lead" doctor, and it wasn't the cardiac surgeon. I didn't really care who did the communicating, I just wanted to know what was going on. Again, I asked for copies of Andrew's records and was told someone would get them to us, but I got a strange feeling from the nurse's reaction when I asked. Was that a forbidden subject?

Early on, my sister and her family started visiting every Sunday. They lived north of Denver about seventy miles. They brought our dog (whom they were taking care of for us) and a homemade crock-pot meal (or sometimes pizza) and came to sit with us for the afternoon. It was literally the one thing our whole family looked forward to each week. Our dog was a very quiet Border Collie, so the hospital staff never minded that he came right into the room, and Andrew *loved* having the dog there! We'd turn on the Sunday afternoon football game and enjoy ourselves. That was about as good as it could get, considering the situation.

The number of doctors and nurses that we were dealing with kept growing and growing. I had been planning to write thank you notes to everyone, but I soon became overwhelmed by the sheer number of doctors. How could I remember all these people? We interacted with four ICU doctors, the cardiac surgeon, two cardiologists, two plastic surgeons, two vascular surgeons, the limb preservationist, the infectious diseases doctor, the wound care team, the general surgeon, the physical and occupational therapists, two orthopedic surgeons, and, of course, all the fabulous nurses in the ICU as well as on the floors. We also had two doctors on each floor.

It was eight long weeks, four additional surgeries and more pain than any of us ever imagined from the day we walked into the hospital until the day we were told Andrew was going to be discharged. We would have to stay close by for a couple of days, but we were ecstatic.

I asked again about the records. It had become obvious that there was something going on there, but we didn't know how to handle it. We couldn't think about taking care of Andrew, getting him home and settled, and at the same time think about the issues surrounding the botched surgery. At first, I just wanted to see the records to get details about dates and surgeries, so I could be accurate for his scrapbook. I'd taken plenty of pictures and planned to document what had happened so that Andrew could look back and see what he'd survived, but we began to think the hospital and doctors were assuming we wanted to see the records for legal reasons and were trying to cover their tracks.

We finally got word that we were going to be allowed to see the records—two hours before we were to be discharged! Someone led us into a conference room where probably ten people sat around the table watching as Tom and I looked through the enormous stack of papers, most of it complicated lab reports and hard-to-read information that meant absolutely nothing to us. It was very intimidating, and we couldn't really make anything out of it all; it was like trying to read a foreign language. We spent about fifteen minutes looking at the records, then someone ushered us out, and that was it. We didn't know what questions to ask, and no one offered any explanations. Neither Tom nor I knew what to think or what to do next, so we gathered our belongings and left the hospital with our son.

Andrew had come so far and was improving each day. He seemed to be nearly back to his normal self, albeit twenty pounds lighter. It was almost surreal that the time had finally come to leave. I was scared to be leaving the protection of the nurses and assuming all the responsibilities for his care on my own. He was fine though and appeared to be doing great, or so we thought. I guess it's all relative. In retrospect, I know now that our perspective was warped because of the "hospital glasses" we'd been wearing. You start to judge how well a person is doing based on his or her condition the day before. Any improvement is a huge re- lief—but you aren't comparing the patient to a healthy person that isn't in the hospital at all. We learned that the hard way.

Since Andrew hadn't celebrated (or even remembered) his birth- day, he asked if we could all go out to dinner and celebrate the day he got discharged. A chance to eat something besides hospital food? We thought it was a fabulous idea! However, it turned out to be the worst evening ever. Even though we dropped him off at the door, Andrew was so weak he could barely crutch his way through the restaurant to the table. He thought he was hungry, but then he had no appetite. He couldn't even eat the special birthday dessert they brought for him. He was miserable, and so were the rest of us. In the end, we finish hurriedly just to get out of the restaurant, longing for our own beds but unable to leave the immediate area for a few days. All five of us were crammed into the one room at the Ronald McDonald House, feeling as if we'd crossed the finish line together, overwhelmed and exhausted, but alive. We helped Andrew get comfortable on the bed, then the rest of us col- lapsed randomly on the floor and blow-up mattresses.

I don't remember falling asleep, but I do know that I slept fitfully and awoke several times with a rather uncomfortable crick in my neck. Morning came shining in way too soon, and I asserted that I hadn't slept much at all. That, however, was the topic of a heated family debate, with my kids going on and on very dramatically about how loudly I had snored all night long.

Twenty-six

Meanwhile, the moment we get tired in the waiting, God's Spirit is
right alongside helping us along. If we don't know how or what to
pray, it doesn't matter. He does our praying in and for us, making
prayer out of our wordless sighs, our aching groans.
– Romans 8:26 MSG

I am so weak that I can hardly write, I cannot read my Bible,
I cannot even pray, I can only lie still in God's arms
like a little child, and trust.
– Hudson Taylor

FINALLY. HOME. I wanted to hug our house. My kitchen, the family room, I took it all in and finally collapsed joyfully on my own bed! It was heavenly. Now what? I knew we had to move forward in Andrew's recovery, but I had no idea which way to turn. We were used to being told what to do: he needs surgery on his leg, he will have physical therapy at three o'clock this afternoon, the wound care team will assess his wound tomorrow, etc. Now, it was up to me. No one was giving us direction or even suggestions. I had the name of a rehab specialist, so I called her to make an appointment before making an appointment with Andrew's primary care physician. Then, I called a physical therapist friend and asked if he could come to our house and assess Andrew's situation. I was grasping for help from anyone.

First, we saw Andrew's primary care physician which was incredibly disappointing. I assumed that this doctor would be the epicenter for all that needed to happen from here on out with Andrew, and that he would communicate with the other doctors—physical therapy, wound care, etc. But that was not to be. He was very busy and apparently uninterested in taking on the challenge. He didn't say that exactly…it was more like, "Okay, his leg looks pretty good. I think you need to just keep on doing what you've been doing."

What? Is he kidding? His leg looks terrible! The doctor basically handed the problem back to me. Over the next week we saw the rehab doctor, the physical therapist and a wound care specialist—but I wasn't getting the responses we needed from any of these professionals.

Finally, my friend Sheri referred us to a pediatric orthopedist, Dr. MaryBeth Deering. I wasn't sure an orthopedic doctor would want to help us, but I made the appointment out of desperation. The first time we met, I could tell she actually cared and *did* want to help. This was one doctor that didn't look at us with a pasted-on bedside manner. She listened to our story and registered genuine shock about what had happened up to that point. She took Andrew's situation seriously and made a plan with us, letting us know that she would do everything she could to make things right. I breathed a sigh of relief because I knew she had heard us.

This dedicated woman became a part of our life *almost daily* for a while—and then we saw her regularly for a couple of years. She was the go-to doctor that Andrew so desperately needed, someone who could see the big picture and was willing to go above and beyond to make things happen. And although he had struggled with his feelings towards doctors in general, Andrew developed a real affinity for Dr. Deering. Like kindred souls, she teased him about getting "out there," shooting hoops, skiing and mountain biking. And she was stern with him about staying off his leg when he needed to. Keeping Andrew down was nearly impossible—as you can imagine. Since Dr. Deering loves being active herself, she knew how Andrew felt being sidelined from the sports he loved and lived for; she understood how intensely frustrating it is to be on crutches for months at a time and how desperately he longed to be "normal" again. Though I'm sure she does the same for all her patients, she made us feel like we mattered to her. In the end, *she* was the one who mattered to us. She became someone we really cared about and trusted. We adored her; she was—and is—a remarkable doctor.

Everything had changed for our family. We were back at home where we had longed to be, yet it felt foreign—none of us knew how to act or what to do. We fussed around with this and that and went through the motions, but all the regular stuff that we normally would have done together was no longer an option. Underneath the surface, we were numb and confused. Our identity as a family had changed, and we found ourselves wondering which way to turn. It was like we'd been fed into a meat grinder as one thing and came out ground up, altogether different in every way. We didn't know who we were anymore, and we hadn't been prepared to hash out a new identity.

We'd always spent a lot of time being active outdoors, but hiking or playing basketball, racquetball, football…all those activities were out now. Well, everyone besides Andrew could still do all those things, but no one wanted to. It didn't feel right without Andrew. *What does this new family do for fun? How do we relate to each other? Let's see, shall we watch TV? Rent movies? Read? Play board games?* We needed to figure it out, but that required emotional energy we simply didn't have at the time.

Tom found solitaire and Sudoku to be the escape he was looking for, and he started playing games whenever he wasn't working. For him, not having to talk or interact with people was a relief. He was trying desperately to keep his business afloat and to provide for our family, but the stress was overwhelming. By playing games on the computer, he could stay in the background while I handled the communication part of family life. Without meaning to, Tom and I began to drift apart.

Our family needed an anchor to hold onto together when everything around us seemed shaky. That anchor was God. He was still there, and I knew that. But He *felt* far away—not close and caring like I'd expected. I thought I'd be able to feel Him in the midst of the darkness, but everything had gone quiet spiritually. Each of us was on our own emotionally, in survival mode, and it was hard to connect with each other, or with anyone else for that matter. At least we had all been together at the hospital. We had eaten together and spent our waking hours in the same room. Now, our family was all over the place, and we avoided feeling or talking or interacting except on the most basic of levels. How could we have survived all that had happened with Andrew just to fall apart in the aftermath?

In the midst of our struggle, we received another blow. We got word that Taylor was not doing well. He was showing signs of graft vs. host and was failing. He had been such a fighter, but he just couldn't continue his fight any longer. Taylor died nine months after his bone-marrow transplant, just two weeks after we'd arrived home from the hospital. Andrew was still barely walking with crutches when we drove to Denver for the funeral. Taylor had been such a bright light in our lives—and in the lives of everyone that had known him—since the day he was born. He was funny, game for any kind of adventure and always a hundred percent in the moment. I couldn't believe he was gone. His death left a gaping hole in our hearts that will never be filled and threw me into an on-again/off-again wrestling match with God.

I had prayed so hard for Taylor. So many people had prayed for him, prayed that he would be healed and yet God said no. At least, He said no to the way I wanted Taylor to be healed. Of course he was healed because he was now in heaven and didn't have to suffer anymore, and I was glad for that; but I was mad that God didn't choose to answer my prayers the way I wanted. *Why did we have to lose Taylor? Did You not hear our prayers? And why did You choose to save Andrew's life and not Taylor's? You could have saved them both, but You didn't.* Both Andrew and Taylor's lives had been in God's hands, and I felt guilty that my son had lived while my nephew hadn't. I didn't know how to reconcile that in my heart. I didn't know if I could love or trust God after that.

Financially, we were overwhelmed with bills. Tom was self-employed, so we had no health insurance. Andrew had been on the state health insurance program for children, so we had purposely chosen for his surgery to take place while he was eighteen and still covered. If things had gone as we'd expected, he would have been out of the hospital before he turned nineteen when he would no longer be covered by insurance. However, he had four more surgeries and a month and a half more in the hospital after his birthday. Now he needed physical therapy, evaluations of the nerve and muscle damage, wound care and possibly braces for his legs to help him walk. Most doctors want at least some money up front, and I understand that—but we truly had no money left.

I wish I could say all this trauma drew us closer together, but it didn't work that way for us. Tom and I barely talked to each other. We tried marriage counseling, but it was a major issue because we couldn't afford it. So then we'd argue about the money. Tom's business was not doing well, and that caused incredible stress for us both. When we sat down and looked at the numbers that summer, we realized we couldn't afford for him to continue with his own business. He needed to look for a job, and for that matter, so did I—but how could I work and also be available to care for Andrew, who couldn't drive himself to appointments or even accomplish some of the most basic life skills on his own. We couldn't pay our bills, and we had exhausted our savings. We had already received financial help from friends and family that went over and above what could be considered normal. We also knew that we either had to sell our house or lose it—and the thought of it made us sick. "There's just no other choice," Tom shared one afternoon when we all got together for a family meeting. "We aren't making ends meet. We can't pay the bills." My throat was tight with tears. I knew it was just a house. After what we'd been through, you'd think a house wouldn't matter that much—after all, you hear people talk about how having each other is all that really matters. So I don't know why, but the house did really matter to me. Maybe it was so hard *because* of all we'd been through—perhaps the house was our link to happier times. But we had never not paid our bills, and we now had *mountains* of bills. I wish we could have waited just a bit longer to sell the house, but we didn't—we couldn't.

Friends from church came over to help us clean the house the night before the realtor walk-through. I had been out running errands, and the first thing I saw when I walked in the house was our good friend—who also happened to be our pastor—standing on a stool, cleaning the blades on the living room ceiling fan. Another friend had replaced our worn-out bedspread with a beautiful new comforter. Although they didn't know it at the time, it was our friends that kept us going. Just when things were at their worst and it seemed like it wasn't worth trying anymore, someone would call to encourage us. Or I'd run into someone in the grocery store who would mention praying for us. Or someone would bring a meal or send money in the mail.

David was particularly sensitive to our financial plight, and he worried about things way more than a son should. One day Tom and I were sitting at the kitchen table discussing the bills and the groceries and our lack of money. David walked into the room, obviously upset—he had apparently been listening to our conversation—and asked, "How can you be so sure that God is going to provide?"

"I know He is because He promises to provide for us," I replied.

"Yeah, but when there is nothing there…how can you just keep on trusting?"

"I don't know *how* He is going to provide, but I know He will." And that was true. I really didn't know. I wasn't talking based on how I felt; my feelings were almost non-existent. It was all faith. I looked at David with tears in my eyes. "I trust Him because He is the only solid thing I have to hold onto." David was silent. I wanted to believe, but my feelings weren't cooperating. I reminded myself that faith isn't based on feelings. You have to be willing to believe even when you *don't* feel it. "I want to believe regardless of these circumstances," I told him. I really didn't know where we were going to get enough money to make it through the month. We had paid the bills and had nothing left. I said, "David, there's nothing else to put your trust in. You can't trust in jobs or money because they may be here one day and not the next. There is only God. He is it."

A little while later, I brought in the mail and opened a letter from some dear friends that we hadn't heard from in ages. Inside was a check for two hundred dollars. I couldn't believe it! I called David in and showed him that God keeps His promises, and He *will* provide. In fact, He provided over and over again just when we needed it most—money from the church, money from family, money from friends. Yet, there were also situations when His provision didn't appear, and we had to step forward into what seemed like the best choice under the circumstances. Having to sell our house was one of those decisions, and Tom closing down his business was another.

You'd have thought all that evidence of God's care and love would have been more than enough to quench my doubt and fear, but the elation I felt at one moment was easily eroded and flattened by discouragement the next. I was fragile. It wasn't that my faith was hitting bottom, but my emotional reserves were drained. I wanted to be strong and bold and confident; I wanted to tell of all God's amazing works and miracles, but I felt stripped down and vulnerable.

We'd had two different doctor friends look over Andrew's hospital records to try to determine if there was even a slight possibility for a malpractice suit. Both doctors concluded that we should pursue it. We were not interested in getting money for money's sake, but we knew that Andrew would need therapy, braces and probably more surgery on his legs. We thought it would be wise to try to cover his future expenses that resulted from the surgical mistakes, so we hired a reputable lawyer from Denver and met with him one wintery day in December. He listened to the story, looked at Andrew's leg and took copious notes.

This attorney didn't take many cases and accepted only the ones he felt were true situations of medical malpractice, so we were overjoyed when he decided to take Andrew's case. He started by ordering the hospital records, but he received a censored version, one that was missing the most important piece of the puzzle—the nurse's report from the surgery. He kept trying but was never able to secure the missing notes and files. His next step involved finding an expert witness who would be willing to review the records and testify in court. To qualify as an expert witness meant that this person had to be a pediatric cardiac surgeon who had performed this surgery before. Only a handful of surgeons across the country fit that profile. Our lawyer sent the records to one doctor clear across the country and received word back after a month or so that the doctor would not testify. Evidently he felt that our surgeon had performed heroically just to keep Andrew alive, that he had done an amazing job. While we were so very thankful that Andrew's surgeon had kept him alive, what about now? Andrew could barely walk. He was in tremendous pain all the time. That had to count for something, so we decided to try again. So the lawyer found another expert witness in another part of the country and sent the information to him. A couple months later, the story was the same. He wouldn't testify. We tried a third time with the same disappointing results.

We didn't know what to think. Were these doctors simply protecting their own? We couldn't keep looking for an expert witness—it cost us about two thousand dollars every time we did, and we had drained our retirement savings to do what we had done thus far. We didn't have any more money to try again. We had no choice but to let it drop. I couldn't believe it, and I was angry. *How could a doctor in good conscience turn his back on this situation? What is Andrew supposed to do? He has his whole life ahead of him. Where will the compensation for braces and surgeries and therapies come from? Will Andrew even be able to work?* So many questions poured out with nowhere to go. Then the door slammed shut for good when, after two years, the statute of limitations ran out. We had to make our peace with things the way they were.

Like a wounded bird, I sought shelter and found it in my faith in God. Psalm 91 has been a favorite of mine, and I love verse four, which says, *"...under your wings we will find refuge."* We had a tan blanket that felt like the soft down of a bird's feathers on one side and smooth leather on the other. Sometimes I'd wrap myself in that blanket with the soft side next to my skin and just lie there and cry. I'd pretend that cozy blanket was God's arms of love and protection. It's a bit dramatic, I know, but I didn't care.

It was hard for me to talk to people, even people I knew well. It was just too gut wrenching to talk about our situation, and I was afraid that I'd end up in tears and not be able to stop. Life was crashing down around us. We were in such a horrible place emotionally that one night I made Tom promise he wouldn't kill himself, and he made me promise the same thing in return. Our promises helped us make it through that night.

Thoughts from Andrew

My first semester of college was awesome! I started out at Mesa State College (now Colorado Mesa University) with my two best friends, David Skaff and Todd Foley. I remember thinking, *This is what college is all about—meeting new people, going to sporting events, getting involved with campus clubs, playing on as many intramural sports teams as I can and, of course, the whole part about learning.* I did it all. I played intramural volleyball and indoor soccer, as well as flag football. My good friend Skaff and I took a basketball class together—every class was like a scrimmage. It just doesn't get much better than that! Life was great, and I was loving every minute of it.

Early in my first semester I went with Todd and some other friends to climb one of the "fourteeners" here in Colorado—Mount Sherman. It was one of the most difficult days of my life. It started out well, but before long I was having trouble breathing. I knew something wasn't right. My pace slowed, and everyone else went on ahead. I tried, but I couldn't push myself any faster. I could barely catch my breath. One of the dads who was climbing with us stayed and walked with me step-by-step to the top. He knew I was embarrassed and frustrated and yet determined to make it to the summit. He was so encouraging. It took us forever, but we made it. I cannot even begin to say how much it meant to me that he gave up climbing with his family to stay with me. I know I never would have made it without him.

When we got home that night, my mom was worried because the climb had taken so much longer than we'd expected. She thought something terrible had happened. We made an appointment to see the cardiologist and found out that I needed another heart surgery. It wasn't an emergency, so I was able to make the decision when to have surgery. I could push it back until after the spring semester, or I could have it during Christmas break. I thought that it would be nice to just get it over with as soon as possible, so I decided to have my fourth open heart surgery over Christmas break. I would need to take the spring semester off, but I would be ready to go again in the fall. I had been here before, and I knew the routine; I would be in and out of the hospital before I knew it.

As I was being rolled into the operating room, I said to my brother and sister, "I will see you guys on the other side." Well, you know what happened. While I was in the hospital, I went from being nearly dead to thinking I would never walk again to having to completely re-learn how to walk. After I got out and was back home on the road to recovery, I was in a crazy amount of pain. The weird thing was that I couldn't feel my leg or foot in a normal way—in fact, I couldn't move my foot at all. It just hung there. But the pain was there, like a million needles stabbing my foot and leg all the time. Not only was the pain constant in that leg, but my other foot wasn't that great either. I'd lost the muscles that controlled the ability to lift my foot up and down and side to side, so every time I took a step, I had to lift my whole leg up and then set my foot down—and that was the good leg. I found out that what I had was called foot drop, and it made walking a major ordeal.

I was crushed and devastated and totally mad at God for allowing this to happen. I was supposed to be having the time of my life in college and here I was fighting just to be normal. I was angry at the doctors. *How could they screw up so badly? I went in for heart surgery and now I can barely walk?* I wrestled with my feelings, back and forth—*Yes, they saved my life, but how can I live like this?* Some days were so hard that I wished I had died right there on the operating table. It would have been way easier. I would be in heaven now. Instead, I was going through hell, every minute dealing with intense pain and the frustration that goes hand-in-hand with not being able to do even the simplest tasks.

Little things I used to take for granted were no longer possible. I hoped the physical therapy would help eventually, but so far it hadn't.

Every day the excruciating pain kept me company while I was trying to cope with my limitations, go to college and live my life. I could not work or run around playing sports with any of my friends. I wondered if I would ever have a normal life again or ever be able to play the sports that I love so much. In my anger, I ended up becoming very depressed. I remember asking God why He allowed this to happen and pleading with Him to restore my leg. I prayed over and over again, but God never did heal my leg. I knew He could, but for some reason He didn't. That prayer was answered with a, "Not now."

I was bound to the couch. It took all the energy I had just to make it from physical therapy back to the house. When school started that fall, I was still on crutches. I was thankful I attended a fairly small campus, but it was not a cake walk. It sucked having to crutch around all the time. I hated trying to explain to everyone what had happened. To get from one class to another on time is hard enough when you can walk. On crutches, I was constantly late. When it was snowing or raining, slushy and muddy, well, you can imagine. Trying to maneuver myself up and down the stairs with a backpack full of books and a leg that didn't work was tiring. I have total respect and awe for everyone out there that relies on crutches all the time. That's got to be challenging.

I remember coming home from class and propping up my leg after popping ibuprofen, and my mom would get ice packs for me. That became my daily routine: get up, go to class, crash on the couch for the evening. I did that for about two and a half years, and I felt like I was being cheated out of life.

I had tons of problems with my foot developing sores and then infections. The pain was almost more than I could bear. All I could do was retreat into myself to deal with it. It seemed that my entire world was falling down around me, and I wasn't dealing with just my own issues. During this same time, three of my family members passed away—my cousins Kendall and Taylor as well as my grandfather. We also had to move from the house we all loved into a townhome, and my dad was out of work. My whole family was grieving these losses, and we each dealt with this grief in our own way, struggling to connect with each other. It seemed that all was lost—like there was no use in even trying anymore.

God really was putting my faith and the faith of my family to the test. This experience for me was like waking up in the midst of a blazing fire. It hurt, I couldn't see a way out, and I didn't know if I was going to make it out alive. When I was in the fire, it was almost impossible to step out of the situation and see things for what they really were. It was difficult to see, but God really had not abandoned me; He was with me, walking beside me and would help me get through it. It was a very trying time. I am so thankful that my friends and family never gave up on me. Most of all, I am thankful to God for His protection during those painful days.

Twenty-seven

Even youths grow tired and weary, and young men stumble and fall; but those who hope in the LORD shall renew their strength; they will soar on wings like eagles; they shall run and not be weary; they shall walk and not faint.
– Isaiah 40:30-33 NIV

Courage doesn't always roar. Sometimes courage is the quiet voice at the end of the day saying, "I will try again tomorrow."
– MaryAnne Radmacher, *Courage Doesn't Always Roar*

"HEY, MOM, could you take a look at the bottom of my foot? I have a spot."

"A spot? What do you mean, a spot?" I asked, walking across the living room of our townhome to the couch where Andrew was sitting, one leg crossed over the other. Checking his foot regularly had become part of our routine since he couldn't *feel* it, *move* it or, because of the pain and lack of movement, even see it very well. It was an odd situation—although he couldn't feel his foot, in some areas it was hyper-sensitive to even the slightest touch. I often rubbed lotion all over it and massaged the parts that didn't hurt, imagining that a massage might help stimulate the nerves and muscles. It was vital that he take care of that foot and stay alert to any changes. It would be easy to develop a sore area that could get infected without him even realizing it.

"Riiiight there," he said, pointing to the ball of his foot, between his third and fourth toes.

I bent over to get a good look. "Ummm, hmmm," I murmured, evaluating what I saw. It didn't look good, and my internal red flag team was immediately marching in formation. The nickel-sized spot was bright red and warm to the touch, but the skin was broken, yellow and caving in at center. I knew it hadn't been there a couple of days ago, so I thought we could probably just wash it extremely well and use antibiotic ointment on it, but I knew I'd feel much better if we got a second opinion before spending the afternoon at the ER for no reason.

"Let's go see what Sheri thinks," I suggested, "She's just finished teaching her class over at the co-op. I bet she's still there."

We hopped in the car and drove a mile to meet Sheri. "Hey, I'm glad we caught you," I greeted her, then I explained what was going on as Andrew peeled off his shoe and sock.

"Um, yeah," she said, looking at the bottom of his propped-up foot. "I'd take him in. The red is starting to move up his foot right here." We both bent over and looked closely at his foot, and I saw the slight red mark shooting out from the infected spot—I didn't remember seeing that at home. We both agreed that he probably needed an oral antibiotic.

So, we were off to the ER again and, wonder of wonders, they weren't busy! We were shown to a bed-space right away, and a nurse came in, looked at his foot, started to get a cleaning tray out for him, but then left. She came back a minute later and said we needed to change spaces. They brought a wheelchair for Andrew, and I grabbed his shoes and socks and crutches and followed them down the hallway. We were shown to a supply room in the very back of the ER.

The doctors and nurses started donning yellow surgical gowns, caps and even shoe coverings and masks before they came in. It seemed like a little overkill for just a little spot on his foot, especially since I was in my regular clothes, sitting right there next to Andrew. I almost asked if I was underdressed for the occasion. *What's wrong with this picture, I thought. Do they know something I don't?* They checked the spot, washed it, checked it again and then ordered a rush on the biopsy and blood samples they took and sent to the lab.

Finally, the doctor spoke into the silence. "It looks like it could be MRSA, but since we won't know for sure till we get the lab results back, we have to take every precaution."

"Well," I said, "He's had MRSA before. Is it possible he still has it… that he never really got rid of it?"

"It's possible, or maybe he picked it up again," the doctor said. "He might even be a carrier. We will find all that out from the lab results."

A carrier? How could that be? It began to dawn on me that I had been unaware of the actual dangers of MRSA. No one ever sat me down and said, "This is really bad, and you need to do this and this and this…" I'd been naively powering along, never imagining that MRSA was something to be worried about. *Could he have picked it up again? Or has he had it all this time? My mind was racing. Why didn't they ask me to put on scrubs? Am I already infected? Is he contaminating everything and everyone around him?*

I didn't know enough about MRSA to really know what was appropriate, and all this bustling about in what seemed almost like hazmat suits while I was still in my regular clothes made me wonder if I should be more concerned. The last few months, ever since returning from Denver, I had been taking care of Andrew's leg wound and foot without gloves or any other safety measures. No one ever told me I should take special precautions.

The ER doctors put Andrew on super heavy-duty medications, and we went to see Dr. Deering every day for a week. Then it was every other day, and then once a week. She would use a black sharpie pen to draw around the outside of the red area to gauge if it was getting worse or better. She would drain the center of the wound and bandage him up until the next time. Gradually the redness diminished. It took about three months of intensive wound care and meds to get over the infection, but then he developed another spot.

He was giving it all he had, and I didn't know what to tell him. I wanted to fix it, I really did, but I didn't have any answers. I felt like throwing up my hands and walking away. What else could I do? *God, help me! I'm so frustrated with all this. I don't know where to turn or how to help him.* I was amazed that he kept going to classes, doing his homework. We had suggested more than once that he take a break from school, but he stubbornly refused. In a way, I think school kept him going and gave him a reason to get up in the morning.

I read online that having open-heart surgery is the medical equivalent to getting hit by a truck. For Andrew, that was followed by the leg injury, four additional surgeries and skin grafts which shaved the top layers of skin off his thighs—just about the only part of his body that didn't already hurt. Throw in a couple of serious infections, exhausting physical therapy work and living life on crutches, and that would have been a daunting list even for Superman. Although he wasn't whining about it, I could see that everything was taking its toll. His lively personality was fading to dim. As resilient and determined as he was, even Andrew had a breaking point—and he was getting close.

It was a couple of months later on a rainy afternoon that it happened. He crutched his way down the hall and into the living room. I still remember everything about that day. I looked across the room as he struggled to find the words.

"I'm going to get my leg amputated, Mom. I've decided to do it. I can't take it anymore," he declared.

Wiping my wet hands on a kitchen towel, I walked into the living room where he stood. "Are you sure, Andrew?" I said. "Really and truly sure?"

"Uh-huh. I'm sure."

Thoughts from Andrew

I WAS incredibly tired of battling infection after infection. I'd been working hard every day at therapy, but I felt like I was stuck and not making progress. Sometimes I could walk on my own, but only for short distances. Most of the time I was on crutches because of the countless infections on my foot. It became obvious that I was never going to be able to return to a normal life—it just seemed that would never be a reality. There had to be another option. How does a person go from incredibly active and full of energy to barely being able to walk? I desperately needed to get back to being able to play sports and run around with my friends, go mountain biking and skiing and just be my normal self. I missed the fun and the freedom that sports had always provided me.

We looked into other options, but they were more limiting than amputation. We considered fusing the bones in my ankle, but I would still be dealing with infections and pain—not to mention being basically limited to walking, No more running or skiing or biking meant that option was out right away as far as I was concerned. Another option was just letting time run its course. But for me, it had been long enough. If the nerves and muscles in my leg were going to start coming back, we would be seeing signs of it by now. I felt like I was running out of time.

I was mad at God for allowing this to happen. I had gone from being extremely energetic and always on the go, to nothing more than a couch potato. I was a totally different person than who I had been my whole life. I was dealing with insane pain levels, and I was dangerously depressed. I felt like I might as well be dead.

I remember telling my mom one day, "That's it, Mom, I'm going to get my leg amputated. I think that might be my best option." Mom was hesitant at first, but we discussed it then made an appointment to talk with Dr. Deering. After that appointment, I was completely convinced that amputation was definitely the best option. At worst, it would relieve my pain; but at best, with a prosthetic, I'd be able to return to a pretty normal life. *More normal than right now anyway*, I thought. Even if the only thing that came out of the amputation was the pain relief, that would be enough for me. It would make a huge difference.

I made up my mind I was going to do it, and I wanted to do it soon. Most people have said to me, "That must have been such a hard thing to do." But in all honesty, it was an amazingly easy decision. I should have done it way sooner. Looking back, I am so glad that I decided to amputate. I know without a doubt that it was the best choice for me.

Twenty-eight

So we do not lose heart. Though our outer self is wasting away,
our inner self is being renewed day by day...For the things that
are seen are transient, but the things that are unseen are eternal.
– 2 Corinthians 4:16, 18 ESV

The reason why many are still troubled, still seeking, still
making little forward progress is because they haven't yet come
to the end of themselves. We're still trying to give orders and
interfering with God's work within us.
– A.W. Tozer, *The Pursuit of God*

Tom AND Andrew and I arrived at the hospital long before sunrise on a chilly Wednesday morning in May. We registered at the front desk, and a nurse led us down a hallway to a bed space in the pre-surgery area. Andrew donned the requisite hospital gown, and we settled in to wait for the seemingly endless stream of professionals that would stop by to check in with us.

I really wanted to look at Andrew's leg while there was still time, but he had the blankets pulled up around him, and I didn't want to ask. After all, he wasn't three years old. It would have been strange to say, "Honey, could I look at your leg one last time?" He would have rolled his eyes and been irritated at my motherly desires. I knew he was nervous, and

I didn't want to make him feel worse. There was no point in it, anyway. I knew what his leg looked like. All the skin grafts and scars, the foot drop and the removal of muscle tissue had given it kind of a patchwork look, thin and markedly different from his right leg. I had watched as his leg morphed from normal, healthy and strong into a weakened limb that hindered and hurt. But it was still his leg. It was the only left leg he'd ever had, and it was going to be cut off forever this morning. I would never see it again, and I just wanted one last look.

My mind replayed the conversations we'd had for weeks now, about how his leg would never be healthy again. If he kept it, he would always deal with infections that could be life-threatening. Plus, I knew his pain was almost unbearable. How could anyone really go on with life in a normal way when wracked with constant pain? He had tried. He was so determined and so brave, but I had seen his bubbly personality slipping away during those months of pain. It was a battle just to make it through each day. Tears suddenly pooled in my eyes. I was truly sad for what he had endured these last eighteen months, sad that he could never again have his own healthy, strong leg. For my son—my athletic, outdoorsy, life-loving son—this loss had taken a massive toll. In one sense, when his leg lost blood supply on the operating table and the muscles became useless with no feeling and movement, it was as if his leg had been removed already.

Part of me wondered if we waited just a little longer, would medical advances in the future allow nerves and muscles to regrow in a situation like Andrew's? Could nerves and muscle tissue be transplanted into his leg? Might it someday be possible to actually create feeling and movement in a limb that has been so wounded? Would it be better to keep the leg and at least have something to work with? We didn't know. He was only twenty—was this a choice he would someday regret? It was so hard as his mom to watch him go through this, and I knew what a difficult choice it had been; but Tom and I stood by him a hundred percent, and we trusted his decision completely. It was going to be tough, that was for sure, but we knew Andrew was in God's hands and that God had promised to walk through this trial with us.

I was hopeful that the amputation would be a new start for Andrew—that this decision would free him from the painful prison in which he'd been living and open doors for an active life again. The thing was—and, of course we all knew this —that after this surgery, he couldn't go back. There would be no changing his mind, no reattaching his leg. It was very, very final. We didn't know anyone else who had actually opted for amputation. It was so drastic. But his pain and the risks involved if he didn't do this were drastic, too.

Sometimes just making the decision is the hardest part. I thought back to Andrew's infancy when we were faced with the choice of where to go for his first surgery and which surgeon to use. The decision was agonizing because we knew our choice could possibly be the difference between life and death. We talked to the doctors; everyone had his own opinion. We prayed and asked God for direction. We weighed the pros and cons, but we finally just had to step out in faith and choose.

When facing life-changing decisions like this, we pray that God will give us wisdom, we seek counsel from others, and then we have to go ahead and make a choice. We can't look back or second guess the decision. This is the time to cling to faith and hold tight to what we do know—that we asked for His direction, He led us to this decision and we stepped forward. It wouldn't be faith if we knew the outcome in advance. What we do know is God's character. We know He loves us and has promised He won't leave us alone. We can be confident in Him even if we are unsure of the future.

It seemed bizarre to think that I would have a son with a prosthetic. I didn't even know anyone with a prosthetic. Planning an amputation seemed counter to everything we'd been working towards. I wanted him to do it—I knew it was the right thing to do, but there were other feelings mixed in, too. Just going through another surgery meant preparing myself for the job of caregiving. Staying at the hospital, being ready for an emergency, preparing our home for his needs—all these things fell on my shoulders. I also felt like the emotional aspects of this surgery would be significant, and I didn't know what that would look like for Andrew or any of us.

Dr. Deering came into the pre-surgery room, smiling and cheerful. She was her usual encouraging and upbeat self. "Are you ready for this?" she asked, looking at Andrew as she pulled a permanent marker out of her pocket. We all nodded and commented that we were very ready. I really wasn't worried about the surgery itself—just the aftermath. She joked with Andrew about messing up and cutting off the wrong leg. Then she wrote a big YES on his left leg and NO on his right leg. "I'll keep you guys posted," she said. "It should take only about two and a half hours."

The night before the surgery had not gone well. I wanted to scream from the emotional pressure. My mom and dad were staying with us, and the phone rang constantly. I wanted to keep the atmosphere kind of fun and light, thinking we could have an enjoyable dinner together and just relax. The reality was that I felt discouraged and weighed down. There was too much to do, too many people to attend to, and nothing felt normal. How could my son be getting his leg actually *amputated*? I pushed down my own feelings to deal with later, but then every little thing started to stress me out. Just when I should have been the strong one for my family, I…well, I wasn't in the running for Mother of the Year that night, or anything close to it.

But as Tom and I walked into the surgery waiting area after sending Andrew into surgery, we were blessed to see a packed house. Andrew has many dear friends—which shouldn't be a surprise since he's such a people person—and I truly felt surrounded by their love. When word got out that he was going to have his leg amputated, he had a ton of support. One of his friends, Casey, a graphic artist, created a t-shirt design with Andrew's favorite scripture verse from Isaiah 40:31, *"But those who hope in the* LORD *will renew their strength. They will soar on wings like eagles; they will run and not grow weary, they will walk and not be faint."* She also handed out iron-on transfers to friends and family so that everyone could make matching t-shirts to wear the day of his surgery. Andrew was going to need this show of friendship.

After finding a seat in the waiting room packed with our friends and family, we prayed together for Andrew and for the doctors and nurses. I believed God was directing their hands. I knew, too, that there were many more prayers being said by those who couldn't physically be with us at the hospital. They were holding us closely in their hearts. For once, I relaxed and let go of my usual fear of having to take care of the crowd.

The surgery went perfectly. By late morning, Dr. Deering met Tom and me in a small room off of the waiting area. She said the nerve and muscle damage in Andrew's leg was much worse than she had suspected. She was able to really take her time as she worked on him so that he would hopefully have minimal problems with phantom pain. We went back out to the waiting room to deliver the good news, then we gathered our belongings and headed up to Andrew's room.

In the elevator on the way to his room, I remember feeling much different than I had thought I would. I was hoping for happy and calm, maybe relieved. But mostly I felt numb and scared and nearly sick to my stomach. *We've been through this hospital routine so many times; when will it start to get easier?* I wondered. Pushing back the curtain at the door of his room, I stopped—out of fear, I guess. I was holding on to that curtain, and I had to make myself walk forward. *Breathe, you can do this. Take a deep breath.* First, I went to the head of the bed, bent down and kissed his forehead and breathed in the smell of his skin and hair mixed with that pervasive smell of anesthesia. I was thankful he had survived and was lying there alive. I stood up rather slowly and allowed my gaze to travel the length of his body, all the way down to his legs—I mean, leg.

It was a shock to see the covers dip down just past his knee where his left shin should have been. His right foot poked up like a tent pole under the blanket, but there was only the one foot—and that seemed bizarre. His other leg was just…not there anymore. I know that sounds stupid. Of course his leg was not there. It's not as if I hadn't known what was happening. We had talked and talked, researched and gotten other opinions. We had decided, along with his doctor, that this was the absolute best choice for Andrew. And Andrew himself had had the final say. But as a mom, is there any way to prepare for this, really? Is there a book titled, *What to Expect When You're Expecting Your Son's Leg to Be Cut Off?* Was I supposed to act like it was a normal procedure? As if everyone goes through this kind of thing and it's not that big of a deal? It was a very big deal to me.

I had all kinds of questions running rampant through my brain. *What did they do with his leg? Did they see any signs of infection in that leg? How is he supposed to take a shower with only one leg? How does a prosthetic stay on?* I was trying to remember that this was what he wanted, but I felt like I might throw up. *This is my son lying there, the kid who was born running and climbed his way through toddlerhood, the one who has loved anything and everything to do with sports since he was barely walking. And now he has one leg? My son? God, I need You. This is not how it was supposed to turn out. Help me trust that You can turn this horrible, sickening thing into something good because right now I'm not feeling like that's even a remote possibility.* I tried to focus on being happy that Andrew was alive. I held his hand and smoothed his forehead.

"Hi, Andrew," I said quietly as his eyelids fluttered open and closed.

His voice was slow and halting as he asked with a frown, "Were there any complications?"

"No, Andrew, everything went as planned." I squeezed his hand. "Dr. Deering said you were the perfect patient, so don't you worry about a thing. You can go right back to sleep." I felt so bad that he had been worried about the possibility of complications. He hadn't said anything about that before the surgery, so I didn't even know he was concerned. But how could I have not known? Of course he'd be worried. Who wouldn't be after what he'd been through?

Dr. Deering came to check on him. Andrew had gone back to sleep, but she checked his pulse and IVs, and then said to us, "Have you had a chance to look at it yet?" Until that moment, I'd kind of ignored what was the obvious elephant in the room.

I shook my head and looked at Tom. We both said, "No, not yet" or something like that. She pulled back the blanket like a magician, and it was suddenly no longer possible to deny what we'd known. His leg wasn't there. I had thought about this moment and imagined what it would be like, and I had tried to prepare myself. But actually seeing half a leg where there used to be a whole one was shocking. It was hard to breathe, like the wind had been knocked out of me. I tried to act normal, but I don't remember anything the doctor said or who else was in the room. I just remember staring at Andrew's leg—his new half-leg wrapped in white gauze bandages that ended just below his knee. It was starkly vivid and incredibly unsettling. My eyes were seeing it, but my brain wasn't processing it accurately yet. *Later, maybe it will seem normal, but not now. Oh, God, not right now.* I sat back down and tried to look casual, but I shook to the marrow of my bones.

By the time the anesthesia had begun to wear off and he was a bit more alert, Andrew's spirits were flying high. "My pain is completely gone," he said with that kind of dopey still-partly-under-anesthesia smile. I had gotten a grip on my emotions by then, telling myself, *This is normal now.* How could I have known that even years down the road I would still sometimes catch myself being surprised by that missing leg?

I was amazed at Andrew. He seemed genuinely happy, cracking jokes and laughing with his friends; we saw glimpses of his old self shining through again. Obviously, he was thrilled. His pain was completely gone—well, except for the pesky little surgical pain one would have if one had just had his leg amputated—but other than that pain, he said he was good to go. I'm pretty sure he was so excited he could have done a high-wire act on his one good leg if we'd let him up out of bed. In fact, I think he said something to the effect that he was feeling *"outstanding."* Then he said, "Get it? Out-*stand*-ing?" And he grinned, "I know, I know, it's a *lame* joke." And we all rolled our eyes and laughed. That was just like Andrew. The fact that he was still drugged up and laughing hysterically at his own jokes made it all the funnier.

A whole troupe of friends gathered in Andrew's hospital room that night to encourage him. We were touched by their honest outpouring of support—probably a little too much support if you asked the nurses. Those nurses about fell over when they walked into his room and saw it filled to the brim with his friends. There must have been fifteen or more college-age kids, and the nurses were uncomfortable, to say the least. Luckily, he had the biggest room on the far end of the hallway, and even though it was pushing the outer edges of sensibility, the nurses looked the other way for a couple of hours, and it meant the world to Andrew to be surrounded by all his friends.

The kids brought pizza and a movie and, promising they'd be extra quiet, settled on the floor around Andrew's bed. They took turns hopping up and down to get Andrew whatever he needed. As I watched from the back of the room, I knew that what he had needed most was all of them being there. Of course, the main reason that it happened at all was because he had the best nurse of all, my good friend, Sheri, who had taken an extra shift just so she could be his primary nurse that night. Sheri bent the visiting rules, and she remarked to me with a knowing smile, "Sometimes stepping outside the box is exactly what is needed." Andrew dozed on and off during the movie, and I don't know if he even ate any pizza, but that didn't matter. Having the loving support of his friends made all the difference in his healing, both emotional and physical.

Thoughts from Andrew

I HOPED that having my leg amputated was going to be a new start. It was a turning point, for sure, but I'm not going to lie—I was a little nervous. I remember thinking, *What if they cut off the wrong leg?* And I remember that a little bit of doubt crept into my mind as I asked myself more than once if this was really the best decision. But I had made up my mind, and there was no turning back. I was on the way to becoming my old self. As I laid on the bed waiting to be rolled into the operating room, my incredible surgeon, Dr. Deering, came in to talk with me and make sure I was as comfortable as I could be. She took out a permanent marker and I asked, "What's that for?"

"It's to mark the correct leg so I don't mess up and take off the wrong one." She smiled and started to mark my right leg.

I shouted, "No, not that one!" Then, when I saw her face, I started laughing. She was always messing with me—that's what I liked about her. She treated me like a regular person, not a person with this terrible problem. She saw past what was happening to me and just saw me. "Just kidding," she reassured me, laughing. "Don't worry, Andrew, I've got this. It's all under control."

The next thing I remember is waking up in the hospital room. Instantly, I realized that the horrible, agonizing pain I'd experienced for the last year and a half was no longer there. It was gone completely. I knew then that I'd made the right decision.

After the amputation, when the focus wasn't so much on managing the pain and infections in that leg any longer, we realized that more damage had been done to my right leg and foot during the heart surgery than we originally thought and that limb needed some major repair. I had a severe case of foot drop, now even more pronounced because it was my "good" leg and foot. Foot drop is when the muscles that allow you to control and lift your foot up and down don't work. It's hard to walk without a brace that holds your foot and ankle in one place. Needless to say, a brace would have been very constricting, so I needed a tendon transfer in my foot and ankle to try to make that foot work. That would involve more physical therapy and teaching myself to move my foot in a whole new way. In addition, a vascular problem needed to be addressed. I couldn't walk very far at all because the blood flow to my legs was hindered, so I needed to have that repaired as well. These surgeries would require about an eight-month recovery. I braced myself again. I knew that hard work and determination and pain lay ahead—but I also knew that I had to get through it.

What a long and hard road it was! It took nearly three full years of hard work and physical therapy and persevering and never giving up. Without God and my family and my excellent doctor and therapists, I know this story would have had a very different ending. I don't know how people make it who don't rely on God to get them through.

AFTER YOU get your leg amputated, you don't just get a prosthetic and begin walking around. It's a long process. Your muscles atrophy where the limb has been cut off so there is a waiting period while those muscles shrink to their new smaller size, and then you get a starter prosthetic to try out. Learning to walk again involves many elements. It's all about using your muscles in ways you haven't before, and it definitely isn't easy. It took me several months before I felt comfortable walking around.

My prosthetic had been harder to get used to than I'd anticipated, but after wearing it for a few weeks, I figured it was high time to up my game and try something new. I thought a bike ride sounded good, so I announced to my mom that I was going to get out my bike and go riding. "I'll be back later," I said. I didn't think it was a big deal, but, just like a mom, she wasn't so sure. She wanted to follow me in the car just in case something happened. I responded with, "Mom, come on, that is ridiculous. Nothing is going to happen." When she insisted, I didn't wait for her—I just took off. I figured she could catch up easily enough.

It felt amazing to be zipping along on my bike again. It seemed like ages since the last time I had been on a bike. It was great! I was just riding through the neighborhoods, but I didn't care—it felt like my own Tour De France.

I was riding free and feeling so good when, all of a sudden, I felt something slipping. I looked down to find that, sure enough, my prosthetic was sliding off. I remember thinking, *Uh-oh, this can't be good. What am I going to do?* I slowed the bike and tried to reach down and grab ahold of it, but it was too late. My prosthetic slipped all the way off, flew ahead of the bike and bounced a couple times down the sidewalk. Now I was really in trouble. *How do I stop this bike and stay upright with only one leg? You need to just stay calm, very slowly come to a stop, then lean over to your right side.* So, I did. *Now what?* I balanced awkwardly on my one leg as I tried to hold onto my bike. *Now how wiill I reach my prosthetic? Should I try to hop over to it?* I was contemplating what to do next when Mom drove up. She parked the car and retrieved my leg while I sat down on the grass next to the sidewalk. Well, that adventure did not go as planned, but I was okay. (Thanks, Mom.) We laughed hysterically, thinking about how the drivers in passing cars must have done a double take when they saw a leg go flying through the air.

In reality, that was only the first of many funny incidents that happened because of my prosthetic leg. I soon learned that keeping a sense of humor is the key.

Later in the summer, I had the opportunity to work at an awesome camp in Missouri. Camp Barnabas serves people with mental and physical handicaps, and I loved my time working there. They have a great high ropes course complete with a long, fast zip line. One extremely hot, humid day when there were no campers, the staff got to try out the ropes course, and I was one of the last staff members to take a turn. I scaled the rock wall and made it to the first platform. Next, I had to walk across a series of wires. I made it across the wires, but it was tough. At that point I was tired and sweaty but looking forward to the exhilarating feeling of flying down the zip line. When I was all hooked up and ready to go, I gathered my courage and launched myself off the platform. I was zooming along when I felt it. My prosthetic was losing its grip on my leg, and I knew it was about to go flying off. I couldn't reach down to it, so I just had to let it fall. It hit the ground hard and bounced along for a while. Once everyone realized that I was okay, we all broke out in boisterous laughter.

Then one time while playing for my summer softball team, I hit a huge line drive to left field and took off running. I was half way to first when my leg slipped off, and I went flying. I fell forward onto my hands and knees and heard everyone gasp, but I wasn't about to let that great hit go so easily. I crawled the rest of the way to the base and made it before the ball arrived. Someone brought my leg to me, and I slipped it back on—no worries. That was a pretty good play.

I've skied basically my whole life, but the first time I went skiing after getting my prosthetic, I decided to take a lesson so I could adjust to skiing with the new leg. Well, I took a pretty nasty fall as I headed down the slope, and my prosthetic twisted around completely so that the foot was facing backwards. In fact, the whole ski and ski boot were backwards, still attached to my prosthetic. I couldn't strip down right there to adjust everything, so they had to call the ski patrol to take me down on a stretcher—one leg and ski still facing the completely opposite direction from the other. I'm quite certain that looked pretty painful to anyone who was looking my way.

I also find it amusing when little kids see my prosthetic and don't know how to react. Most of the time, they've never seen a prosthetic before, so they don't even have a point of reference. They usually think I must be a robot or something. When the Transformers movie was in the theaters, I was at Taco Bell in shorts on a hot summer day. A little boy came up and very sweetly asked, "Are you a Transformer?"

I told him, "No, my leg just got hurt so the doctors made it look like I was a Transformer, and now it doesn't hurt anymore."

He replied, "Cool," and that was the end of that.

Right after my amputation, I decided to go watch a baseball game with friends one summer afternoon. I was crutching my way into the stadium because I didn't yet have my prosthetic. It was probably only a couple of weeks after my amputation and my leg still hurt like crazy. The only covering on my stump was a piece of cloth, kind of like a sock, so I was nervous about using crutches in the crowd. As I was trying to navigate my way through everyone, a middle-aged woman straight out asked me, "Young man, is there something wrong with your leg?"

I felt like getting all sarcastic on her and saying, "No, no, my leg is fine." Or pretending that I had no clue that my lower left leg was missing and saying, "Why, what's wrong with my leg?" then looking down at it and saying, "Oh, my gosh! When did that happen?" But I just replied that I had hurt it a while back and ended up getting it amputated. I still just shake my head and laugh at that one. Why would anyone ask such an obvious question?

Life is full of valleys and mountaintops, and often while we are in a valley it is nearly impossible to take a step back and answer the question, "Why? God, why is this happening?" But in reality, that's not even the right question. We can't answer the "why" because at the time, right in the middle of the trauma, we can't wrap our minds around anything bigger than the immediate moment. We just have to get through that.

What I believe is that God is not putting us through tests as a punishment. Rather, God is allowing us to go through tests because He wants to see our faith grow. He knows everything, and He will never put us through anything that we can't handle. He's on our side. But it is hard to see the reason or reasons for the tough times when we are right in the middle of it.

We've got to remember that God never said that it would be easy to follow Him. In fact, just the opposite is true. This path we're on as Christians isn't something we enter into lightly. It's a serious decision because it means we give it our all—100%. It's not like we're choosing a topping for ice cream. We're making a life choice that will ultimately affect everything.

Following Christ is a narrow path, full of hurdles and hard places, and we have to look to God to get us through each and every one. Sometimes we think we're the only ones going through trials, but that's not true. I believe that God allows us different experiences according to what we need.

———

Think back to some of the great men and women you've ever known—or heard about. Did they have to endure tests? You bet they did. I think of men and women in the Bible—so many suffered and endured and were ultimately strengthened.

Remember Job? He was, *"...blameless and upright; he feared God and shunned evil."* He had a large family, seven sons and three daughters. He was a very rich man, the "greatest man among all the people of the East." The Bible says that Satan came to God and said that Job had faith only because of all the riches he had, but God knew that Job loved Him no matter what. So God allowed Satan to take away all those things and do whatever he wanted to try to make Job turn away from God. Satan caused Job to lose all of his possessions and even had the roof collapse and kill all of his sons and daughters, yet Job still praised God. No matter what circumstances Job was confronted with, he still trusted God and followed Him. His faith was simply not conditional to his situations. Neither is mine.

Twenty-nine

Let the morning bring me word of your unfailing love, for I have put my trust in you. Show me the way I should go, for to you I entrust my life.
– Psalm 143:8 NIV

The experiences of our lives, when we let God use them, become the mysterious and perfect preparation for the work He will give us to do.
– Corrie ten Boom

*A*NDREW HAD a cardiology appointment last week. Like everyone born with a serious congenital heart defect such as Truncus, he's had a cardiology checkup every two weeks or every month, every three months, every six months or once a year for his entire life so far. This appointment was different, though, because he went without me. I wasn't there to hear what the doctor said or to watch as the nurse placed the sticky leads all over his chest for his EKG. I wasn't cheering him on as he agonized through the stress test or sitting in the dark watching intently as the ultrasound screen revealed the deepest corners of his heart, searching for unusual movement, mixed blood flow, thinning or thickening or narrowing of tissues. I wasn't there to talk through the results with him—whether good or bad—in the car on the way home.

I had called Andrew the day before, and he assured me everything would be okay. It's funny how, after all these years of me reassuring him, now he's the one reassuring me. I've been this mom—the mom of a child with a congenital heart defect—for so long that I'm not sure I know how to transition into the mom of the adult version of my son. I'd peppered him with instructions before the big day. "Be sure you ask how the valve sounds compared to last year, and whether there's any leakage," I said.

"I will, Mom. Things are fine. I feel fine, and there are not going to be any surprises."

"Are you having an ultrasound?"

"I think so."

"Well, just try to remember everything he says so you can tell me."

"I will. I'll call you right after, okay?"

"Okay," I agreed. "Bye."

My heart is a mom's heart, and I can't just turn off my emotions and forget all that we have been through together. I remember how anxiously I awaited the sound of his first cry, and how I have begged God so many, many times on my knees, pleading that Andrew's life would be spared. I was there through the most devastating and painful situations, and I cried with him and held him as he cried. I held his little hands as he took his very first steps, and I was there to help him when he had to learn to take those steps again with a painful leg that had no sensation, and then again with a leg of titanium. How could I possibly forget any of it? But I don't want to be forever remembering; I must keep moving forward.

Sometimes I'm afraid I won't be able to get through the next one. There will always be another surgery because the homographs don't last forever, and the thought of that looks like a dark cloud on the far horizon. I don't know when or where it will be, but I know that God will be there, holding Andrew close every step of the way no matter what happens. I am haunted sometimes by frightening memories that sneak up and overwhelm me, a type of PTSD (Post-Traumatic Stress Disorder) flashback that sometimes grips my whole being. It would be easy to be paralyzed by my fear. But if I can't put it in God's hands, or if I refuse to let go of all that we've already lived through, I'm definitely not going to be able to appreciate where we are now. Or where we're going. I believe there's joy out there, and I want to live in joy.

God is both unchanging and surprising. He is almighty and personal, He is creative and structured, all at the same time. Since I am created in His image, these contrasting qualities co-exist in me as well. When this realization hit me, I saw how it might be possible to experience joy again. These last few years have been messy for sure. But they have shown me that sorrow and joy can be friends living happily side by side, accepting and appreciating the strengths of the other. I used to think the goal was to grab hold of as much joy as possible and get rid of any sorrow and pain. But it's not like that—one fits together with the other. The losses I experience will always be a fundamental part of who I am; the joys I experience are also mine forever. So I don't have to choose one or the other, pain or joy—in fact, I *can't* do that. It is bittersweet, but it is possible to live with both. My little ducks have learned to fly, whether all lined up in a nice neat row or scattered like stars in the sky…sparkling stars.

Before this happened, I really thought I was doing right trying to keep myself and our family all "put together"—having the proper manners and the right clothes, serving the healthiest meals, choosing the best schools and most popular activities. I kept hoping that when I did it all correctly, everyone would be very pleased with me, and we'd all live "happily ever after." Isn't that what living a Christian life is all about? I was so wrong. Being a Christian is not about impressing or trying to please anybody. It isn't about working hard enough to please God, either. It's simply about me and God, choosing to love Him and accept His love and grace.

I'm not thrilled that our family has had to live through this carousel of experiences, and I'm *certainly* not happy about what Andrew's had to endure. But if we hadn't been through the valley, how would we know God is faithful? If we hadn't needed a miracle, how would we know that miracles really do happen? If everything in this world filled up the spaces in our hearts, how would we really know *Him*? I'm sure it is different for each of us, but for me, the pain of my circumstances showed me that He is all that matters, and He alone sustains me. It's not my well-planned schedule, controlled routines and traditions that keep me going every day. It isn't about praying in the right way with enough faith so that God will do it the way I want Him to. God is God, and I am me, and I am not in charge. It is God who sets the wind in motion and hangs the stars in their places, and He knows all the days of my life, and I can trust Him. What He has planned for me may be far different from what I've imagined, but because of my faith, I believe that it is tremendously better than anything *I* could ever organize or plan.

God created this amazingly beautiful (and sometimes frightening) world. He *made* us, and He's going to be with us regardless of the situations we encounter. Until heaven, we will experience tsunamis and white-outs and earth-shattering breaks that pierce us to the marrow. Everything we've hoped for may have gone horribly, excruciatingly wrong, leaving our deepest heart exposed in a profoundly painful way. But in the midst of the devastation, He is still there, and He covers us with His wings. We must look at His face, let go of any longing for this world, and whisper *Hallelujah* through our tears. Then, with our hand tightly in His, we take just one brave step and then one more, then another and another, and we try to never let go. If we do, He's there to catch us and bring us back to love. It's not a perfect faith; it is a living faith. And it moves us forward toward hope.

Thoughts from Andrew

"THE CHALLENGE of my life is to see how far I can take it." This comment from a commercial for an energy drink really made me start thinking. The commercial shows some of the best athletes in the world doing amazing physical feats. That seems to be a big deal here in the U. S. But what if, instead of living their lives to gain physical prowess, challenging themselves to achieve more than the last guy, people lived totally opposite of that?

When we try to have control of our lives, we eventually fall flat on our faces and have nowhere to turn. If we let God have control of our lives, sure, we will still have ups and downs, but when we do screw up, we can turn to a loving God. He's there.

I am so thankful that I have a God who loves me, a God of mercy and grace who longs to have a deep and meaningful relationship with me, and with each one of us. Psalm 139 tells us that He understands us—He knows us better than anyone. It often seems that when we're in our worst state, we try to hide from friends and from God. We are ashamed of our sins, and we are afraid of the judgment that we think is going to come. On the outside we seem perfectly normal, but inside we are trapped in a deep, dark pit of sin or depression that we try to hide from everyone.

What if we lived like we knew that we weren't perfect but there was no reason to hide—as if we knew we were forgiven and it was okay? What if we let go of trying to prove ourselves and let go of the shame and fear that Satan throws on us so hatefully? Could we ever just give it up to God? The Lord already knows all our sins, so why should we try to hide from Him? We are like Adam in the Garden of Eden, trying to be invisible before the God of the universe. That's just silly. God *loves* us.

Despite our meaningless efforts and our fear and shame, God does love us. All our energies trying to make things right fail because we do in fact need His love to cover our weaknesses and fear and sin. That covering is Jesus. That's why He died. His love covers all the bad stuff that tries to hide in corners deep down inside. His love conquers all and is everlasting, and He will love us the same today, tomorrow, next week and twenty years from now. No matter what. He is longing for us to call Him our Father and leap into His arms of love.

I've always been up for a challenge, but I have no interest in proving myself physically or in any other way against someone else just for the recognition. I am nothing in my own power, but I have a very powerful God. If it were up to me, I'd change that commercial to say instead, "The challenge of my life is to see how far God will take it." No matter what happens in my life, that's how I want to live.

My phone jangled loudly on the counter, pulling me back into reality. "Hello?"

"Hi, Mom," Andrew's voice came through the receiver.

"Hey, Andrew, how's it going?"

"Good." His standard response.

"What's new?"

A short pause, then, "Well, Mom…I've pretty much decided I'm going to go to Kenya and work at that orphanage I told you about."

I can hear the excitement in his voice, "Wow, that's great, Andrew." I'm thrilled for him and bursting with questions, but I wait, giving him space to tell me first.

"Yep. I talked to the director, and I'll be heading to Kenya in February."

"Really? That's fantastic!" I listen as his happy words bubble over, one sentence into the next. I'm not at all surprised by his decision. The experiences Andrew has lived through have impacted his life in every way. He gets it when others are hurting; his compassion runs deep, and he wants to do something about it. He is driven to live life to the absolute brim, spilling over with adventure, forgetting about the personal cost, because what would be the point? Like most people who have had a near-death experience, Andrew realizes that his life is part of a bigger story, God's story, and there is nothing to fear. Life is too short and far too fragile for fearful living. It's about giving what you have to those you can. It makes absolute sense that he would be off on another life-changing journey because that's exactly who he is.

This new path Andrew has been called to may be unfamiliar, but I'm confident that he'll be safe in God's hands, wherever he is. I'm sure it will be a wild ride, scary and unpredictable at times, but he's used to that, and so am I. It's the same in my life; no matter what may happen from here, I know I'm safe in God's hands, and I don't say that frivolously. I may need reminding sometimes because I'm human—forgetful and fickle as a two year old—but I do trust Him, and, in my heart, I will always belong to Him.

Our lives never seem to skip down the road quite as easily as we think they will, no matter how much planning we do. I look back now and smile at my fervent efforts to control and schedule my life, realizing it was never really mine to control in the first place. Trusting God is a process, and we just can't force it—we have to grow through it and take one step of faith at a time.

There's no denying that my life has been vastly different than I anticipated. I could not have imagined it happening this way even if I'd tried. I'm glad I don't worry so much anymore about following the rules and caring what everyone else thinks, because I found out that is exactly what weighs me down. God knew I needed to steer clear of Main Street and walk my own road. He knew I needed to confront my fears and worst nightmares in order to realize that He will never leave me.

The changes I've seen in myself (and those I continue to work through every day) and every single experience God has allowed in my life have made it quite an unexpected journey...unexpectedly spectacular.

Meet Cathy Atkinson
(and family)

I LIVE in Western Colorado with my husband, Tom, and our beloved flat coated retriever/mutt, Abby. I have a "day job" as an academic advisor to elementary homeschooled students. I love my job, my students and their families. I'm honored to work with such an amazing staff. Next to writing, working with kids has always been my happy place. I am an artsy-crafty kind of gal; I love knitting, sketching, scrapbooking, and doing pretty much anything creative.

Tom works from home. He keeps the sanity levels within a somewhat normal range and regularly reminds me that I just might be over-reacting to _____ (fill in the blank). He still enjoys a good nap, trash talking sports with the boys, or watching an old television western.

Our kids are grown up (or at least they pretend to be) and, lucky for us, they all live within sixty miles. David is the scientist and trivia king of the family, keeping the Atkinson geek-gene alive with his collection of vintage thesauruses. Andrew is a fabulous cook, loves to go fishing, and is never without his trusty sidekick, Jax, a golden retriever. He lives nearest to his gram and occasionally finds himself talked into an afternoon of playing cards with her lady-friends (all over the age of eighty), keeping them in stitches—ever the good sport. We weren't a bit surprised when Amy decided to become a nurse. (Was it because she spent so much time at hospitals in her early years?) She's currently tending to the tiniest of babies in a newborn intensive care unit—a place that will always be very near and dear to our hearts. She married a remarkable man, Cheyne, and right off the bat, Tom and I knew we'd hit the son-in-law jackpot. But when the grandbabies came along, we discovered the best prize of all was the unimaginable joy of being a grandparent. Our grandkids fill our world with laughter and adventure. Both our grandson, Luke, and Daisy, his little sister, are absolutely perfect in our unbiased opinion.

I blog at www.theunexpectedspectacular.com. Come on over and say "Hi!" I'd love to hear from you.